1001 Kansas Place Names

1001 Kansas Place Names

Sondra Van Meter McCoy
and Jan Hults

Illustrations by John Gruber

 University Press of Kansas

© 1989 by the University Press of Kansas
All rights reserved

Published by the University Press of Kansas (Lawrence, Kansas
66045), which was organized by the Board of Regents and
is operated and funded by Emporia State University, Fort Hays
State University, Kansas State University, Pittsburg State University, the University of Kansas, and Wichita State University

Library of Congress Cataloging-in-Publication Data

McCoy, Sondra Van Meter.
  1001 Kansas place names / Sondra Van Meter McCoy and Jan Hults;
illustrations by John Gruber.
      p.   cm.
  Includes index.
  ISBN 0–7006–0392–1.   ISBN 0–7006–0393–X (pbk).
  1. Names, Geographical—Kansas.   2. Kansas—History, Local.
I. Hults, Jan.   II. Title.   III. Title: One thousand one Kansas
place names.
F679.M38   1989
917.81'003–dc20   89–8885
                                                                CIP

Printed in the United States of America

10   9   8   7   6   5   4   3   2

To Donald R. McCoy and Donald Stamford Hults

Contents

Introduction

For thousands of years, people have named mountains, rivers, valleys, seas, and towns. Place naming in the United States has been done within the last few hundred years by Indians, explorers, surveyors, settlers, post office employees, and railroad officials.

According to onomastician George Stewart, place naming falls into ten major classifications: descriptive, associative, possessive, incidental, commemorative, commendatory, coining, transfer, folk etymology, and mistake. In Kansas, the majority of names fit into three of the categories: descriptive, transfer, and commemorative. The descriptive includes Smoky Hill, Pretty Prairie, and Saline. Transfer names include the names migrants brought from their former home states or from foreign countries. Americans brought Pittsburg, Erie, Oberlin, and Manhattan to Kansas. Foreign immigrants brought Toronto, Liebenthal, Clyde, Alexanderwohl, and Smolan. As elsewhere in the United States, by far the greatest number of names fits into the commemorative category, with places named for resident Indians, postmasters, landowners, railroad officials, military heroes, local politicians, and nationally prominent senators, judges, and presidents.

Place naming in Kansas falls into three major time periods. The first period encompasses exploration, Indian occupation, the territorial period, and early statehood. Until 1854, when Kansas became a territory, the Indians, French, and Spanish had named rivers, creeks, other landforms, and villages. From 1854 through 1869, the eastern half of the state was settled. During that time, legislators named counties for themselves, their friends, and admired politicians. Later territorial legislatures did likewise. After the Civil War, the 1867 legislature honored many of the Kansas military war dead by naming counties in their memory. During this period, 1854–1869, over 730 post offices were established, with personal and transfer names predominating. Often a post office had the nucleus of a town, such as a general store, a blacksmith shop, and a residence or two. Horace Greeley observed: "It takes three loghouses to make a city in Kansas, but they began calling it a city as soon as they have staked out the lots" (*History of Marshall County*, p. 205).

In the second period, between 1869 and 1889, town promotion boomed, with the state's population quadrupling from 364,400 to 1,428,100, and the number of post offices increasing by 3,297. It was also a period of major railroad construction. "Throughout Kansas, the railroad, more than any other economic organization, was responsible for the pattern of small town development. The main concern in developing these towns was to channel agricultural products on the company's rails for transportation" (James E. Sherow, "Rural Town Origins in South Reno County," *Kansas History*, vol. 3, no. 2, Summer 1980, p. 99). Between 1886 and 1889, the Chicago, Rock Island, and Pacific Railway Company alone established over eighty-five towns in Kansas. According to historian John Rydjord, "the Atchison, Topeka and Santa Fe left the largest number of railroad names on the map" (*Kansas Place Names*, University of Oklahoma Press, 1972, p. 449).

The third period encompasses the years after 1890. A few new towns were established in the 1890s, but by 1910, place naming had run its course in Kansas. According to Kansas University onomastician Karl Rosen, of the 4,281 post offices established (this number includes many proposed and actual towns), only 777 remained in 1916 ("Community Names from Personal Names in Kansas," *Names*, vol. 21, no. 1, March 1973, p. 28).

The decline in post offices meant a decline in official place names. Rural free delivery of mail, school consolidation, and a decreasing rural population have taken away many of the delightful names of yesterday. Gone are Nonchalanta, Monotony, Discord, Cosmosa, and Hourglass.

Time and technology weren't the only agents robbing Kansas of interesting place names. The federal post office screened, simplified, and approved all names. Hungarian immigrants could not use the name "Pesth," nor could Americans keep "Shoo Fly City." Although the Kaw River is widely referred to, its Washington-imposed name is the Kansas River. Officials based in Washington occasionally named Kansas post offices after themselves or family members.

Place naming was once the special privilege of the explorer, the pioneer, the first on the land. Since 1910, place naming has been the domain of the real estate developer, who uses names commending the property to prospective buyers. These names suggest a peaceful, pastoral atmosphere, such as Prairie Village, Mission Hills, and Grandview Plaza.

For this book, we have selected slightly more than 1,001 of the over 11,700 Kansas place names. (Actual count of entries is 1,068.) We have included all 105 counties and their county seat towns and all 629 incorporated places as listed in the 1980 United States census. The remaining names have been chosen because of historical interest or geographic or geological significance. Some places are rich in historical background; others existed as named places for only a few months before disappearing. We consulted historians for specific Indian tribal names. In all cases, we have made every effort to be accurate in discerning the source of the name. Vague or differing reasons have been checked back to the original source where possible.

Most of the name sources are from recorded history, such as county histories, newspapers, manuscripts, maps, and numerous publications. Any corrections that readers supply will be considered in revisions to be made for future editions of this book.

The entries include the following information:

a. The place name.
b. Pronunciation of unusual names.

c. County where located.
d. Body of the entry, wherein the origin of the name is given. Attempts have been made to eliminate the unlikely story, but sometimes such a story deserves telling. Occasionally we have grouped two or more places under the same name.
e. Post office information showing the opening and closing dates of the post offices. This is often an indicator of the date of the beginning of a town.
f. Population figures as derived from the 1980 census data and the *1987 Commercial Atlas*.
g. Designation of county seat with CS.

The pronunciation guide is based on: *A Pronunciation Guide for Kansas Place Names*, edited by Donald W. Hansen (The Radio and Television Laboratories, University of Kansas, 1962).

Acknowledgments

Several works have been essential to compiling *1001 Kansas Place Names*. Lists of all the known names are in the *National Gazeteer of the United States* (1984) and *Kansas Geographic Names Alphabetical Finding List* (1981). Robert Baughman's *Kansas Post Offices* (1961) lists all the post offices to 1961. His work has not been updated. The *Rand-McNally 1987 Commercial Atlas* lists current postal information as well as population based on the 1980 United States census figures. A. T. Andreas's *History of Kansas* (1883) is a comprehensive early history of Kansas. *Kansas Place Names* (1972) and *Indian Place Names* (1968), both by John Rydjord, are invaluable sources, as is "County and Community Names in Kansas" (1962) by Wayne E. Corley. Huber Self and Homer Socolofsky's *Historical Atlas of Kansas* (1972) also provides important information.

Other publications consulted include Henry Gannett, *American Names* (1947 reprint); George R. Stewart, *Names on the Land* (1970); William E. Koch, "Kansas Place-Name Scholarship" (n.d.); and Karl M. Rosen, "Community Names from Personal Names in Kansas" (1973).

The periodicals *Kansas Historical Collections, Kansas Historical Quarterly, Kansas History,* and *Names, Journal of the American Names Society* were essential. Without other relevant publications, clippings files, and manuscript material in the Kansas State Historical Research Center, the task would have been impossible. The county histories used at the Kansas Collection of the University of Kansas were equally important. The staffs at the Kansas Collection and the library at the Kansas State Historical Research Center were very helpful.

For general historical information we turned to the following: Robert Richmond, *Kansas, Land of Contrasts* (1974); William Frank Zornow, *Kansas, A History of the Jayhawk State* (1957); John Bright, *Kansas, The First Century* (1956) and *Kansas: A Guide to the Sunflower State* (1939); Nyle Miller and the staff of the Kansas State Historical Society, editors, *Kansas, The Thirty-Fourth Star;* and numerous other publications dealing with Kansas history.

Information on population statistics came from the United States census, 1980, and the *1987 Commercial Atlas.*

A comprehensive bibliography for this place names book has been placed in the Kansas Collection, Spencer Library, University of Kansas, Lawrence, Kansas, and the library of the Kansas State Historical Society Research Center, Topeka, Kansas.

Pronunciation Key

The following key to vowel sounds and consonant combinations is used throughout this guide.

a	is like the a in cat
ay	is like the a in gate
ah	is like the a in arm
e	is like the e in bet
ee	is like the ea in beat
i	is like the i in bit
eye	is like the i in ice
o	is like the o in rot
oh	is like the o in go
oo	is like the oo in boot
<u>oo</u>	is like the oo in foot
uh	is like the u in cut
u	is like the u in use
er	is like the er in farmer
k	is like the c in cap
j	is like the g in ledge
g	is like the g in gun
ow	is like the ow in cow
oy	is like the oy in toy
aw	is like the aw in caw
air	is like the air in lair

Consonants not listed have their usual sounds. Syllables to be accented are in capital letters.

1001 Kansas Place Names

Abbyville *(Reno)*

When local leaders decided to organize a town, they would sometimes name it after the first baby born in their community—in this case Abby McLean.
PO: June 1, 1866–; Pop. 123

Abilene *(Dickinson)* [A-buh-leen]

Wild cowtown, "Greyhound Capital of the World," the boyhood home of President Dwight Eisenhower—all refer to Abilene. Before fame came to the town, a new settler, Mrs. T. F. Hersey, suggested the name of *Abilene*. The Biblical name from Luke 3:1 referred to the ancient tetrarchy Abilene, which was located about forty miles north of the Sea of Galilee. The word means "grassy plain."
PO: December 6, 1860–; Pop. 6,572; CS

Ada *(Ottawa)*

Jacob B. Lane took charge of the first post office at Ada and named the place for his wife.
PO: September 26, 1872–; Pop. 125

Admire *(Lyon)*

This town was named after Jacob V. Admire, who had served as a captain in Company E of the Sixty-fifth Indiana Infantry during the Civil War. After the war Captain Admire became a lawyer and newspaperman in Topeka and Osage City and served in the Kansas legislature in 1887.
PO: November 15, 1886–; Pop. 158

Agenda *(Republic)*

Before the town was platted, the nearby post office and railroad station were known as *Agenda,* from the Latin word meaning "things to be done."
PO: February 1, 1874–September 4, 1883; April 19, 1888–; Pop. 106

Aggieville *(Riley)*

The city of Manhattan has two business districts, one downtown and the other adjacent to the campus of Kansas State University. The latter has been called *Aggieville* since the time the college was known as the Kansas State Agricultural College and its students were called the "Aggies."

Agra *(Phillips)*

Organizers named the town after the daughter of the president of the Chicago, Rock Island, and Pacific Railroad.
PO: December 7, 1887–; Pop. 294

Albert *(Barton)*

Albert received its name from its local store owner, Albert Kreisinger.
PO: August 20, 1887–; Pop. 236

Alcove Spring *(Marshall)*

This spring below the waterfall at the Independence Creek Crossing was named in 1846 by emigrants on the Oregon Trail, who carved the name on the surrounding rocks and trees. Thousands of thirsty travelers on their way to Utah, Oregon, and California in the 1840s and 1850s camped near the spring.

Alden *(Rice)*

Land promoter Alden Speare, an official of the Santa Fe Railroad, managed to have his hand in several town promotions, including this one.
PO: February 13, 1882–; Pop. 214

Alexander *(Rush)*

Scottish emigrant Alexander Harvey was with Lt. Col. Custer's 7th U.S. Cavalry in 1868. Afterward he built a trading post known as *Harvey's Ranch* on the Fort Hays–Fort Dodge Trail. It became the nucleus of the small town of Alexander.
PO: February 13, 1874–; Pop. 116

Alexanderwohl *(Marion)* [AL-eg-ZAN-der-vol]

Except for seven families, the entire village of Alexanderwohl, Russia, emigrated to North America seeking religious freedom and economic opportunity. Six hundred of the German-Russian Mennonite emigrants bought land in western Marion and eastern McPherson counties in 1874 and settled in eight related villages that altogether were known as the *New Alexanderwohl* community. The origin of the name goes back to the year 1821, when a large group of Mennonite colonists met Russian Emperor Alexander on the road. He asked where they were going; they said to a new settlement in Russia; he wished them well. Thus, Alexander inspired the name of their Russian village—*Alexander well*, or *Alexan-*

derwohl. The communities within New Alexanderwohl were Gnadenfeld, Gnadenthal, Blumenfeld, Blumenort, Hochfeld, Gruenfeld, Springfeld, and Emmathal. Although Alexanderwohl never incorporated as a town, it continues to be a viable religious community.

Allen *(Lyon)*

Charles H. Withington, the "first settler in Lyon County," kept a store in Council Grove from 1851 to 1854. He then moved to the point where the Santa Fe Trail crossed One Hundred Forty-two Mile Creek; there he built a log cabin, established a stage station and post office, and opened a general store and a "house of entertainment" for travelers. The place was named for Allen McGee of the noted McGee family that was prominent in business and political circles in Kansas City, Missouri, in the 1850s.
PO: February 26, 1855–October 28, 1856; February 19, 1857–; Pop. 205

Allen County *(Established August 30, 1855)*

Allen County, established on land once reserved for the New York Indians, was named after Ohio Democratic Senator William Allen. Allen, a proslavery sympathizer, was said to have originated the fiery phrase "Fifty-four Forty or Fight" in reference to the Canadian-U.S. dispute over the Oregon territory.
Pop. 16,200

Alma *(Wabaunsee)* [AL-muh]

This town was named either for a city in Germany from which some of the first settlers had come or for the stream Alma in the Crimea, where western European allies defeated the Russians. The German word *alm* means "a pastureland on the mountainside." There are no mountains around Alma, but the pastures are abundant.
PO: April 17, 1863–; Pop. 925; CS

Almena *(Norton)* [al-MEE-nuh]

Supposedly Mrs. James Hall, a resident of Norton County, wished to have a town named for her own hometown of Alma, Michigan. Since this name was already taken, Mrs. Hall accepted the diminutive *Almena*, a name close enough to satisfy her.
PO: June 10, 1872–; Pop. 517

Alta Vista *(Wabaunsee)*

Alta Vista, Spanish for "high view," is appropriately named, since it is located on the high divide between the Kansas (Kaw) and Neosho rivers.
PO: March 22, 1887–; Pop. 430

Altamont *(Labette)*

Altamont was originally named *Elston* for the family who settled there. Elston lost its bid for the county seat, and subsequently its Illinois settlers renamed the town *Altamont* for Altamont, Illinois.
PO: February 1, 1875–; Pop. 1,054

Alton *(Osborne)* [AWL-tun]

When General H. C. Bull and Lyman T. Early came to Osborne County, each man wanted to name the town site. Unable to agree on a name, they flipped a coin. Bull won the toss and named the town *Bull's City*. After Bull and three companions were killed by Bull's pet elk, residents petitioned to rename the town *Alton*, after Alton, Illinois. They succeeded—with the aid of a few forged signatures. The horns of the murderous elk hung in a small shop on Alton's main street for many years.
PO: May 31, 1871–February 27, 1885, as Bull's City; February 27, 1885–; Pop. 135

Altoona *(Wilson)*

I. N. Spencer named this coal-producing community after Altoona, Pennsylvania.
PO: April 11, 1870–; Pop. 564

Americus *(Lyon)*

The Americus Town Company, organized in 1857, named the town from the Latin version (Americus Vespucius) of the name of the explorer Amerigo Vespucci. In its early history, Americus was known for its manufacture of cheese.
PO: November 19, 1866–; Pop. 915

Ames *(Cloud)*

Located on the south side of the Republican River, the town was developed in the spring of 1883. The source of the name remains unclear, but it could be a person, Ames, Iowa, or Ames, New York.
PO: May 28, 1878–; Pop. 50

Amy *(Lane)*

J. R. Bruner once owned the site on which the newly designated post office stood. Officials in the federal Post Office suggested that it be named for his daughter Amy.
PO: January 22, 1906–May 31, 1954

Andale *(Sedgwick)*

Two locally prominent families, the Andersons and the Dales, coined the name *Andale* when the Wichita and Colorado Railway needed another station on the route between Wichita and Hutchinson.
PO: January 16, 1889–; Pop. 538

Anderson County *(Established August 25, 1855)*

This county was named after Joseph C. Anderson, speaker pro tem of the Kansas Territorial House from the Fort Scott District.
Pop. 8,749

Andover *(Butler)*

Originally named *Minneha*, residents renamed this town after Andover, Massachusetts.
PO: June 7, 1880–; Pop. 2,801

Anness *(Sedgwick)* [AN-nes]

W. H. Wilson left Arcade, New York, to acquire land in the wheat belt of Kansas. In exchange for granting a town site to the Santa Fe Railroad for a station, Wilson was permitted to name the town for his wife, Ann S. Wilson.
PO: February 25, 1887–January 31, 1952

Antelope *(Marion)*

Pioneer George Morrell observed that pronghorn (often referred to as antelope) grazed in the meadows near the town. These pale tan animals, distinguished by their broad white throat bands, have been clocked at speeds up to 40 miles per hour.
PO: July 25, 1870–

Anthony *(Harper)*

While he was governor, George T. Anthony had authority to locate the county seat for Harper County. To show their appreciation, the residents named the town for him. Anthony is

known for its dog and horse races, held at Anthony Downs
each July since 1904.
PO: June 14, 1878–; Pop. 2,661; CS

Arcadia *(Crawford)*

First called *Findlay City* for George Findlay, a coal contractor,
the residents renamed the town for the district of Arcadia in
ancient Greece.
PO: April 23, 1867–; Pop. 460

ARCADIA

Argentine *(Wyandotte)* [AHR-juhn-teen]

The location of the Atchison, Topeka, and Santa Fe Railroad
transfer depot with its side tracks, roundhouse, coal chutes,
and sheds largely determined the site of the town. Many
workers and businesses built near the depot. In 1880, the
same year the town was platted, the Kansas City Smelting
and Refining Company began receiving ore from mining districts in the western mountains. The company processed the
ore into lead, gold and silver. This smelting activity led to the
town being named *Argentine*, from the Latin word meaning
"silver."
PO: June 17, 1881–July 1, 1903; part of Kansas City

Argonia *(Sumner)* [ahr-GOHN-i-uh]

The town is named after the ship *Argo* in Greek mythology. In 1887, Argonia voters elected Mrs. Susanna Salter to the office of mayor. She is said to be the first woman in the United States elected to a mayoral position.
PO: June 17, 1881–; Pop. 587

Arkansas City *(Cowley)* [ahr-KAN-zuhs]

This early rendezvous for horse thieves was first called *Walnut City*, then *Adelphi*, and next *Creswell*. On June 10, 1872, the town incorporated as *Arkansas City*, mainly because it was built on a hill close to the Arkansas River.
PO: May 16, 1870–; Pop. 13,201

Arkansas River *(Western Central Kansas)* [ahr-KAN-zuhs]

Spaniards first called this river *St. Paul and St. Peter*, after arriving there on that Catholic holy day in 1541 in the expedition of explorer Francisco Vasquez de Coronado. Later, Spaniards called it by the Indian names of *Rio Napeste* or *Napestle*. Indians also referred to the Arkansas as *Ne Shuta*, which means "red water." The later name of *Arkansas* came from French explorers who named the river for the Arkansa Indians. In 1806, James Wilkinson, governor of the Louisiana Territory, called it the *Arkansaw*. The Arkansas may be the only river whose pronunciation changes as it crosses state lines. From the mouth of the river to the Oklahoma-Kansas line, it is called the *Arkansaw*. From Arkansas City, Kansas, through Kansas, the river is called the *Arkansas*. Again from the Kansas-Colorado border to its headwaters near Leadville, Colorado, the name assumes the pronunciation *Arkansaw*.

Arlington *(Reno)*

Arlington received its name from Arlington Heights in Massachusetts. The small town was located on the Sun City Trail, a major trade route through the area.
PO: February 7, 1878–; Pop. 631

Arma *(Crawford)*

The town site was first known as *Rust*, a small coal camp in the center of a rich bituminous coal deposit. Upon incorporation, the town's name changed to *Arma* for W. F. Armacost, who owned most of the land northeast of the camp.
PO: May 13, 1891–August 31, 1906; February 17, 1908–; Pop. 1,676

Armourdale *(Wyandotte)*

The meat-packing industry flourished in the Kansas City area in the late nineteenth and early twentieth centuries. The Armour family established a meat-processing plant not far from the stockyards, and the city of Armourdale developed around it. The company that organized the town site included the notable Boston capitalists Charles Francis Adams, Jr., John Adams, and Nathaniel Thayer.
PO: June 16, 1882–March 31, 1891; part of Kansas City

Arrington *(Atchison)*

Young Mary Arrington of Ohio planned to marry Thomas Hoops of Atchison County, Kansas. He died before the marriage could take place, so that she never saw the town and spa named for her. In the 1880s health enthusiasts flocked to bathe in the "highly magnetic waters" of the Arrington Mineral Springs. Chemists from St. Louis stated: "This water is highly recommended for the following: liver and kidney complaints, rheumatism, scrofula, gout, dropsy, hemorrhoids, chlorosis, hysteria and general debility." For over twenty years, the Springs brought prosperity to Arrington, but a large fire in 1917 and the coming of World War I ended the health resort era. The post office used the name *Arrington* from 1862 to 1879.
PO: September 15, 1879–; Pop. 30

A R R I N G T O N

Arvonia *(Osage)* [ahr-VOHN-i-uh]

Welsh immigrants "zealous for the cause of the Savior and of Welsh literature" started the settlement of Arvonia in April 1869. "Several famous poets and writers" lived in Arvonia, according to R. D. Thomas in his *A History of the Welsh in America*, 1872. The name *Arvonia* was modified upon its

transfer from the old country. In Wales, in the county of Caernarvon, is the area called Arvon (Arfon in Welsh).
PO: June 30, 1869–March 15, 1901

Asherville *(Mitchell)*

Asherville claims to be one of the oldest villages in the Solomon Valley. It began on part of the homestead of John Rees, a man born in Liverpool, England, who came to America as a child, served in the Union Army during the Civil War, and then moved to Kansas. Asherville was located in Asherville township and on Asher Creek.
PO: November 15, 1869–; Pop. 75

A S H R O C K

Ash Rock *(Rooks)*

One of the first settlers, Henry F. Olds, found a portion of a petrified ash tree when cutting firewood along the South Solomon River and brought it home with him. The name *Ash Rock* was first used to identify a post office established at Olds's residence on September 19, 1876. The original rock—two feet long and several inches wide—was used by Olds for a cornerstone in his house. A piece of the ash rock has been preserved and placed in the Rooks County Historical Society in Stockton. The name *Ash Rock* is used for a township, a rural school, a church, and a cemetery, in addition to the town.
PO: September 19, 1876–June 29, 1885

Ashland *(Clark)*

In late 1885 a group of Winfield men organized this town, naming it after Henry Clay's home in Kentucky.
PO: June 26, 1885–; Pop. 1,096; CS

Assaria *(Saline)* [uh-SAYR-i-uh]

South of Salina, Swedish settlers named their town *Assaria* after their church name, which meant "In God is our help." Originally the term *Assaria* was derived from the Hebrew term *Azariah,* meaning "Yaweh helps."
PO: September 3, 1879–; Pop. 414

Atchison *(Atchison)* [ATCH-i-suhn]

When he visited Atchison in 1859, the Republican abolitionist Horace Greeley called it a "Border Ruffian nest." If Greeley had come in 1854, proslave fanatics might have coated him with tar and feathers, or worse. In that year Missouri Senator David R. Atchison and friends selected the town site on the west bank of the Missouri River, expecting it to be the gateway through which proslavery forces could enter and take control of the newly opened Kansas Territory. On the morning of the sale of town lots, Senator Atchison told the assembled crowd that "he would hang every abolitionist who dared show his face there."
PO: March 15, 1855–; Pop. 11,407; CS

Atchison County *(Established August 25, 1855)*

The county of Atchison, established after the town, took its name from the town.
Pop. 18,397

Athelstane *(Clay)* [ATH-el-stayn]

In 1869 and 1870 large numbers of English colonists settled in the southern part of Clay County in Athelstane and Exeter townships. The city of Athelstane in southwest England is named for Aethelstan, king of the English from 924 to 939.
PO: January 31, 1872–May 31, 1898

Athol *(Smith)* [AY-thuhl]

The name has five possible sources: a railway official's wife and daughter, Atholl in Scotland, Athol, Massachusetts, or Athol, New York.
PO: February 9, 1888–; Pop. 90

Atlanta *(Cowley)*

The town-naming committee could not agree on a name until fifteen-year-old Mary Higgins suggested *Atlanta.*
PO: August 14, 1885–; Pop. 256

Attica *(Harper)*

Richard Botkin named this Kansas town after a province in ancient Greece. The name is synonymous with "great culture" in Greece.
PO: July 21, 1880–; Pop. 730

Atwood *(Rawlins)*

Town founder J. M. Matheny named the town after his son. The first spelling contained two *t*'s in 1879. One *t* was dropped in 1881.
PO: October 11, 1881–; Pop. 1,665; CS

Auburn *(Shawnee)*

Before the town was incorporated as *Auburn,* the settlement was called *Brownville.* Auburn aspired and expected to be the capital of Kansas, but Topeka had more commercial advantages. Onomastician Wayne Corely says the town was named for Auburn, New York.
PO: March 1859–; Pop. 890

Augusta *(Butler)*

Shamleffer and James opened a log cabin trading post on the town site in 1868. C. N. James named the town *Augusta* after his wife. The log structure still stands and now houses a historical museum.
PO: October 12, 1868–; Pop. 6,969

Aurora *(Cloud)* [uh-RAWR-uh]

French-Canadian immigrants obtained grants to land sixty miles northeast of Salina in Cloud County. They arrived in 1870 but did not establish the village of Aurora, named after Aurora, Illinois, until later. The French word *aurore* meant "dawn" or "daybreak."
PO: April 16, 1888–; Pop. 130

Axtell *(Marshall)*

After a day of hunting game, Dr. Jesse Axtell, an official of the St. Joseph and Grand Island Railroad, and his companions discussed starting a town. Subsequently, the town was named for him.
PO: December 20, 1871–; Pop. 470

Bala *(Riley)* [BAH-luh]

Members of a Welsh colony, organized in the state of New York, came to Kansas in 1870 and named their town and

township *Bala* after a town in northern Wales. The original
name, *Y Bala, Yn Powys,* was shortened to *Bala.*
PO: February 24, 1871–

Baldwin City *(Douglas)*

An eccentric reformer and a master architect and builder have
made their marks on Baldwin City. John Baldwin, the town's
namesake, came from Berea, Ohio, to construct a saw and
gristmill in 1857, but his broader purpose was to build "a different state of society through Christian education." Baldwin
usually wore blue overalls and a striped hickory shirt that
was seldom buttoned in front. He often went bareheaded and
barefooted. Architect Joseph Spurgeon built numerous
houses and business and Baker University buildings in the
late 1800s, many of which remain to give Baldwin City much
of its charm. Thousands of visitors enjoy Baldwin's Annual
Maple Leaf Festival each fall.
PO: May 22, 1862–; Pop. 2,829

Barber County *(Established February 26, 1867)*

Free-stater Thomas W. Barber was murdered near Lawrence,
Kansas, on December 6, 1855. Friends attending his funeral
feared for their own safety and dressed like women so they
could not be recognized. The naming of the county became
the martyr's memorial.
Pop. 6,548

Barnard *(Lincoln)* [BAHR-nahrd]

Locals were so favorably impressed with visitor J. F. Barnard,
a branch manager of the Atchison, Topeka, and Santa Fe
Railroad, that they named their end-of-the-line town for him.
PO: May 22, 1888–; Pop. 163

Barnes *(Washington)*

This small town may have been named for A. S. Barnes, a
publisher of U.S. history; or for A. F. Barnes, a railroad stockholder; or for A. S. Barnes, who built and operated the first
lumber yard here. Near Barnes, in 1984, Texaco drilled the
deepest well ever drilled in Kansas. No oil was found, but the
11,300-foot-deep well is rich in geologic history.
PO: February 5, 1887–; Pop. 257

Bartlett *(Labette)*

Robert A. Bartlett began selling part of his land in 1886 for the
purpose of establishing a town.
PO: September 15, 1886–; Pop. 163

Bartlett Arboretum *(Sumner)*

Just outside Belle Plaine stands Bartlett Arboretum, a
twenty-acre tract planted with more than 4,000 varieties of
trees, shrubs, and other plants. Beginning in 1910, Dr. Walter
E. Bartlett, physician, developed the garden with a lagoon,
stone walkways, retaining walls, and terraces. His son,
daughter-in-law, and granddaughter have continued to
maintain an English rock garden, a Rocky Mountain section,
a cactus section, a wild woods section, and a Japanese section. New plants have been added each year since the beginning. Thousands visit the arboretum each year, many people
coming when the tulips are in bloom.

Barton County *(Established February 26, 1867)*

Kansas honored the famous volunteer Civil War nurse Clara
Barton by naming the county for her. She went on to or-
ganize and serve as the first president (1881) of the American
Red Cross. This is the only Kansas county named for a
woman.
Pop. 31,343

Basehor *(Leavenworth)* [BAY-suhr]

One could say that a certain well in Lawrence made Basehor
possible. The well provided refuge for Ephraim Basehor during Quantrill's raid on Lawrence in 1863. The Basehor
brothers, Ephraim and Reuben, had come west from
Pennsylvania to settle in Kansas in the 1860s. Ephraim
worked as a hired hand until he accumulated enough money
to buy the land on which the town was located. He opened a
post office and built the Basehor State Bank in 1901.
PO: April 17, 1888–; Pop. 1,483

Bavaria *(Saline)*

Ernest Hohneck first settled here in 1871, serving as postmaster at *Hohneck*. In the 1880s, a large colony from Ohio bought
land in the area. For a reason now unknown, the name
changed to *Bavaria* by 1880. It appears that this is the only
populated place called *Bavaria* in the United States. It may
have been named from one of the political divisions in Germany.
PO: January 8, 1880–; Pop. 100

Baxter Springs *(Cherokee)*

Captain M. Mann and V. V. Barnes named the town after its
first settler, A. Baxter, and for the springs nearby. His friends
called Baxter a universalist missionary; others called him a

"cantankerous infidel." During the 1860s and 1870s, Texas cattlemen drove thousands of cattle to the pastures around the town. For a while the high-spirited cowboys and gamblers made Baxter Springs "the toughest town on earth."
PO: January 5, 1867–; Pop. 4,773

Bazaar *(Chase)*

Several families from Illinois settled Bazaar township in 1857. Mary Walton Leonard, wife of the first postmaster, is said to have suggested the name *Bazaar,* meaning "market place," although for almost two years the name *Mary* was used in her honor. The small trading center is located in the Flint Hills cattle range country.
PO: April 16, 1860–July 20, 1876, as Bazaar; July 20, 1876– March 19, 1878, as Mary; March 19, 1878–; Pop. 30

Bazine *(Ness)* [bay-ZEEN]

Tradition holds that Bazine was named after General Achille François Bazaine, a French general in the Franco-Prussian War of 1870. The Post Office Department lost the second *a* in *Bazaine,* leaving *Bazine.*
PO: June 22, 1874–; Pop. 385

Beattie *(Marshall)* [BAY-tee]

Mayor A. Beattie of St. Joseph, Missouri, visited the town site with railway officials and announced: "I want to give this town my own name." The area is sometimes known as the "Milo Capital of the World."
PO: July 10, 1871–; Pop. 316

Beaumont *(Butler)* [BOH-mahnt]

This Flint Hills town was once a thriving shipping point on the St. Louis and San Francisco Railway. Rancher J. C. Squier, who owned 2,000 acres near the town, flew his personal airplane to oversee his livestock operation. Squier later purchased the Beaumont Hotel and Cafe and put a landing strip next to it. The restaurant is now closed and for sale. *Beaumont* means "beautiful mount" in French.
PO: June 3, 1880–; Pop. 100

Beecher Bible and Rifle Church *(Wabaunsee)*

Among the organized groups that came to help establish a free state was the Connecticut Kansas colony that founded the community of Wabaunsee. The church they organized and built became known as the Beecher Bible and Rifle

Church when the famous abolitionist preacher Henry Ward Beecher and his eastern congregation contributed Sharps carbines and Bibles to the Kansas group. The old stone church, completed in 1862, is on the National Register of Historic Places.

Beeler *(Ness)*

One of America's greatest scientists, George Washington Carver, was only twenty-two years old when he built a sod house on land he homesteaded near Beeler. Two years later he mortgaged his claim to raise money to go to college. Carver's work at Tuskegee Institute revolutionized agriculture in the South. A Mr. Beeler founded the small village.
PO: April 19, 1888–

Belle Plaine *(Sumner)*

This town, laid out in 1871, was given the descriptive name meaning "beautiful plain."
PO: April 17, 1871–; Pop. 1,706

Belleville *(Republic)*

The county seat of Belleville was named after Arabelle, the wife of A. B. Tutton, one of the founders of the town site.
PO: February 18, 1870–; Pop. 2,805; CS

BEECHER BIBLE AND RIFLE CHURCH

Beloit *(Mitchell)* [buh-LOYT]

First known as *Willow Springs*, the town became *Beloit* when Timothy Hersey of Beloit, Wisconsin, moved to Kansas with Aaron A. Bell and renamed the site.
PO: May 16, 1870–; Pop. 4,367; CS

Belpre *(Edwards)* [BEL-pree]

Belpre is an abbreviation of the French phrase for "beautiful meadow." This name was transferred from Belpre, Ohio, by Ed McKibben who founded the Kansas Belpre.
PO: July 7, 1879–; Pop. 154

Belvidere *(Kiowa)*

Once known as *Glick*, Belvidere was founded by two wealthy ranchers, Iowa Watson and C. P. Fullington. Their wives named the town, choosing the Italian word *belvidere*, meaning "beautiful view." Near Belvidere is an outcrop of rock called Champion shell bed, which contains numerous marine fossils deposited during the Cretaceous Period.
PO: April 26, 1890–; Pop. 40

Belvue *(Pottawatomie)*

Located on the main branch of the Kansas Pacific, halfway between St. Marys and Wamego, Belvue started as a small village and station in 1871 in Belvue township. The name appears to be descriptive, a shorter version of the French word *bellevue*, or "beautiful view."
PO: May 31, 1871–; Pop. 212

Bendena *(Doniphan)*

It is said that in 1886 the first Rock Island Railroad agent at the station named it for his girlfriend, who later jilted him. The farming community of Bendena then established a post office in 1888, with Victor Ladwig as the first postmaster. Ladwig's father had immigrated from Mecklenburg, Germany, in 1852, coming to Wolf River township in Doniphan County in 1862.
PO: January 19, 1888–; Pop. 150

Bender Mounds *(Labette)*

The Bender family—John, his wife, his son, and his daughter Kate—lived close to the natural mounds that bear their name. They built a small house there in 1871, partitioned by a canvas cloth into two rooms, one a kitchen and the second a bedroom with a trap door above a pitlike cellar. Kate, an attractive, voluptuous self-proclaimed healer and spiritualist, was the leading spirit of her murderous family. Because the Bender house was located on a main road, travelers stopped for meals. After several disappeared and suspicions pointed to the Benders, the family fled. A search of their property disclosed eleven bodies buried in the garden, skulls crushed by hammer blows.

BENDER MOUNDS

Benedict *(Wilson)*

The source of the name remains a mystery. It may have been named after a person or after the Catholic Order of Saint Benedict. Benedict Creek in Coffey County took its name from the Benedict family who first settled the area.
PO: August 17, 1886–; Pop. 111

Bennington *(Ottawa)*

At Bennington in Bennington County, Vermont, the colonists won a battle against the British during the American Revolution. Immigrants from New England brought the name to Kansas.
PO: July 16, 1864–; Pop. 579

Bentley *(Sedgwick)*

Located in northern Sedgwick County, the town was named for O. H. Bentley, secretary-treasurer of the board of the Kansas Midland Railroad, which became part of the Frisco

line. Bentley compiled a comprehensive early history of
Sedgwick County.
PO: March 6, 1888–; Pop. 311

Benton *(Butler)*

Thomas Benton Murdock served in the Kansas legislature
and was founder and editor of the *Walnut Valley Times* in El
Dorado.
PO: June 12, 1872–; Pop. 609

Bern *(Nemaha)*

Swiss settlers remembered Bern, Switzerland.
PO: October 10, 1888–; Pop. 220

Berryton *(Shawnee)*

In 1888, when George W. Berry built a store, he named the
site after his father, George Washington Berry, one of the
first settlers in Monmouth township. It was said that Berry
was related to Abraham Lincoln and Daniel Boone.
PO: May 7, 1888–; Pop. 40

Beulah *(Crawford)* [BU-luh]

Methodists from Iowa, Illinois, and Pennsylvania formed a
town company in 1874 to survey land in Kansas for a colony
to be composed exclusively of Methodists. Upon arrival in
Kansas, they stopped to dine in a Girard restaurant where
they sang "Beulah Land." The Biblical name *Beulah* refers to
a land in which Jehovah reigns.
PO: December 31, 1874–March 15, 1955; Pop. 70

Beverly *(Lincoln)*

The town, platted on the homestead of Volany Ball, was
named after his birthplace, Beverly, West Virginia.
PO: April 29, 1886–; Pop. 171

Big Basin *(Clark)*

The undrained depression, or sink, measures a mile in diameter and is one hundred feet deep. The sink is the result of
the dissolution of thick subsurface deposits of salt and gypsum. Big Basin is geologically similar to Little Basin and St.
Jacob's Well in the same county. There is also a *Big Basin* in
McPherson County.

Big Blue River *(Northeast Kansas)*

This 300-mile-long river at one time was referred to locally as the "Merrimack" of Kansas because it furnished abundant water power, thus reminding the early settlers from New England of the Merrimack River in Massachusetts. The Big Blue River originates in Hamilton County, Nebraska, and empties into the Kansas River at Manhattan, Kansas.

Big Springs *(Douglas)*

The constantly flowing springs in the vicinity led to the community name of *Big Springs*. The Big Springs settlement dates from 1854, making it one of the first in Douglas County. The rural village was the site of the first Free-state Convention, which met September 5, 1855. Later, in 1856, one of the first temperance meetings in the territory was held there. While flames engulfed one whiskey barrel, one temperance speaker after another stood on a second barrel, shouting against the evils of "demon-rum."
PO: January 7, 1856–April 7, 1894; Pop. 75

Bird City *(Cheyenne)*

Originally called *Bird Town*, Bird City was named either after John Bird or after Benjamin B. Bird, editor of the *Bird City Times*.
PO: October 28, 1885–; Pop. 546

Bismarck Grove *(Douglas)*

Kansas' most popular nineteenth-century campground hosted numerous picnics, parties, church encampments, Chautauquas, fairs, and temperance meetings during the late nineteenth century. In 1867, the Union Pacific Railroad built shops two miles northeast of Lawrence, calling them Bismarck Shops. Just north of the shops was a grove of trees that railroad employees used as a picnic ground. By 1878, the railroad phased out the shops, and Bismarck Grove became a pleasant place to hold large public meetings. Bismarck Grove may have been named for Otto von Bismarck of Germany.

Bison *(Rush)*

The mighty buffalo once ranged over this town site. Judge John Butler of La Crosse was so impressed with the formidable creatures that he named the site *Buffalo*. The federal Post Office turned down the name, saying that a *Buffalo* already was on its list. The name was switched to the more accurate

BISON

zoological name for the American buffalo, that of *Bison*, in 1873.
PO: May 7, 1888–; Pop. 279

Black Jack *(Douglas)*

Mexican traders traveling on the Santa Fe Trail named the creek *Black Jack*, possibly for the blackjack oak trees in the area. The village of Black Jack, begun in 1857, was the site of numerous robberies in the early 1860s. It was also the site of a battle between proslavery forces led by H. Clay Pate and the victorious free-state forces led by John Brown. The "Battle of Black Jack" is staged each year as part of the Baldwin Maple Leaf Festival.
PO: May 15, 1858–January 31, 1895

Bloom *(Ford)*

Immigrants from Bloomsburgh, Pennsylvania, named the town. The *-sburgh* ending was later dropped.
PO: December 23, 1885–; Pop. 75

Blue Mont *(Riley)*

Explorer John C. Frémont once camped on the high hill with its magnificent view of the Big Blue River Valley. Bluemont College, which preceded Kansas State University, was opened in 1860 within a few miles of the summit.

Blue Mound *(Linn)*

The town was given the name after the nearby hill that distinguishes it.
PO: January 31, 1886–; Pop. 319

Blue Rapids *(Marshall)*

Colonists from New York established the town in 1869. They constructed a dam near the Blue River rapids, thus developing a superior source of water power. Early entrepreneurs built a woolen mill; flour, paper, and gypsum mills; a foundry; and a machine shop.
PO: March 14, 1860–; Pop. 1,280

Bluestem Pasture Region *(East Central Kansas)*

This region is named for the predominant grass that grows in a narrow oval two counties wide and covering some four and a half million acres in an area between Oklahoma and Nebraska. These pastures comprise the last large segment of true prairie that once stretched from the forests of the east to the Great Plains. The region is also known as the Flint Hills, but a more accurate name includes the bluestem grass that grows throughout. *(See* Flint Hills.)

Bluff City *(Harper)*

The village took its name from nearby Bluff Creek.
PO: January 28, 1890–; Pop. 95

Bogue *(Graham)* [BOHG]

The Union Pacific Railway rejected the town's original name of *Wild Horse*, renaming the site *Bogue* to honor the engineer of the first Union Pacific train through the town.
PO: September 19, 1888–; Pop. 197

Boicourt *(Linn)* [BOY-cort]

A man named Boicourt owned several thousand acres of pasture land in the area and gave his name to the post office and community.
PO: July 9, 1886–; Pop. 20

Bonner Springs *(Wyandotte)*

Bonner Springs claims the honor of being the first commercial center in Kansas. Fur traders Francis and Cyprian Chouteau developed the first trading post, known as the *Four Houses*, between 1812 and 1821. The post stockade was laid out in a square with a house at each corner. A town company platted Bonner Springs in November 1855, naming the town for Robert Bonner, editor of the *New York City Ledger*. The *Springs* referred to the plentiful springs in the area.
PO: July 9, 1886–; Pop. 6,266

Boot Hill *(Ford)*

The famous burial ground, where cowboys were buried with their boots on, was used from 1872 to 1878 when Dodge City made history as the "Wickedest Little City in America."

Bourbon County *(Established August 25, 1855)* [BER-buhn]

Samuel A. Williams, member of the first Kansas legislature, recommended the name of his home county in Kentucky.
Pop. 15,969

Brainerd *(Butler)*

On May 15, 1871, Elisha B. Brainerd located the claim he wanted in Butler County. Fourteen years later he platted a town on part of it. He and other landowners agreed to name it *Brainerd* since he had sold the most acreage for the town site.
PO: January 25, 1886–August 31, 1907; Pop. 60

Brewster *(Thomas)*

The railroad station and town were named after L. D. Brewster of Illinois, a director of the Rock Island Railroad.
PO: September 17, 1888–; Pop. 327

Bronson *(Bourbon)*

Ira Bronson came to Kansas in 1857 and engaged in the lumber business. After serving in the Union Army from 1861 to 1865, he expanded his lumber interests into several Kansas and Missouri counties. Bronson, who lived in Fort Scott, was a director of the St. Louis, Fort Scott, and Wichita Railroad; his name was given to a station.
PO: October 3, 1881–; Pop. 414

BOOT HILL

Brookville *(Saline)*

The Kansas Pacific Railway platted and surveyed the town site in April 1870. The descriptive name of Brookville possibly refers to the small brook that meanders through the town. The historic Brookville Hotel restaurant, in operation since 1874, attracts several thousand visitors each year to its family-style chicken dinners.
PO: February 2, 1870–; Pop. 259

Brown County *(Established August 30, 1855)*

The brilliant but very eccentric Orville H. Browne, member of the 1855 territorial legislature, wanted a county named for him. The *e* was dropped in 1857.
Pop. 11,955

Brownell *(Ness)*

This town was named after an attorney for the Denver, Memphis, and Atlanta Railroad. The railroad was later purchased by the Missouri Pacific Railroad.
PO: May 1, 1888–; Pop. 92

Buckeye Township *(Dickinson)*

Two hundred colonists from Ohio were so pleased with Dickinson County that they selected land north of Abilene. When the township organized in 1873, the colonists from the "Buckeye State" had a name ready.

Bucklin *(Ford)*

The prairie town was named for a railroad official whose last name was Bucklin. Parents of the first boy born in Bucklin named him Glenn Bucklin Sparks.
PO: August 5, 1887–; Pop. 786

Bucyrus *(Miami)* [bu-SEYE-ruhs]

Settlers who came from Bucyrus, Ohio, brought the name with them.
PO: May 14, 1887–; Pop. 140

Buffalo *(Wilson)*

The millions of buffalo that grazed on the Kansas prairies were remembered in a town name. Kansas also has a Buffalo River.
PO: September 6, 1867–; Pop. 386

B U F F A L O   B I L L'S   W E L L

Buffalo Bill's Well *(Rice)*

William Mathewson, the original "Buffalo Bill," worked at
the Beach Valley Ranch at Cow Creek Crossing beginning in
1858. From that base, Buffalo Bill killed as many as eighty
buffalo a day. The hand-dug well at the ranch, which dates
back to 1858, is about forty feet deep and walled from top to
bottom with sandstone slabs. It became known as Buffalo
Bill's Well after Mathewson bought the place in 1864. A small
park supported by the Rice County Historical Society and the
Lyons Kiwanis Club surrounds the well.

Buhler *(Reno)* [BU-ler]

Some 15,000 Mennonites moved to the valleys of the Little
Arkansas and Cottonwood rivers in the 1870s. Russian-born
Mennonites led by Elder Bernard Buhler founded the Hebron
Mennonite Church and Buhler northeast of Hutchinson.
PO: October 20, 1888–; Pop. 1,188

Bunker Hill *(Russell)*

Settlers from Ohio may have chosen this name for the Ohio
towns of Bunker Hill or Bunkerhill or for Bunker Hill, Massachusetts.
PO: June 21, 1871–; Pop. 124

Burden *(Cowley)*

Organized in September 1879, Burden was named after the
president of the town company, Robert Burden.
PO: May 19, 1884–; Pop. 518

Burdett *(Pawnee)*

This trading center surrounded by wheat fields and cattle pastures was the boyhood home of Clyde Tombaugh, the astronomer who discovered the ninth planet, Pluto, in February 1930. The settlement was called *Brown's Grove* between 1875 and 1887 before being changed to *Burdett* after author and humorist Robert J. Burdette. The final *e* was dropped.
PO: April 29, 1887–; Pop. 275

Burlingame *(Osage)*

Planned in New York City by the American Settlement Company in 1854, the Kansas town was first called *Council City*. The heavily used Santa Fe Trail went down the 150-foot-wide main street of the town. Council City was renamed in 1870 for Massachusetts Senator Anson Burlingame, an early free-state advocate, abolitionist, and U.S. minister to China.
PO: January 30, 1858–; Pop. 1,239

Burlington *(Coffey)*

As with Council City, interested parties organized the town company, named it, and then sent members out to locate the site. The Burlington Town Company was organized in Lawrence, Kansas, in February 1857, under the leadership of O. E. Learned, former resident of Burlington, Vermont.
PO: February 16, 1858–; Pop. 2,901; CS

Burns *(Marion)*

The town site was originally called *St. Francis City* by the German Roman Catholic St. Boniface Homestead Association of Cincinnati, Ohio, who planned the town on their land purchase. Because Kansas already had a town named *St. Francis*, the name was changed to *Burns* in the early 1880s for a Florence, El Dorado, and Walnut Valley Railroad Company official named Burns.
PO: November 30, 1880–; Pop. 224

Burr Oak *(Jewell)*

The town of Burr Oak and the township took their names from the bur oaks that grew in the area.
PO: June 3, 1871–; Pop. 366

Burrton *(Harvey)*

The Arkansas Valley Town Company named the site after I. T. Burr, vice president of the Atchison, Topeka, and Santa Fe Railroad.
PO: June 3, 1873–; Pop. 976

Bushong *(Lyon)* [boo-SHONG]

When the Missouri Pacific Railroad wanted a station in northern Lyon County, Joseph Weeks donated twenty acres to them. The station went by the name *Weeks* until it was changed to *Bushong*. The origin of *Bushong* remains unknown, but some say the town was named for a baseball player, Albert "Doc" Bushong, who played for six major league teams from 1875 to 1890, including Cleveland, St. Louis, and Brooklyn.
PO: January 31, 1887–; Pop. 62

Bushton *(Rice)*

The attractive row of bushes extending from one edge of the site to the other was responsible for the town's name.
PO: April 29, 1887–; Pop. 388

Butler County *(Established August 25, 1855)*

Encompassing 1,445 square miles, Butler County is 231 square miles larger than Rhode Island. As the largest county in Kansas, it has been called the "State of Butler" and the "Kingdom of Butler." The 1855 pro-South territorial legislature named the county for Andrew P. Butler, who was U.S. senator from South Carolina, from 1847 to 1857. Extensive oil drilling beginning in 1914, especially the heavy showing at Stapleton No. 1, made Butler County the "Queen of all county oil booms." New oil towns such as Midian and Oil Hill were established in the middle of oil fields, each attracting over three thousand workers and their families, but now oil production has substantially decreased and the towns are gone.
Pop. 44,782

Byers *(Pratt)*

This small village was named for O. P. Byers of Hutchinson, Kansas.
PO: April 12, 1915–; Pop. 47

Cairo *(Pratt)* [KEYE-roh]

Could the name go back to its Egyptian ancestor? Hardly. The South Fork of the Ninnescah looked nothing like the Nile. More likely, settlers brought the name from a previous home in one of several states—probably Illinois.
PO: February 9, 1887–January 14, 1922; Pop. 20

Caldwell *(Sumner)*

In 1871, the year in which Leavenworth's successful businessman Alexander Caldwell became a U.S. senator from

Kansas, a border town on the Chisholm Trail was named for him. For a few years, Caldwell flourished as a "cowtown" and was known from the Rio Grande to Dodge City as the "Border Queen."
PO: May 29, 1871–; Pop. 1,401

Cambridge *(Cowley)*

The popular name Cambridge, taken from the English university town, appeared in several states before it came to Kansas.
PO: January 30, 1880–; Pop. 113

Camp Forsyth *(Geary)*

The former cavalry replacement training center at Fort Riley officially became Camp Forsyth in 1942. Maj. General James W. Forsyth, West Point graduate, Civil War officer, and a cavalry major at Fort Riley, participated in several Indian campaigns. He became commandant at the fort in September 1887.
Pop. 2,054

Canada *(Marion)*

A publication based in Manitoba, Canada, invited Canadians to move to Kansas "where the land is beautiful, the climate is

CANADA

healthful and temperate, and the winters short and mild!''
Canadians began arriving in Marion County in September
1873. Many who came were of German or Dutch ancestry.
PO: February 20, 1884–February 28, 1954; Pop. 20

Caney *(Montgomery)* [KAY-nee]

The town takes its name from the Caney River and from the
canebrakes that grew near the town site in 1871. Caney
claims to be the first glass manufacturing town in Kansas,
beginning in 1902.
PO: May 16, 1870–; Pop. 2,284

Cannonball Highway

In the 1880s D. R. Green ran one of the fastest, most efficient
stage lines in Kansas—in fact, the spectacular speed of his
stagecoaches won for him the nickname Cannonball. He was
a striking figure, over six feet tall, big and bronzed, flam-
boyantly dressed, and carrying rolls of cash. His route west
of Wichita to Greensburg became U.S. Highway 54,
nicknamed the Cannonball Highway.

Canton *(McPherson)*

Once called by the Polish name *Ostrog,* the town was renamed
by residents after Canton, Ohio. The *Canton* in McPherson
County is the only *Canton* out of four to survive in Kansas.
PO: October 1874–; Pop. 926

Capioma *(Nemaha)*

Chief Kapioma of the Kickapoo tribe signed the Washington
Treaty of May 18, 1854, which reduced the Kickapoo reservation in Kansas. Kapioma's name survives in a township. The
word is now spelled with a *C* instead of a *K*.

Carbondale *(Osage)*

The coal town was first called *Carbonhill.* The name was
changed as the Atchison, Topeka, and Santa Fe Railroad built

C A N N O N B A L L   H I G H W A Y

through the area. Carbondale, Pennsylvania, may be its namesake.
PO: September 20, 1869–; Pop. 1,518

Carlton *(Dickinson)*

The blacksmith who operated the post office when the town came into being was named Carlton.
PO: February 21, 1872–; Pop. 49

Carneiro *(Ellsworth)* [kahr-NAIR-oh]

The name *Alum Creek Station* changed to *Carneiro* when E. W. Wellington, a sheep rancher, laid out a town on property belonging to Henry McManes. *Carneiro* is Portuguese for "sheep," and it was said that a large number of sheep were shipped from here to the eastern states in the late nineteenth century.
PO: June 14, 1882–September 30, 1953

CARNEIRO

Carona *(Cherokee)* [kuh-ROH-nuh]

The place was first given the descriptive name *Carbona*—an *a* added to *carbon* to indicate a place name—because of the coal in the vicinity. For some unexplained reason the *b* was dropped, leaving *Carona*.
PO: March 13, 1905–; Pop. 130

Cassoday *(Butler)*

An attorney for the Santa Fe Railroad who studied law under John B. Cassoday, a chief justice of the Wisconsin Supreme Court, chose to name the new Kansas town after Cassoday.
PO: July 9, 1906–; Pop. 122

Castleton *(Reno)*

Brothers W. E. and C. C. Hutchinson laid out the town site in 1872. They named it after Castleton, Vermont, the birthplace of C. C. Hutchinson's wife.
PO: December 6, 1872–June 28, 1957; Pop. 30

Cathedral of the Plains *(Ellis)*

The most impressive and best known of the Ellis County Catholic churches is St. Fidelis, also known as the Cathedral of the Plains, the name given to it by William Jennings Bryan, the well-known American orator of the early twentieth century. The cathedral was designed for the 225-member Victoria parish, whose members constructed the church between 1907 and 1911. The pastor assessed every man in the parish over twelve years of age forty-five dollars, and required him to haul six loads of stone and four loads of sand to the building site. The rock had to be hauled seven to eight miles in flatbed wagons pulled by horses. The church, which incorporates Romanesque and Renaissance Revival elements, has been named to the National Register of Historic Sites because of its architecture and historic significance.

CATHEDRAL OF THE PLAINS

Catharine *(Ellis)*

Catholic Volga-German settlers to western Kansas bought land from the Kansas Pacific Railroad, established the town on April 8, 1876, and named it after their former Russian

home of Katharinenstadt. The term *Volga-German* referred to Germans who had settled along the Volga River in Russia.
PO: November 23, 1882–July 1, 1938; Pop. 120

Cato *(Crawford)*

The first village in the county was started by John Rogers in 1854. If the name was taken from Roman history, it could refer to Cato the Censor or Cato Uticensis, both noted for being severe and inflexible or perhaps it was named for Sterling G. Cato, an associate justice of the Kansas Supreme Court from 1855 to 1858, during the territorial period.
PO: July 30, 1858–July 31, 1905

Cawker City *(Mitchell)*

Each of four friends—E. H. Cawker, Huckell, Ride, and Kshinka—wanted to name the town after himself. They agreed to let the winner of a poker game name the town; Cawker won. Some time later *City* was added.
PO: June 30, 1870–; Pop. 640

Cedar *(Smith)*

Eastern red cedar trees, commonly called cedar, grew throughout much of Kansas, leading to the frequent use of the name *Cedar* for places: thirteen post offices and—

CAWKER CITY

according to *Kansas Geographic Names*—nineteen *Cedar Creeks*
and thirteen *Cedar Bluffs*.
PO: May 19, 1906–; Pop. 53

Cedar Crest *(Shawnee)*

Cedar Crest is the name given to the governor's mansion in
Topeka, the state capital.

Cedar Point *(Chase)*

French-born Francis Bernard arrived in Kansas in 1857; he
had planned to start a French settlement but concentrated on
farming instead. A large number of French immigrants, however, did settle in the Cottonwood Valley in the 1870s, with
Cedar Point being a trade and social center. According to a
local historian, the French celebrated life: "Love of compan-
ionship, of good music and dancing, more than any other
characteristic, set these people apart from their American
neighbors. . . ."
PO: June 23, 1862–; Pop. 66

Cedar Vale *(Chautauqua)*

J. R. Marsh named the town for the trees located in the valley
of Cedar Creek.
PO: May 2, 1870–; Pop. 848

Centralia *(Nemaha)* [sen-TRAYL-ee-uh]

The settlement of Centralia came into being as early as 1859.
The name may have been brought from Illinois or Missouri or
may have referred to the location in the center of the township.
PO: March 27, 1860–; Pop. 486

Centropolis *(Franklin)*

Perry Fuller envisioned a town site that would be the territorial capital of Kansas. He used the contraction *Centropolis*,
standing for "central metropolis," to denote his town.
*PO: August 4, 1858–November 2, 1859; December 8, 1865–
January 14, 1930*

Chanute *(Neosho)* [shuh-NOOT]

Chanute owes its name and existence to a track-laying race
between the Leavenworth, Lawrence, and Galveston (LL&G)
and the Missouri, Kansas, and Texas (KATY) railroads in the

early 1870s. At the junction where the two lines crossed, town promoters planned three towns: *Tioga, New Chicago,* and *Chicago Junction.* The two railroad rivals schemed and fought for dominance. Finally, after two years, rivalry-weary leaders cooperated to plat a fourth town, *Alliance.* This solution failed, so they agreed to consolidate all the towns and call the conglomerate *Chanute* after Octave Chanute, the LL&G chief civil engineer who later became a pioneer aeronautical engineer. Osa Johnson, the explorer, was born in Chanute; the Martin and Osa Johnson Safari Museum containing photographs and artifacts is located here.
PO: April 29, 1873–; Pop. 10,506

Chapman *(Dickinson)*

Chapman is located on the north bank of the Smoky Hill River, about one-half mile west of the spot where Chapman Creek empties into the river. Early settlers applied the name *Chapman* to the community, but the source of the name is unknown.
PO: May 16, 1872–; Pop. 1,255

Chase *(Rice)*

Just after the Santa Fe Railroad built through the area, the town was platted and named for Mr. Chase, one of the railroad's officials.
PO: September 5, 1881–; Pop. 753

Chase County *(Established February 11, 1859)*

Samuel W. Wood, who came to Kansas from Marion County, Ohio, admired Ohio Governor Salmon P. Chase and named the new county for him. Chase later became chief justice of the U.S. Supreme Court.
Pop. 3,309

Chautauqua *(Chautauqua)* [shuh-TAW-kwuh]

The town used the same Iroquois Indian name as the county in which it is located.
PO: October 3, 1881–; Pop. 156

Chautauqua County *(Established March 3, 1875)*

An immigrant from Chautauqua County, New York, named the Kansas county.
Pop. 5,016

Cheney *(Sedgwick)* [CHEE-nee]

The town was named for Benjamin P. Cheney, Sr., of Boston, a director of the Santa Fe Railroad from 1873 to 1894, who later made a desperate seventy-nine-hour train ride from California to Chicago to be with his seriously ill son. The story was worked into Rudyard Kipling's *Captains Courageous.*
PO: September 20, 1883–; Pop. 1,404

Cherokee *(Crawford)* [CHAIR-uh-kee]

When the territory opened to white settlement, town builders thought they were in Cherokee County and named their town *Cherokee.* Actually, they were in Crawford County.
PO: August 12, 1870–; Pop. 775

Cherokee County *(Established February 18, 1860)*

The county was first known as McGee after A. M. McGee of Kansas City, a noted early day proslavery leader. In 1866, the Kansas Legislature changed the name to *Cherokee* for the Cherokee Indians.
Pop. 22,303

Cherokee Strip *(Southern Kansas)*

The Cherokee Strip (Cherokee Indian Reservation in the 1840s and 1850s) on the southern border of Kansas Territory was about 3 miles wide and more than 200 miles long.

CHEROKEE

Cherryvale *(Montgomery)*

The Kansas City, Lawrence, and Southern Railroad laid out the town site in March 1871, naming it after the black cherries and chokecherries that grew wild in eastern Kansas.
PO: August 24, 1894–; Pop. 2,769

Chetopa *(Labette)* [chuh-TOH-puh]

The settlement of Chetopa dates from January 1857, when members of the Powhattan Agricultural Association of Powhattan, Ohio, organized to establish a colony in Kansas. They named it after the Osage Chief Chetopa, who lived nearby.
PO: April 15, 1867–; Pop. 1,751

Cheyenne Bottoms *(Barton)* [sheye-AN]

The 19,000-acre shallow freshwater inland lake and basin was often dry before the Kansas Fish and Game Commission diverted Arkansas River water to it. Representative Clifford Hope (Garden City) introduced a bill in 1927 to create the wildlife refuge and work began on it in the 1940s. Not only does the shallow lake with its marshes attract thousands of migrating cranes, snipes, gulls, and other waterfowl in the spring and fall, but over three hundred species of birds also nest there. Long before the bottoms became a wildlife refuge, the Cheyenne Indians defeated the Pawnees in battle here—hence the name.

CHEYENNE BOTTOMS

Cheyenne County *(Established March 20, 1873)*

For many years the Cheyenne Indians lived and hunted in this high plains country.
Pop. 3,678

Chikaskia *(Sumner)* [chuh-KAS-ki-uh]

The Pawnee Indian name (whose meaning unfortunately is unknown) is applied to a town and three townships as well as the river flowing through the county. In 1984 Chris Madson, a naturalist, called the Chikaskia "one of the most beautiful and pristine" rivers in Kansas.
PO: October 19, 1871–February 26, 1886

Chingawassa Springs *(Marion)* [CHING-a-wah-suh]

The healing, invigorating mineral springs at Chingawassa attracted many visitors in the late nineteenth century. Sometime between 1873 and 1888 the name of the springs was changed from *Carter's Mineral Springs* to *Chingawassa* for an Osage chief whose name meant "handsome bird." After five Kansas State Agricultural College (now Kansas State University) faculty members visited the spring in 1888, they suggested that the springs could possibly become a famous health resort rivaling the Hot Springs of Arkansas. Marion County entrepreneurs promoted the health spa successfully until the 1890s, when interest declined and a nationwide financial depression closed down the Chingawassa Railroad.

Chisholm Trail *(South Central Kansas)* [CHIZ-uhm]

In trading with Indians, Jesse Chisholm traveled between the North Canadian River in Oklahoma and present-day Wichita. Joseph McCoy, the Illinois stockman who built cattle yards at Abilene, suggested that the trail Chisholm used be extended south to the Red River, the southern border of Indian Territory. The Chisholm Trail in Kansas ran roughly parallel to the present-day locations of U.S. Highway 81 and I-35 from Oklahoma to Wichita, then north through western Marion County and on to Abilene. At least a million cattle made it to Abilene over this trail.

Cimarron *(Gray)* [SIM-uh-rahn]

This western Kansas town is located near the Cimarron Crossing of the Santa Fe Trail, where one branch of the trail headed south to the Cimarron River. Here is a case of the destination giving the name to the town. The same was true for the Santa Fe Trail, which went from Missouri to Santa Fe.
PO: March 28, 1878–; Pop. 1,491; CS

Cimarron National Grasslands *(Morton)*

During the 1930s, much of this land was overcultivated and became severely wind eroded. The U.S. Forest Service has taken 107,000 acres out of cultivation and is attempting to restore the natural short-grass prairie.

Cimarron River *(Southwest Kansas)*

In Spanish, *cimarron* means "wild" or "unruly." The Cimarron River begins in New Mexico, cuts across a corner of Colorado, and meanders through far southwest Kansas. According to one historian, the only thing the Cimarron lacked was water!

Circleville *(Jackson)*

When the town was formed, it was named after the former home of a local resident, Mr. Cook—Circleville, Ohio. Until that time the unofficial name had been *New Brighton.*
PO: July 27, 1861–; Pop. 164

Claflin *(Barton)* [KLAF-lin]

Once known as *Giles City*, Claflin was renamed for founder O. P. Hamilton's wife, whose maiden name was Claflin. Her first husband, Roswell P. Gould, was the brother of railroad magnate and financier Jay Gould.
PO: May 27, 1887–; Pop. 764

Clark County *(Established March 7, 1885)*

First established February 16, 1867, the county was abolished in 1883, then recreated in 1885. The county took its name from Captain Charles Clarke of the Sixth Kansas Cavalry, who died in Memphis in 1862. The Kansas legislature dropped the final *e*.
Pop. 2,599

Clay Center *(Clay)*

Clay Center is the centrally located county seat of Clay County.
PO: July 3, 1862–; Pop. 4,948; CS

Clay County *(Established February 27, 1857)*

The county was named after the distinguished Kentucky legislator Henry Clay.
Pop. 9,802

Clayton *(Norton)*

The village was called *Cameron* until a town storekeeper thought the name should reflect the fact that clay was plentiful in the area.
PO: March 31, 1879–; Pop. 102

Clearwater (Sedgwick)

The Osage-Siouan word Ninnescah means "spring water," "running water," "good water," and "clear water." This town uses an English version.
PO: April 5, 1871–; Pop. 1,684

Clifton (Washington)

Clifton was named for a well-liked government surveyor who was once on the site. The township took the same name.
PO: August 26, 1862–; Pop. 695

Climax (Greenwood)

The community used the name Bell Grove until it was re-named Climax because of its elevated location near the head-waters of the Fall River.
PO: September 8, 1880–; Pop. 81

Clinton (Douglas)

Now located on a peninsula in Clinton Lake, this town was one of the pioneer communities of Douglas County. Immigrants named it for their former home in Clinton, Illinois.
PO: August 30, 1858–November 30, 1927; Pop. 30

Clinton Lake (Douglas)

The lake and state park, containing approximately seven thousand acres, were opened to the public in 1980.

Clonmel (Sedgwick) [KLAHN-mel]

Between 1872 and 1876, a group of Irish families emigrated from Johnson County, Iowa, to homestead on Osage Trust Lands in Sedgwick County. They brought the name Clonmel from a town in southern Ireland.
PO: March 14, 1905–June 30, 1938

Cloud County (Established May 27, 1867)

In a light-hearted mood, a member of the committee on coun-ties in the 1860 territorial legislative session suggested nam-ing a county for Jane Shirley, a "notorious Leavenworth pros-titute" known to all "the boys." Joining in on the joke, the majority voted for Shirley. (The name Sherman, for John Sherman, had been suggested, but lost to Shirley.) The name Shirley remained until county representative John B. Rupe, angry at the "stigma and burlesque" attached to his county's name, introduced a bill substituting the name of Cloud, in

honor of Colonel William F. Cloud of the Second Kansas. Rupe considered Cloud one of the "noblest and bravest of the state's heroes," a man and a name of which the people could be proud.
Pop. 12,494

Clyde *(Cloud)*

David Turner, Sr., one of the town's founders, spent much of his boyhood enjoying the beauty of the River Clyde in Scotland before moving to Kansas. The town company had considered *Elkhorn, Shirley,* and *Colfax* before deciding on Clyde.
PO: November 30, 1868–; Pop. 909

Coats *(Pratt)*

Town-site owner William A. Coats named the town for himself.
PO: June 7, 1887–; Pop. 153

Coffey County *(Established August 25, 1855)*

The county was named after Asbury M. Coffey, a member of the first Kansas territorial legislature. Despite the fact that Coffey was a southern sympathizer and a colonel in the Confederacy, the county retained the name.
Pop. 9,370

Coffeyville *(Montgomery)*

In July 1869 James A. Coffey built a house and trading post near the present intersection of Fifteenth and Walnut streets. Early Coffeyville depended on trade with the Osage Indians and cattlemen. In 1892, the Dalton Gang, who lived near Coffeyville, raided the town and tried to rob two banks, but an alert citizenry shot three of the robbers. Another claim to fame is that internationally known political figure and presidential candidate Wendell Wilkie taught U.S. history at the high school in Coffeyville in 1914.
PO: December 13, 1869–; Pop. 15,185

Colby *(Thomas)*

Early settler J. R. Colby published the first Thomas County newspaper.
PO: April 8, 1881–; Pop. 5,544; CS

Coldwater *(Comanche)*

Two parties seeking a town site were surveying land in the same area near Cavalry Creek. C. D. Bickford of Coldwater,

Michigan, offered to abandon his claim if the other party named the town *Coldwater*.
PO: October 17, 1884–; Pop. 989; CS

Collyer *(Trego)* [KAHL-yer]

The trading center was founded in 1878 by a soldier and sailor colony from Chicago. Rev. Robert Collyer was president of the organization.
PO: May 3, 1878–; Pop. 151

Colony *(Anderson)*

A colony of settlers from Ohio and Indiana could not think of anything more imaginative than the name *Colony* for their town.
PO: April 3, 1872–; Pop. 474

Columbus *(Cherokee)*

This county seat is located almost exactly in the geographical center of Cherokee County. In 1868 A. L. Peters named the town *Columbus* after his home town in Ohio.
PO: June 24, 1869–; Pop. 3,426; CS

Colwich *(Sedgwick)*

The name was coined from the first syllables of the Colorado and Wichita Railroad on which the town was located.
PO: December 18, 1885–; Pop. 935

Comanche County *(Established February 26, 1867)*

The Comanche Indians once hunted throughout this county as well as all of western Kansas and eastern Colorado.
Pop. 2,554

Concordia *(Cloud)*

Two communities agreed to organize Concordia in 1869 in order to enter the county seat contest. Concordia got the most votes, yet it was no more than a name on a piece of paper. To ensure that the county seat would remain where planned, the mastermind of the Concordia movement built a road at his own expense from Junction City to Concordia and used political influence to get the Land Office there in 1871. The late Frank Carlson, former Kansas governor, U.S. representative, and U.S. senator, was from Concordia.
PO: June, 1870–; Pop. 6,847; CS

Conway *(McPherson)*

Located by the Santa Fe Railroad in 1880, the town was named Conway after a railroad official.
PO: June 29, 1880–; Pop. 75

Conway Springs *(Sumner)*

Early settlers enjoyed the sparkling clear spring water at the site. J. L. Johnson, a local resident, named the town for his old home town in New Hampshire and for a favorite author, Moncure D. Conway.
PO: October 13, 1864–; Pop. 1,313

Coolidge *(Hamilton)*

Thomas Jefferson Coolidge, former president of the Atchison, Topeka, and Santa Fe Railroad, left his name on this town.
PO: July 5, 1881–; Pop. 82

Copeland *(Gray)*

A secretary-treasurer of the Santa Fe Railroad, E. L. Copeland, gave his name to this community.
PO: October 26, 1912–; Pop. 323

Corning *(Nemaha)*

New York businessman Erastus Corning, president of two railroads and a director of eight others, promoted railroads in northeast Kansas. For that reason his name was put on one of the stations of the Atchison and Pike's Peak Railroad (Missouri Pacific branch).
PO: September 23, 1868–; Pop. 158

Coronado Heights *(Saline)* [KOR-oh-NAH-dah]

The idea that Spanish explorer Francisco de Coronado stood on the highest of the Smoky Hill Buttes is derived more from fancy than from fact. Early settlers of the area called the prominence *Smoky Hill,* it being one of many hills in the Smoky Hills highlands in central Kansas. The name changed in the 1930s to the historically appealing *Coronado Heights* when Saline County obtained Works Progress Administration funds to construct a medieval-style sandstone shelter house, twelve picnic units, and a serpentine road to the crest. The grand panoramic view from the summit spans large tracts of farmland, the town of Lindsborg, and the Smoky Hill River Valley.

Cottonwood Falls *(Chase)*

Cottonwood Falls and Strong City are known as the "twin cities" of Chase County. The older, Cottonwood Falls, began when three Dunkard families settled near Jacob's Creek and Isaac M. Alexander laid out a town overlooking a falls in the Cottonwood River. In 1872, the Santa Fe Railroad built a line a mile from Cottonwood Falls and put in a station they called *Cottonwood Station.* That name was changed to *Strong City* in 1881 for W. B. Strong, then president of the Santa Fe Railroad. The "twin cities" were connected by an interurban track in the early days. Cottonwood Falls, the county seat, has the oldest courthouse building in Kansas, a majestic French Second Empire–style structure built between 1871 and 1873.
PO: September 16, 1858–; Pop. 954; CS

Cottonwood River *(East Central Kansas)*

The river arising in Marion County was called the Cottonwood as early as 1844. The cottonwood tree grows throughout Kansas and is the state tree.

Council Grove *(Morris)*

In 1825 growing traffic on the Santa Fe Trail brought about a government survey and right-of-way treaties with certain Indians. George Sibley, a member of that survey party, wrote: "As we propose to Meet the Osage Chiefs in council Here, to negotiate a Treaty with them for the Road cc. I suggested the propriety of naming the place 'Council Grove.' " The grove refers to a large grove of trees in which the council met. The name *Council Grove* was carved on a "venerable" large white oak tree.
PO: February 26, 1855–; Pop. 2,381; CS

Countryside *(Johnson)*

In 1937, Frank Hodges looked at the pleasant surroundings of this town site and named it *Countryside.*
PO: none listed; Pop. 346

Courtland *(Republic)*

The name *Courtland* was probably after Cortland, New York.
PO: January 30, 1888–; Pop. 377

Cow Creek Crossing *(Rice)*

Where the Santa Fe Trail crossed Cow Creek, Asahel Beach and his son Abijah established a trading ranch from which

they hunted buffalo, sold hides and meat, traded with the Indians, raised produce, and sold it and other provisions to the Santa Fe travelers. William Mathewson, the original "Buffalo Bill," worked at the crossing after its beginning in 1858 and owned it from 1864 to 1867. Also called Beach Valley; (*see* Buffalo Bill's Well.)
PO: February 10, 1859–June 22, 1866 (Beach Valley)

Cowley County *(Established February 13, 1867)*

Lieutenant Matthew Cowley of the Ninth Kansas Cavalry died in service in October 1864. The Kansas legislature named the county for the war hero.
Pop. 36,824

Coyville *(Wilson)*

Coyville claims to be the oldest town in Wilson County, dating back to 1859 when Albert Hagen opened the first store and began trading with the Delaware Indians. After Oscar Coy and A. P. Steele bought Hagen's store in 1864, they named the village *Coyville*.
PO: May 2, 1866–; Pop. 98

Crawford County *(Established February 13, 1867)*

Both the county and the town of Crawfordville were named for Samuel J. Crawford, governor of Kansas from 1865 to 1868.
Pop. 37,916

Crawford County State Park *(Crawford)*

In 1928, the citizens of Pittsburg, Kansas, purchased 439 acres of land, 80 percent of it abandoned coal strip pits. The land was transferred to the state, which converted the area from an ugly wasteland to a rugged, well-timbered tract with many beautiful narrow lakes.

Crestline *(Cherokee)*

The first settlers named the site after Crestline, Ohio.
PO: July, 1875–; Pop. 135

Crystal Spring *(Marion)*

The largest spring in Marion County has supplied the city of Florence with water since 1920. The spring is located two miles north of Florence.

Cuba *(Republic)* [KU-buh]

Bohemians and Swedes founded the town in 1873, and it was often called the Bohemian capital of Kansas because it had the largest Bohemian colony in Kansas. Swedes, Scots, Irish, French-Canadians, and Americans also settled there. Most likely the founders chose the name of the Bohemian capital of Kuba for their town in Kansas. Americans spelled the name with a *C* rather than a *K*.
PO: March 23, 1868–; Pop. 286

Cullison *(Pratt)*

Mary M. and John B. Cullison deeded land to the original town of Cullison.
PO: August 14, 1885–; Pop. 154

Culver *(Ottawa)*

Lieutenant George W. Culver lost his life in the fight with Indians at Beecher Island, Colorado, in September 1868.
PO: April 14, 1873–; Pop. 167

Cummings *(Atchison)*

Beginning in 1872, the *Cummingsville* post office was named for prominent citizen William Cummings. Residents preferred the shorter *Cummings* and had the name changed.
PO: December 1, 1873–; Pop. 80

Cunningham *(Kingman)*

Farmer James D. Cunningham promoted the town site on his farm by offering two lots to each person who settled there. He planned the town in the form of a cross.
PO: May 29, 1888–; Pop. 540

Dalby *(Atchison)*

The Missouri Pacific named a rail station for James Dalby, one of the railroad's officials. Hetherby Cemetery, the oldest cemetery in Atchison County, is located there.

Damar *(Rooks)* [duh-MAHR]

Possibly named for pioneer land owner D. M. Marr. The settlement has been called the "Acadia of Western Kansas" because many of its people were of French-Canadian descent.
PO: February 5, 1894–; Pop. 204

Danceground Cemetery *(Jackson)*

This cemetery, with its walled graves, is a traditional Potawatomi burial ground. The walls are remnants of grave "houses," apparently built as residences for the spirits of the dead.

Danville *(Harper)*

The settlement was first called *Coleville* from Mrs. E. J. Cole, then changed to *Danville* for her son Dan. The change may also have been influenced by the fact that several residents came from Danville, Ohio.
PO: May 25, 1882–; Pop. 71

Dearing *(Montgomery)*

A Mr. Andrews named the town to honor his neighbor, Mr. Dearing.
PO: January 7, 1888–; Pop. 475

Decatur County *(Established March 6, 1873)*

This western county took its name from Commodore Stephen Decatur, known for his daring attack and victory over the Barbary pirates near Tripoli and his service in the War of 1812. The last Indian raid in Kansas took place in this county at Sappa Creek in 1878. One early settler told why he chose to live in Decatur County: "I first saw the Sappa Valley . . . in September, 1872. . . . Buffalo were plentiful, and at night beavers splashed in the creek. Going to camp from a buffalo killing one evening about sunset, I counted 200 skunks, an occasional deer, antelope or turkey was encountered and wolves were all about, I considered it a hunter's paradise."
Pop. 4,509

Deerfield *(Kearny)*

The town is said to be named for the large herd of deer that grazed in that vicinity in the early days. It could also have been named for Sam Dear, a Santa Fe Railroad official.
PO: March 3, 1882–; Pop. 538

Delavan *(Morris)* [DEL-uh-van]

In order to get the railroad station near his property, Henry Kingman of Delavan, Illinois, donated eighty acres of land for the town site in 1885. Kingman built the first general store and became the first postmaster and the first depot agent.
PO: July 20, 1886–; Pop. 100

Delaware *(Wyandotte)*

The name *Delaware,* used for several places in Kansas, was taken from the Indian tribe residing on the Delaware Trust lands in Kansas. Delaware township is at the southwest corner of the county.
PO: September 10, 1850–February 1, 1856

Delaware River *(Nemaha and Jefferson)*

This river was called the *Grasshopper* as early as 1819. After grasshopper plagues made the name most unpopular, it was changed to *Delaware* for the Indians living in the area.

Delia *(Jackson)*

A station on a branch line of the Union Pacific was named *Delia* for Mrs. Delia Cunningham.
PO: January 12, 1906–; Pop. 181

Delphos *(Ottawa)* [DEL-fus]

Levi Yockey, the first postmaster, named it in memory of his home town, Delphos, Ohio. The word *Delphos* originated from the ancient Greek town of Delphi. This town was platted on land owned by W. A. Kiser in 1869 and 1870.
PO: November 13, 1866–; Pop. 570

Denison *(Jackson)*

A town promoter from Dennison, Ohio, deserves credit for the name.
PO: December 13, 1887–; Pop. 231

DELAWARE RIVER

Denmark *(Lincoln)*

Danish immigrants founded Denmark in Lincoln County in 1869. For many years they operated cooperative dairy farms.
PO: May 2, 1872–February 29, 1904; March 30, 1917–January 31, 1954

Denton *(Doniphan)*

Four Denton brothers from England lived on the site, called *Dentonville* by neighbors for twelve years. The name was shortened to *Denton* in 1905.
PO: March 13, 1888–February 17, 1905, as Dentonville; February 17, 1905–; Pop. 156

Derby *(Sedgwick)*

The second-largest town in Sedgwick County was founded first as *El Paso* around 1871. In 1880, the Santa Fe Railroad changed the name from *El Paso* to *Derby* (after a Santa Fe official) to end any confusion with El Paso, Texas, on its line. *Derby* was commonly used, but legally and officially the name remained *El Paso*. In an unusual move, some Derby residents petitioned to recognize the old name of *El Paso* and forget about *Derby*. Only a citizen vote could change the name and that occurred in 1956 when citizens voted to keep the name *Derby* and a court order made it official.
PO: July 5, 1881–; Pop. 9,786

De Soto *(Johnson)*

Those who laid out the town in 1857 named it after the famous Spanish adventurer, Hernando de Soto.
PO: January 14, 1863–; Pop. 2,061

Devizes *(Norton)* [deh-VIH-zez]

This was the first settlement in the northwest part of Norton County. Homesteader Ruben Bisbee named the community *Devizes* after a post office he lived near in Ontario, Canada.
PO: March 4, 1874–April 15, 1926

Dexter *(Cowley)*

This may be the only Kansas town named for a horse—Dexter, a great trotter owned by Robert Bonner of New York, who paid $35,000 for him. Bonner and the horse Dexter were traveling through the area at the time the town was being organized. During his racing career Dexter ran fifty races, winning forty-eight of them for a total of $67,100. He died in

DEXTER

1888 at the age of thirty. Artists Currier and Ives immortalized Dexter in one of their paintings.
PO: July 14, 1870–; Pop. 366

Diamond Spring *(Morris)*

> They called you "Diamond of the Plain,"
> So great was the far-reaching fame,
> When o'er the prairies heated wild,
> They stopped to taste a beverage mild.
> No water flowed so full and free
> Along the Trail to Santa Fe—
> Dear Old Diamond, Diamond Springs."
> —George P. Morehouse

George Sibley, Santa Fe Trail surveyor, camped near the spring in 1827 and wrote: "This spring is very large, runs off boldly among Rocks, is perfectly accessible and furnished the greatest abundance of most excellent, clear, cold sweet water. It may be appropriately called 'The Diamond of the Plains.' "

Dickinson County *(Established February 20, 1857)*

Daniel S. Dickinson, U.S. senator from New York, introduced a Senate resolution in 1847 respecting territorial government. The resolution embodied the doctrine of popular sovereignty, which affected Kansas settlement and politics during the 1850s.
Pop. 20,175

Dighton *(Lane)*

The county seat was named for Richard Deighton, surveyor of Ness City, county seat of adjacent Ness County. Deighton

had studied and qualified as a civil engineer and as a result was much in demand by new settlers. He spent several years surveying in Rush, Ness, Lane, Scott, Trego, and Pawnee counties. The *e* in Deighton was dropped.
PO: March 26, 1879–; Pop. 1,390; CS

Dodge City *(Ford)*

The settlement was first called *Buffalo City* because of an estimated twenty-five million buffalo in the surrounding territory. When the prospective *Buffalo* postmaster made application for a post office, he was informed that mail was already being delivered to a Buffalo, Kansas; the federal Post Office therefore suggested the town be named *Dodge City*. The name made sense since the town site was adjacent to Fort Dodge Military Reservation. Colonel Richard I. Dodge was the fort commander at the time (1872), and the fort had been named for his uncle, Colonel Henry I. Dodge. Dodge City became the "Cowboy Capital of the World." Between 1875 and 1885 cattlemen drove thousands of longhorns up from Texas and New Mexico. Business flourished while Dodge City became the most notorious of all cattle towns; its notoriety lasted the longest of any of the famous cowtowns on the old railroad frontier.
PO: September 23, 1872–; Pop. 18,001; CS

Donaldville *(Atchison)*

Miners eager to profit from a coal deposit built cabins and shanties along the banks of Whiskey Creek. The community prospered for a while in the 1890s, but when the coal played out, the miners abandoned their shanties. The miners were probably Scottish, because *whiskey* means "water" in Gaelic, but the word had a very different significance in Kansas during prohibition. The name therefore was changed to *Donaldville*. It was Atchison County's one and only mining camp.

DODGE CITY

Doniphan *(Doniphan)* [DON-uh-fuhn]

Town founders had high hopes in 1854 of making Doniphan a major market on the Missouri. But when the land office and businesses moved to more vigorous nearby towns, Doniphan settled back to being a quiet village. Like the county, Doniphan was named after Colonel Alexander W. Doniphan.
PO: March 3, 1855 to August 15, 1943

Doniphan County *(Established August 25, 1855)*

This was the first Kansas county to be named; it took its name from Alexander W. Doniphan, a colonel in the Mexican War of 1846. Bordered on three sides by the Missouri River, the county offered great advantages for markets up and down the navigable river.
Pop. 9,268

Dorrance *(Russell)* [DOR-uhns]

O. B. Dorrance, a superintendent on the Kansas Pacific Railway, was the source for the town's name. All NBA basketball hoops are manufactured here by the Gared Tossback Company.
PO: July 9, 1883–; Pop. 220

Douglas County *(Established August 25, 1855)*

The name of Illinois Democratic Senator Stephan A. Douglas, author of the Kansas-Nebraska bill that opened Kansas to settlement and enlarged the slavery controversy by opening Kansas and Nebraska to popular sovereignty, is perpetuated in the county's name.
Pop. 67,640

Douglass *(Butler)*

The town site was on land originally part of the Osage Reserve, a tract of land in southern Kansas originally set aside for the Osage Indians but later opened to settlement by anyone. Joseph W. Douglass was the pioneer merchant and postmaster who owned the town site.
PO: September 24, 1868–; Pop. 1,450

Dover *(Shawnee)*

Early settlers may have chosen the name *Dover* from Dover, New Hampshire, or from Dover, England. There were several English immigrants living in the township of Dover, which preceded the village.
PO: April 16, 1863–; Pop. 135

Downs *(Osborne)*

The village was named for Major William F. Downs, land commissioner and general superintendent of the western division of the Missouri Pacific Railroad.
PO: September 10, 1879–; Pop. 1,324

Dragoon Creek *(Osage and Wabaunsee)*

A U.S. soldier—a dragoon—died on the western bank of this creek.

Dresden *(Decatur)*

On May 23, 1888, Dresden was chartered by a group of eastern Kansas land promoters. German settlers named it for their home in Saxony.
PO: October 3, 1888–; Pop. 84

Dubuque *(Barton)* [duh-BUK]

Polish immigrants left Wisconsin, Illinois, and Indiana for this settlement in Kansas. Following them was a colony of Luxemburgers from Minnesota, Wisconsin, and Iowa. This last group named the town for Dubuque, Iowa.
PO: February 17, 1879–April 30, 1909

Dunlap *(Morris)*

Indian trader and agent Joseph Dunlap founded the town in 1874 and built the first house. In 1878 approximately three hundred freedmen located a colony adjacent to the town, making Dunlap one of Kansas' larger black settlements at that time.
PO: April 20, 1874–; Pop. 82

Durham *(Marion)*

Before ranchers brought pedigreed cattle to Kansas, cowboys drove the lean, bony, wild Texas longhorns to Kansas to fatten. In an effort to improve the quality of the herds, Albert Crane and other ranchers introduced blooded cattle and sometimes crossed them with the longhorns. In the 1870s, Crane imported domestic and foreign bred shorthorns, often called Durhams for their origin in Durham County, England. Crane's Durham Park herd reportedly had the "highest priced blood lines in the world." When he sold his ranch in the 1880s, part of it went to the town company that platted Durham.
PO: September 19, 1887–; Pop. 130

Dutch Avenue *(Harvey and Reno)*

A large number of German-Russian immigrants settled in Harvey and eastern Reno counties. Along the road from Hesston to Buhler, German-named landowners prevailed, giving rise to the term *Dutch Avenue (Deutsche Strasse)*. The names of Goering, Jantz, Schrag, Schmidt, Lorhentz, Wedel, Toevs, Harder, Fast, Ratzlaff, and Ediger still predominate.

Dwight *(Morris)*

Land for the town site was purchased from Dwight Rathbone and Jessee Hammer, judge of the Probate Court.
PO: March 19, 1887–; Pop. 320

Earlton *(Neosho)*

Earlton, established in 1884, was named for a settler known as Mr. Earle.
PO: July 3, 1877–October 1, 1950, as Earleton; October 1, 1950–; Pop. 79

Eastborough *(Sedgwick)*

This enclave of the well-to-do of Wichita originated in the mind of real estate developer Alton Smith, who envisioned a

DUTCH AVENUE

residential community with winding roads, parks, and beautiful houses. His company, Eastborough Estates Company, built five houses in 1926. The economic depression slowed development until the late 1930s and the 1940s. Although once a mile east of Wichita, Eastborough is now surrounded by Wichita but remains an unincorporated third-class city that excludes commercialism. In 1985, Eastborough ranked as the third-wealthiest city in Kansas, with a per capita income of $47,096.
Pop. 910

Easton *(Leavenworth)*

The town was originally named *Eastin* for its founder, Lucian J. Eastin, a proslavery man. Within a year the spelling was changed to *Easton,* the name of Kansas Governor Reeder's home town in Pennsylvania.
PO: December 21, 1855–; Pop. 460

Edgerton *(Johnson)*

Town founders chose the name *Edgerton* for the chief engineer of the Santa Fe Railroad.
PO: July 14, 1871–; Pop. 1,214

Edmond *(Norton)*

A merchant named Weaver wanted a town named for him, but there was already a *Weaver* in Kansas. Jack Edmond, a smooth, fast-talking salesman, offered Weaver forty sacks of flour if he would name the town *Edmond.*
PO: June 3, 1879–; Pop. 56

Edna *(Labette)*

Who could claim the honor? Edna Prouty? Edna Brink? or Edna Gregory? Local historians favor Edna Prouty, daughter of William Prouty.
PO: April 4, 1878–; Pop. 537

Edson *(Sherman)*

Ed Harris and his son settled here.
PO: September 12, 1888–; Pop. 50

Edwards County *(Established March 7, 1874)*

William C. Edwards and the Edwards family had extensive landholdings south of Kinsley in the early 1870s. In 1874, while organization of the last of the western Kansas counties

was under consideration, the name *Edwards* seemed appropriate. After all, the Edwards family had been among the first settlers in the area. Furthermore, W. C. Edwards wanted a county to be named for him.
Pop. 4,271

Edwardsville *(Wyandotte)*

The town site is on farmland once belonging to Half Moon, a Delaware Indian. It was named for John H. Edwards, then general manager and ticket agent of the Union Pacific Railroad and afterward a state senator from Ellis County. One of Edwardsville's most illustrious citizens was Junius Groves, the "Kaw Valley Potato King." From his thousand-acre farm, he shipped potatoes by the trainload all over the United States during the early 1900s.
PO: January 9, 1867–; Pop. 3,364

Effingham *(Atchison)*

Effingham H. Nichols was a Boston-based promoter of the Union Pacific Railroad, Central Branch.
PO: January 20, 1868–; Pop. 634

Elbing *(Butler)*

Mennonite immigrants often took place names from their home towns in Europe. One group of Mennonites settling in Butler County chose the name *Elbing,* for a Baltic town in Prussia.
PO: November 2, 1887–; Pop. 175

El Cuartelejo *(Scott)* [el-KWAR-tuh-lay-ho]

The ruins of the only known Indian pueblo in Kansas are in Lake Scott State Park. About 1639, the Taos Indians migrated to the Scott County area to escape the Spanish. They built a seven-room pueblo before returning to what is now New Mexico. Another group came in 1696 and lived here until 1706. *El Cuartelejo* means something like "little barracks."

El Dorado *(Butler)* [EL-dor-AY-doh]

"El Dorado!" exclaimed Joseph Cracklin upon first seeing the site in 1857. Aware that *El Dorado* meant "a place of wealth and abundance," he chose that name because of the site's beauty and golden countryside. Unknown to him, great riches lay deep below the ground on which he stood. That wealth was brought to the surface during the oil boom beginning in 1915 with Stapleton No. 1, the discovery well of the

El Dorado oil field, a part of the vast Mid-Continent field. For several years, Kansas ranked third in oil production in the United States.

PO: November 14, 1860–; Pop. 10,510; CS

Elephant Rock *(Decatur)*

The large rock formation, visible for many miles, has two holes in it, one the "eye" of an elephant and the other the space under the body and beneath the legs.

ELEPHANT ROCK

Elgin *(Chautauqua)* [EL-jin]

"The biggest shipping point in the world!" That's what was said of little Elgin when it was the terminal for all the cattle from the southwest and Texas. L. P. Getman started the town and built the first store. *Elgin* is a Scottish name used frequently for place names in the United States. The largest *Elgin* is in Illinois.

PO: February 27, 1871–; Pop. 139

Elk City *(Montgomery)*

Elk City was located on the already named Elk River.

PO: November 5, 1869–; Pop. 404

Elk County *(Established March 3, 1875)*

The county also took its name from the Elk River.

Pop. 3,918

Elk Falls *(Elk)*

The first town in Elk County derived its name from a nearby spot on the Elk River where the water falls over a projecting ledge of rock 10 feet high and 100 feet wide. One of the town's most famous residents was Prudence Crandall, the woman who had dared to open a school for black girls in Canterbury, Connecticut, in 1833. Townspeople there perse-

cuted both teacher and students until the school had to close. Prudence was jailed; her case reached the Supreme Court of the United States, where it was dismissed on a technicality. Prudence Crandall Philleio (her husband died in 1874) and her brother Hezekiah were living in Illinois when a Kansas man persuaded them to trade their Illinois home sight unseen for land near Elk Falls, Kansas. They moved immediately to their new home. Both Prudence and Hezekiah are now buried in the Elk Falls Cemetery.
PO: May 19, 1870–; Pop. 151

Elk River *(Southeast Kansas)*

The Indians named the river for the great herds of elk that grazed around the headwaters of the river. The English word *elk* was often used for township names, creeks, and other places.

Elkhart *(Morton)*

The "metropolis of Morton County" is located in the far southwestern corner of Kansas, almost on the Oklahoma border. The name was brought from Elkhart, Indiana. The late Glenn Cunningham, holder of the world's record for the mile in the 1930s and a member of the U.S. Olympic team in 1932 and 1936, grew up in Elkhart.
PO: May 9, 1913–; Pop. 2,243; CS

Ellinwood *(Barton)*

This town is said to be named after John Ellinwood, who surveyed for most of the Santa Fe Railroad across Kansas. In the early years, four-fifths of the residents were of German ancestry and gave German names to all north-south streets except for the main street, which they named Washington. For example, there are Wielan, Goethe, Schiller, Bismark, Humbolt, Arndt, Wilhelm, and Fritz.
PO: August 5, 1872–; Pop. 2,508

Ellis *(Ellis)*

This town takes its name from the county name. The automobile manufacturer Walter Chrysler spent his boyhood years in Ellis.
PO: June 27, 1870–; Pop. 2,062

Ellis County *(Established February 26, 1867)*

George Ellis left Pennsylvania for Kansas, where he enlisted in the Twelfth Kansas Infantry. He fought Quantrill's raiders

at Lawrence in 1863 and later lost his life at Jenkins Ferry, Arkansas, on April 30, 1864. Kansas legislators honored First Lieutenant Ellis by naming a county for him.
Pop. 26,098

Ellsworth *(Ellsworth)*

Before either the town or the county was organized, Fort Ellsworth had existed on the banks of the Smoky Hill River. Second Lieutenant Allen Ellsworth had established a small fort in June 1864. Although the fort was abandoned in 1866, the name remained for the town, which was surveyed in 1867. Early Ellsworth prospered from the Texas cattle trade, from railroad construction, and from fifteen hundred soldiers and government employees stationed four miles away at Fort Harker.
PO: July 3, 1867–; Pop. 2,465; CS

Ellsworth County *(Established February 26, 1867)*

The Kansas legislature named the county after Allen Ellsworth, the second lieutenant in command at Fort Ellsworth.
Pop. 6,640

Elmdale *(Chase)*

This community was named after the elm trees abundant in early Kansas.
PO: January 7, 1873–; Pop. 109

Elsmore *(Allen)*

When founded in the early 1860s, the village used the Danish place name *Elsinore* made famous in Shakespeare's *Hamlet*. The village was moved in 1887 when the Missouri, Kansas and Texas Railroad built through the area. When the name of the town was being painted on the new depot, said Wayne Corley, a Kansas place names historian, the painter failed to dot the *i* in *Elsinore* so that it appeared to be an *m* instead of *in*. No one corrected the mistake. In his *History of Kansas* (1883), Andreas used both *Elsmore* and *Elsinore* on the map, *Elsmore* for the township and *Elsinore* for the town.
PO: February 11, 1889–; Pop. 104

Elwood *(Doniphan)*

First called *Roseport* by a town promoter named Rose, who invested ten thousand dollars in the town site in 1856. He persuaded other investors to join him in a town company and

make Roseport a great inland river port. When fellow town company directors discovered that Rose was an ex-convict, they drove him out, put John B. Elwood in charge, and renamed the town for him. Elwood flourished as a river port until a flood on the Missouri River in 1860 cut away a large part of the town. Repeated floods have diminished Elwood even more.
PO: June 10, 1857–; Pop. 1,275

Elyria *(McPherson)* [uh-LEER-ee-yuh]

The original town, named *King City*, began battling for county seat designation in 1875 but lost out to McPherson. Town leaders decided to move the site closer to the railroad; in doing so, they changed the name to *Elyria*, a name suggested by a homesick Ohioan.
PO: February 26, 1887–February 15, 1954; Pop. 75

Emma Creek *(Harvey)*

The daughter of a pioneer family had ridden her horse out one evening to herd cattle homeward when a storm came up. She became lost along the creek bank and was never seen again. Tradition says wild animals killed her. Her name remains on the creek where she disappeared.

EMMA CREEK

Emmett *(Pottawatomie)*

A township and a town were named by Irish settlers after Robert Emmett, an Irish rebel who opposed English rule in Ireland. The hamlet of Emmett boasted of being home to Jess Willard, the world heavyweight boxing champion from 1915 to 1919.
PO: November 25, 1905–; Pop. 223

Emporia *(Lyon)*

According to the Roman historian Polybius, Emporia was a country of great wealth in North Africa under Carthaginian dominion. George Brown, editor of the Lawrence *Herald of Freedom*, recalled from his readings that "the revenue that arose from Emporia was so considerable that nearly all of the Carthaginian hopes were founded on it." Brown had that district in mind when he and others developed the frontier town of Emporia in 1857. Brown gave street names to match: Merchant, Commercial (the main street), Mechanic, Union, and Exchange. Emporia also emphasized education, especially teacher education and Emporia Normal School, which later became Emporia State University. Emporia editor William Allen White attracted nationwide attention through his *Emporia Gazette*.
PO: September 19, 1857–; Pop. 25,287; CS

Englewood *(Clark)*

Colonel C. D. Perry of Englewood, Illinois, named the town. Perry and Wichita capitalists had built the Bucklin to Dodge City railroad. Town boomers advertised Englewood as the "Star of the Western Empire," but others warned travelers to bypass Englewood, calling it a "horse thief town."
PO: February 4, 1885–; Pop. 111

Ensign *(Gray)* [EN-seyen]

G. L. Ensign established the town, naming it for himself. Such street names as Leavenworth, Dodge, Larned, and Zarah recall Kansas military forts.
PO: November 14, 1887–; Pop. 209

Enterprise *(Dickinson)*

Hoffman's Mill, Hoffman Falls, and *Enterprise Mills* were names given to the site on the south bank of the Smoky Hill River that became *Enterprise.* The number of flour millers and other manufacturing establishments that located there was large, considering the town population of only 500 in the 1880s.
PO: January 6, 1873–; Pop. 839

Erie *(Neosho)*

A post office bearing the name *Erie* was established at a trading post on April 6, 1866. *Erie* is an Iroquois name used for other places in the United States.
PO: April 6, 1866–; Pop. 1,415; CS

Esbon *(Jewell)*

Esbon was organized in August 1872, taking its name from a native New Yorker, Ezbon Kellogg. In 1882, the z was changed to s.
PO: June 26, 1874–April 21, 1880, as Esbon; May 31, 1880–June 15, 1882, as Ezbon; September 3, 1887–; Pop. 234

Eskridge *(Wabaunsee)*

Town founder Ephraim H. Sandford named *Eskridge* for his friend Colonel Charles V. Eskridge, Emporia journalist and politician. Colonel Eskridge prospered in Kansas, but the lot he bought for five hundred dollars in Eskridge was sold for taxes.
PO: October 18, 1869–; Pop. 603

Eudora *(Douglas)* [u-DOR-uh]

Long before white people came to the site, Paschal Fish, a Shawnee Indian, built a log house that he used as a hotel. Fish helped a German settlers association obtain an 800-acre town site, and the settlers then named their town after his daughter, Eudora.
PO: September 1, 1857–; Pop. 2,934; CS

Eureka *(Greenwood)*

In search of a town site, Edwin Tucker and M. L. Ashmore were traveling southwest of Burlington when they discovered a spring on the bank of a small stream. Whether they cried "Eureka" or not, this was the place. They organized a town company and proceeded with the development of Eureka.
PO: August 23, 1858–; Pop. 3,425

Everest *(Brown)*

Colonel Aaron S. Everest worked as an attorney for the Central Branch of the Missouri Pacific Railroad. He also represented Atchison County in the state senate.
PO: June 23, 1882–; Pop. 331

Fairmount *(Leavenworth)*

Settlers in the area considered the location on a hill a beautiful one and thus chose the descriptive name. Two post office names preceded Fairmount—*Little Stranger* and *Kelly's Station*.
PO: August 2, 1864–May 17, 1866, as Little Stranger; June 28, 1867–January 15, 1934, as Kelly's Station; Pop. 75

Fairview *(Brown)*

This descriptive place name is used for eleven civil units, eleven schools, five churches or chapels, and forty-two cemeteries in Kansas.
PO: March 23, 1869–; Pop. 258

Fairway *(Johnson)*

In 1938, J. C. Nichols, developer of the Country Club Plaza in Kansas City, Missouri, bought 133 acres in the Kansas City area; he planted hundreds of trees to beautify the new housing development. Nichols named the area *Fairway* because of its proximity to the then existing golf clubs at Old Mission, Mission Hills, and Kansas City.
Pop. 4,619

Fall Leaf *(Leavenworth)*

This small station on the Kansas Pacific Line was named after a Delaware Indian chief.
PO: January 28, 1868–July 31, 1894

Fall River *(Greenwood)*

The town is located on the banks of the Fall River.
PO: January 29, 1880–; Pop. 173

Falun *(Saline)* [FAWL-uhn]

A colony of approximately seventy-five persons, many of them Swedish immigrants, came from Henry County, Illinois, in 1870. Both town and township were named *Falun* after a town 130 miles northwest of Stockholm, Sweden.
PO: February 18, 1870–; Pop. 85

Fancy Creek *(Clay and Riley)*

Early in 1855, Gardner Randolph and his large family settled near the mouth of a creek that they named *Fancy Creek* because of the picturesque valley in which it is located. A township also took the name *Fancy Creek*.

Farlington *(Crawford)*

Farlington was first called *Farleyville* after one of the original settlers, a Mr. Farley. The Kansas City, Fort Scott, and Gulf Railroad changed the name to *Farlington*. Between 1870 and 1874 a large number of Swedes settled around Farlington.
PO: July 14, 1870–; Pop. 100

Farmington *(Atchison)*

At least ten states east of Kansas had a *Farmington* located in a farming area. Settlers from any one of these states may have carried the name with them; most likely they were from Farmington, Illinois.
PO: November 30, 1868–May 31, 1940; Pop. 25

Faulkner *(Cherokee)*

It is thought that this town is named for an official of the Missouri Pacific Railroad.
PO: September 18, 1886–September 1944; Pop. 20

Feterita *(Stevens)* [FET-uh-REE-tuh]

This stop on the Atchison, Topeka, and Santa Fe apparently took the name of a sorghum crop grown successfully in the southwestern part of the state.
PO: October 25, 1919–April 30, 1937

Finney County *(Established March 6, 1873)*

David Wesley Finney was lieutenant governor of Kansas when the legislature named Finney County for him. Originally from Indiana, Finney served in the Civil War and then came to Kansas in 1866. A businessman and politician, he served in the Kansas legislature for several terms.
Pop. 23,825

Flint Hills *(Eastern Kansas)*

The Flint Hills, which extend from Washington County on the north down through Cowley County and on into Oklahoma, are the only extensive area of tall-grass prairie in the eastern great plains. These hills are characteristically rolling, marked occasionally with rock outcroppings. The flint found in the hills is actually nodules on the surface and within the limestone. Many Indian tribes came from western Kansas to find flint for arrowheads, knives, and spears.

Florence *(Marion)*

Governor Samuel J. Crawford was treasurer of the town company that named Florence for his daughter. Florence Crawford married Arthur Capper, who was also an elected governor of Kansas.
PO: March 13, 1871–; Pop. 729

Flower Pot Mound *(Barber)*

This natural cone-shaped mound is located about eight miles southwest of Medicine Lodge. There, according to a story, the last of an ill-fated pioneer colony were burned at the stake.

Flush *(Pottawatomie)*

The settlement was named for Michael Floersch, an early settler in Rock Creek Valley. When the community petitioned for a post office in 1898, the federal government simplified the spelling to *Flush*.
PO: June 20, 1899–November 30, 1927

Fontana *(Miami)* [fahn-TAN-uh]

Located ten miles south of Paola, the town took its name from a spring known as "the Old Fountain." *Old Fontana*, its name in Spanish form, was established in 1858 by Richard W. Shipley and consisted of a house, a one-room store, and a blacksmith shop. In September 1869, J. B. Grinnell established Fontana at its present location, a half mile east of the original site.
PO: June 2, 1873–; Pop. 173

Forbes Field *(Shawnee)*

The large air base just south of Topeka was named for Major Daniel H. Forbes, Jr., who was killed while conducting an airplane test flight. The base was a processing center for B-17, B-24, and B-29 aircraft and crews during World War II. It is now a public airport with scheduled service and also has an Air Force and Army National Guard installation.

Ford *(Ford)*

The town was named after the county.
PO: February 2, 1885–; Pop. 272

Ford County *(Established February 26, 1867)*

This western county was named for Captain James H. Ford of the Second Colorado Cavalry; he was a brevet brigadier general of the U.S. Volunteers.
Pop. 24,315

Formoso *(Jewell)* [for-MOH-suh]

The Formoso Town Company platted the town in December 1887 while the railroad was being built through Jewell County. *Formoso* is a Portuguese word meaning "beautiful."
PO: December 17, 1887–; Pop. 166

Fort Dodge *(Ford)*

The fort was located in 1865 by Colonel James H. Ford under the command of General Grenville M. Dodge. It was named in honor of Colonel Henry I. Dodge, Indian fighter, Wisconsin senator, and uncle of General Grenville M. Dodge. The fort stood about twenty miles east of where the Santa Fe Trail branched, one route following the Arkansas River and the other a dry, but shorter, route. The fort operated until 1882 as a base for protection of travelers, stages, wagon-trains, and railroad survey and construction parties. When the need for a fort ended, the site was converted to a State Soldiers Home.
PO: October 24, 1865–; Pop. 450

Fort Hays *(Ellis)*

The frontier post was established as *Camp Fletcher* in 1865 to protect military roads, defend railroad construction crews, and guard the mail. Major General Hancock changed the name of the post to *Fort Hays* on November 17, 1866, in memory of the late General Alexander Hays, who had once been captain of a Kansas volunteer company and was wounded in battle at Jenkins Ferry. Generals Miles, Sheridan, and Custer were based here at one time. From this post, "Buffalo Bill" Cody earned his reputation while supplying railroad crews with buffalo meat. The fort was abandoned in 1889 and is now a historic site.

Fort Larned *(Pawnee)* [LARH-nuhd]

As early as 1825, the Santa Fe road-surveying party recognized the strategic importance of the fort's future location. Camp Alert was established there in October 1859 for protection of the Santa Fe Trail trade. Its name was changed in June 1860 in honor of Colonel Benjamin F. Larned, then paymaster general. The fort was an important supply base for the Army during the Civil War and the Plains Indian wars of the 1860s and 1870s. One of the best preserved and restored military forts in Kansas, it is now a National Historic Site operated by the National Park Service.
PO: April 4, 1866–September 28, 1881

Fort Leavenworth *(Leavenworth)*

The fort with the "country club air," one of the oldest military posts in the West, was named by Colonel Henry H. Leavenworth, who established it in 1827. First known as *Cantonment Leavenworth,* it served as a base for soldiers protecting travelers on the Santa Fe Trail. Early visitors to the fort, impressed with the natural beauty of the site, compared its grounds to that of "some old English Manor." Indeed, fox hunts became a favorite pastime for soldiers stationed there. Now comprising about 8,000 acres, the fort is home of the Army's Command and General Staff College as well as the U.S. Disciplinary Barracks.
PO: October 19, 1841–; Pop. 950

Fort Riley *(Geary and Riley)*

Established in 1852 as Camp Center because of its being in the center of the United States, the fort was renamed in July 1853 after General Bennet C. Riley. Riley had led the first military escort on the Santa Fe Trail and later served as California territory's last governor. He died in 1853, the year the fort was named in his honor. Fort Riley has remained an active military post for the Army. Seventy-nine percent of the post's total population resides in Riley County and the remainder in adjacent Geary County.
PO: December 20, 1855–; Pop. 2,310

Fort Scott *(Bourbon)*

Provisions were made for a camp between Fort Leavenworth and Fort Gibson, Indian Territory, as early as 1837, but it was not until 1842 that the military built a fort midway between the two and named it after General Winfield Scott. The town of Fort Scott developed on and around it. Fort Scott's buildings are being reconstructed as they were in the 1842–1853 period. Several of these buildings were opened to the public in 1975 and others are under restoration. It is a National Historic Site operated by the National Park Service.
PO: March 3, 1843–; Pop. 8,893; CS

Fort Wallace *(Wallace)*

Indian attacks on travelers over the Smoky Hill Trail to Denver and building of the Union Pacific Railroad through western Kansas led to the construction of Camp Pond Creek in 1865. The name was changed to *Camp Wallace* in 1866 in honor of General William H. L. Wallace, who died from wounds suffered at Shiloh in 1862. From 1865 to 1878 it was the most active post on the Indian frontier. The Army aban-

doned the fort in 1882, and nothing remains of the stone and wood buildings where once as many as 500 men were stationed. Only the post cemetery remains.
PO: October 3, 1866–June 1, 1882

Fostoria *(Pottawatomie)*

Fostoria, Ohio, seems to be the namesake for this Kansas town.
PO: August 14, 1884–; Pop. 50

Fowler *(Meade)*

When George Fowler was looking for homestead land, he refused to be misled by the big cattle companies that ran huge herds and fraudulently claimed that homestead land was all taken. He staked a claim in 1884 and moved his family to Kansas in 1885.
PO: January 13, 1885–; Pop. 592

Frankfort *(Marshall)*

Originally known as *Frank's Fort*, the town soon had the name *Frankfort*. It was named after real estate agent Frank Schmidt, one of the town's ten organizers and the first to build a house there. Frank Schmidt was from the German city of Frankfurt.
PO: December 28, 1869–; Pop. 1,038

Franklin *(Crawford)*

The southeastern Kansas town was named for Benjamin Franklin.
PO: October 27, 1908–; Pop. 500

Franklin County *(Established August 25, 1855)*

The first territorial legislature named the county after Benjamin Franklin, the American politician and philosopher.
Pop. 22,062

Frederick *(Rice)*

After using *Golden City*, then *Kansas Centre* for names, residents finally agreed on *Frederick* for one of the early settlers, Frederick Litchfield.
PO: May 14, 1887–May 15, 1954; Pop. 29

Fredonia *(Wilson)*

Early settler John T. Heath suggested the name *Fredonia* after Fredonia, New York. From 1869 to 1873 Fredonia contested with other towns for the county seat, finally winning by a close countywide vote in 1873.
PO: August 26, 1868–; Pop. 3,047; CS

Freedom *(Butler)*

Often the post office took the name of the postmaster. In this case, however, the federal Post Office preferred the name *Freedom* to that of the first postmaster, Adlah C. Annis.
PO: June 23, 1874–April 14, 1900

Freedom Colony *(Bourbon)*

On March 8, 1897, twelve members of the Freedom Colony mapped a town site and divided acquired land into farm plots. The community cooperatively owned a coal mine. The colonists began feuding among themselves; by 1905 most of the residents had left. The Freedom Colony was one of several unsuccessful attempts for labor reform born in the depression era of the 1890s.

Freeport *(Harper)*

The spirit of liberty may have been on the minds of the town founders when they chose the name *Freeport*. Or it could have been named after Mr. Freeman, who operated a general store here. This village of eleven residents claims to be the smallest incorporated city in the state of Kansas; the residents want to keep it that way. Mayor Ben Brooks told the *Wichita Eagle*, "We just don't want to be in the newspapers." Mary Armstrong, postmistress at one time, said, "Every time we've gotten into the paper, it's brought us trouble"; that trouble came in the form of unwanted tourists!
PO: September 16, 1885–; Pop. 11

Fremont *(McPherson)*

European immigrants, especially those coming in the 1870s, established churches in their rural neighborhoods. Swedish immigrants did this at several locations, including Fremont. After several names had been considered the congregation chose *Fremont* after the American explorer John C. Frémont, who William Johnson said "was the forerunner of civilization in the south-west so we hoped that this church organization would be a fore-runner of Swedish Evangelical Lutheran churches in the southwest." Historian Emory Lindquist states

that the local church was named *Freemount* "in conformity with the action of a Synod . . ." that was not likely to use a political name for a Christian congregation.
PO: January 23, 1895–January 30, 1932

French Ridge *(Coffey)*

For many years French Ridge was one of the liveliest communities in Coffey County, attracting young people from nearby towns to attend dances and other social activities in the dance hall on the Peter Cayot homestead. *French Ridge* referred to a neighborhood whose members had moved from France to Kansas around 1857. French Ridge Cemetery remains in the neighborhood.

Friend *(Finney)*

At one time, German Quakers were among the farmers living around Friend. Quakers are called Friends—hence the name for the place.
PO: August 19, 1887–; Pop. 50

Frontenac *(Crawford)* [FRAHN-tuh-nak]

The opening of Mine No. 1 of the Cherokee-Pittsburg Coal Company was the principal cause of the establishment of the camp called Santa Fe No. 1 in 1886. An official of the coal company, A. A. Robinson, laid out the town of Frontenac on the campsite in 1887. The French name of *Frontenac* may have

FRIEND

GALATIA

been for the colorful, egotistic, and unscrupulous Count
Frontenac, governor of New France (Canada) from 1662 to
1698, or for the French General Louis de Buade Frontenac.
This mining town has been called the melting pot of Kansas
because many of its early inhabitants immigrated from a total
of twenty-one nations. Italians dominated with 45 percent;
Germans and French had 8 percent each; 26 percent came
from seventeen other countries; the rest were of American
birth.
PO: June 23, 1887–; Pop. 2,586

Fulton *(Bourbon)*

Charles Mitchell named this town after Fulton County, Illinois, his former home county.
PO: April 6, 1876–; Pop. 194

Furley *(Sedgwick)*

Prominent Wichita physician and railroad promoter Dr. C. C.
Furley joined associates in naming the town for himself.
PO: September 20, 1887–June 30, 1953; Pop. 75

Galatia *(Barton)* [guh-LAY-shuh]

Before being called by the more cosmopolitan name of *Gala-
tia,* the town had been known as *Dogtrot.* Harry Weber, from
Galatia, Illinois, renamed the town.
PO: June 3, 1889–; Pop. 69

Galena *(Cherokee)*

The discovery of lead and development of lead mines was the
cause for starting the town in 1877. Population surged to
3,000 in two months. Miner shanties, mining excavations,

and slag heaps standing side by side made the town look rough and ugly. Even so, rivalry with the adjacent but older and more stable town of Empire City led to the building of a log wall between the two towns to discourage residents from going to prosperous Galena. The name *Galena* is derived from the mineral galena, which is the principle ore of lead. The name could also have been a transfer from Galena, Illinois. The mines are closed now, but the old part of town still holds reminders of the town's origins.
PO: May 25, 1877–; Pop. 3,587

Galesburg *(Neosho)*

The town was probably named after Galesburg, Illinois. According to historian John Rydjord, "By 1880, Illinois had more settlers in Kansas than any other state and it surpassed all the others as a source for Kansas place-names. . . ." Census figures for 1895 showed that Illinois provided 111,945 emigrants. Ohio was next with 90,354 emigrants.
PO: March 6, 1871–; Pop. 181

Galva *(McPherson)* [GAL-vuh]

A large number of persons of Swedish descent settled in the rural community of Galva. Mrs. J. E. Doyle named it after Galva, Illinois, where her father had lived.
PO: October 1, 1879–; Pop. 651

Garden City *(Finney)*

A traveling tramp who stopped by Mrs. William D. Fulton's house in the summer of 1878 asked her what they called the settlement. She said no decision had been made yet. He looked around, noted that there were no trees, but that the buffalo grass was thick and green. He said: "Why not call it Garden City, as it looks so pretty around here." The Fultons liked the name and filed the original plat of Garden City.
PO: October 8, 1878–; Pop. 18,256; CS

Garden of Eden *(Russell)*

The garden was once the home of S. P. Dinsmoor in Lucas, Kansas. Civil War veteran Dinsmoor wanted the memorial to be "the most unique home for the living or dead on earth." He used 113 tons of cement to build a concrete log cabin and scores of concrete figures. At the front of the cabin, the figures of Adam and Eve form an arch with their outstretched arms; a concrete serpent lies coiled in a treetop above them; a concrete devil leers from a nearby roof. After Dinsmoor died in 1932, his body was placed in a glass-topped concrete coffin he made himself. His coffin and one containing his first wife were placed within a mausoleum. On the roof of the mausoleum is a concrete angel, and above all that is a red, white, and blue concrete flag.

Garden Plain *(Sedgwick)*

Residents wanted their village given a "small town" name. Clinton L. Genoways, one of the settlers, suggested *Garden Plain* because of level land and its suitability for gardening. Formal town platting came in December 1883 when the Wichita and Western Branch of the Santa Fe Railroad came through.
PO: August 19, 1875–; Pop. 775

Gardner *(Johnson)*

Situated on the Santa Fe Trail, ten miles southwest of Olathe, Gardner was settled in 1857 and named for O. B. Gardner, member of the local town company and a justice of the peace. Gardner stood at the fork of the Santa Fe and Oregon trails.
PO: March 18, 1858–; Pop. 2,392

Garfield *(Pawnee)*

James A. Garfield was elected president of the United States in 1880, at the beginning of the real estate boom in western Kansas. The *Garfield* name has survived in fourteen Kansas townships as well as the town located southwest of Larned.
PO: May 28, 1886–; Pop. 277

Garland *(Bourbon)*

From February 1875 to March 1886, this village's post office used the name *Memphis*. Because the railroad had another stop called *Memphis*, a committee formed to rename the town. J. I. Million suggested the name *Garland* after a currently popular brand of stove. The local depot used such a stove.
PO: March 18, 1886–; Pop. 100

Garnett *(Anderson)* [gahr-NET]

Dr. G. W. Cooper explored Anderson County for a town site, then returned to his home in Louisville, Kentucky, where he organized a town company with wealthy businessman, W. A. Garnett as president. Mr. Garnett purchased a flour mill and sawmill for the town and provided other financial support for the new settlement.
PO: July 16, 1859–; Pop. 3,310; CS

Gas *(Allen)*

In the summer of 1898, land owner E. K. Taylor sank a well that developed a flow of gas. He sold sixty acres to a zinc smelter company, laid out part of his land into town lots, and named the place *Gas City*. Other gas wells were opened in the area.
PO: August 25, 1899–; Pop. 543

Gaylord *(Smith)*

This community was named for C. E. Gaylord of Marshall County.
PO: June 2, 1871–; Pop. 203

Geary County *(Established March 7, 1889)* [GAIR-ee]

Prosouthern sentiment dominated the 1855 Kansas territorial legislature when it first named the county for Jefferson Davis, U.S. secretary of war from 1853 to 1857. When pro-North members gained control of the legislature, they wanted to erase vestiges of southern influence. While Kansas troops were fighting on the Union side during the Civil War the people of Davis County hated having their county named for the man who had become the president of the Confederacy. Twice during the war, legislators tried to get another name, but failed. Finally, in February 1889, the legislature changed the county's name to *Geary* in memory of the highly regarded third territorial governor of Kansas, John W. Geary.
Pop. 30,800

Gem *(Thomas)* [JEM]

The Gem Ranch located in Thomas County was responsible for the name of the post office, railroad station, and the town.
PO: December 14, 1885–; Pop. 101

Geneseo *(Rice)* [gen-uh-SEE-o]

Major E. C. Modderwell of Geneseo, Illinois, brought the name *Geneseo* to Kansas.
PO: January 15, 1887–; Pop. 496

Geuda Springs *(Sumner and Cowley)* [GYOO-duh SPRINGZ]

Geuda's seven healing springs were visited first by the Ponca Indians, whose word *Geuda* meant "healing waters." The springs never became as well known as Saratoga Springs in New York or Hot Springs in Arkansas, but they were used as a health resort. A German member of the Dunkard faith who was a missionary to the Indians in 1867 used the German

word *gute* ("good") for the springs. *Gute* and *geuda* were
nearly identical in sound.
PO: June 19, 1882–; Pop. 217

Gilfillan *(Bourbon)* [gil-FIL-uhn]

From this one-industry hamlet, Robert S. Gilfillan used to
ship out thousands of railroad cars full of quarry stone. Some
of the original homes still stand.
PO: February 1, 1882–January 31, 1902

Girard *(Crawford)* [juh-RAHRD]

Girard's most famous citizen, E. Haldeman-Julius, put the
town on the map when he revolutionized the publishing industry with his mass production and advertising schemes.
Before his death in 1951, Haldeman-Julius had used the mails
to sell an estimated 500 million books. He published every-
thing from the classics of Homer to the latest novel of Upton
Sinclair. His mass-produced books, known as the Little Blue
Books, cost only a nickel. The small Kansas town also became
a socialist stronghold in 1908, when Socialist Eugene V. Debs
launched his presidential campaign from the courthouse
steps. The one time socialist "hub of the Universe" had hum-
ble beginnings. In 1868, according to local legend, Dr. C. H.
Strong started from his cabin to obtain supplies and to locate
a new town. At a point where he shot and killed a deer, Dr.
Strong put down a stick, attached some grass to it, and
named the site *Girard* after his home town Girard, Pennsylvania.
PO: September 30, 1868–; Pop. 2,888; CS

Glade *(Phillips)*

Here is another Kansas town named after a railroad engineer.
This time the Missouri Pacific claimed the honor.
PO: July 1, 1908–; Pop. 131

Glasco *(Cloud)*

John Hillhouse, a man of Scottish background, suggested the
name *Glasgow* for a town in Kansas. The postmaster sent in
the name as *Glasco*.
PO: December 13, 1869–; Pop. 710

Glen Elder *(Mitchell)*

The town name came from a combination of *glen*, meaning
"narrow valley" in Scottish, and *elder*, after the box elder
trees common to Kansas. The town began with the building
of a flour mill in 1871. The nearby Glen Elder Dam, one of the

key flood control structures in the Kansas River basin, was completed in December 1968. The 12,600-acre Lake Waconda stands behind the dam. *(See* Waconda.)
PO: July 5, 1870–; Pop. 491

Glenloch *(Anderson)* [GLEN-lok]

The Glenloch Town Company filed its plat for the town on July 20, 1889. The name is from the New York town of Glenloch.
PO: January 26, 1887–February 15, 1913

Goddard *(Sedgwick)* [GAHD-uhrd]

Located fourteen miles west of Wichita in wheat-growing country, Goddard was named for J. F. Goddard, an officer of the town company that laid out the town in 1882. Goddard once served as vice president and general manager of the Santa Fe Railway.
PO: January 10, 1884–; Pop. 1,427

Goessel *(Marion)* [GOS-el]

Around 1895, a German ship sank in the Atlantic. Captain Goessel stayed aboard until the last person was safely off, then he went down with the ship. Dr. Richert of a Mennonite community in western Marion County admired the captain and proposed the name *Goessel* be given to the new post office in the area. The town of Goessel developed at the site.
PO: April 13, 1895–; Pop. 421

Goff *(Nemaha)* [GAWF]

A Union Pacific Railroad, Central Branch, official, Edward H. Goff, had a station named for him.
PO: December 15, 1894–; Pop. 196

Golden Belt *(Central Kansas)*

The term *Golden Belt* refers to the wheat-producing region of central Kansas. For a few years, a post office in Lincoln County had the name *Golden Belt*.

Good Intent *(Atchison)*

Schoolteacher Miss Hattie Dorman, favorably impressed by an Atchison County community, started a Sunday School. Some time later, a newly established post office took the name *Good Intent*. Irish and German Catholic farmers predominated in the Good Intent community.
PO: November 8, 1872–July 31, 1900

Goodland *(Sherman)* [GOOD-luhnd]

One of the influential stockholders in the town company that started Goodland came from Goodland, Indiana.
PO: December 1, 1887–; Pop. 5,708; CS

Gorham *(Russell)* [GOR-uhm]

Elijah Dodge Gorham platted the town of Gorham in 1879.
PO: February 24, 1879–; Pop. 355

Gove *(Gove)* [GOHV]

Settlers from Davenport, Iowa, laid out Gove, the county seat for Gove County.
PO: February 13, 1886–; Pop. 148; CS

Gove County *(Established March 3, 1868)*

Captain Grenville L. Gove had the reputation of having the best drilled company in the Eleventh Kansas. When his Company G drilled, others came to watch. Gove died in 1864.
Pop. 3,700

GOOD INTENT

Graham County *(Established February 26, 1867)*

The legislature named the county for Captain John L. Graham, Company D, Eighth Kansas. He was killed in action at Chickamauga on September 19, 1863.
Pop. 3,900

Grainfield *(Gove)*

Local historians relate that John Beal, a representative of the Kansas Pacific Railroad, was driving down a road with a passenger who noticed the green field along the road and said, "Oh, what a pretty green field." By the time the name discussion for the local community took place, *Grainfield* was the choice. The name fits: "Wheat grows right up to the town's back door."
PO: May 20, 1879–; Pop. 417

Grandview Plaza *(Geary)*

The community of Grandview Plaza developed immediately east of Junction City. *Grandview* is a descriptive name.
PO: January 4, 1895–February 21, 1895; Pop. 1,189

Grant County *(Established March 6, 1873)*

The county is named after Ulysses S. Grant. The county seat is Ulysses. Several townships in Kansas were named after the Civil War hero and U.S. president.
Pop. 7,300

Grantville *(Jefferson)*

The village was first called *Kaw City*. In 1866, however, Dan Kleinhans laid out the town and named it *Grantville* after General Ulysses S. Grant.
PO: October 3, 1866–; Pop. 225

Gray County *(Established March 5, 1887)*

The highly respected Alfred Gray served as the secretary of the state Board of Agriculture from 1873 to 1880. A teacher and a lawyer, he had moved from New York to Quindaro, Kansas, in 1857.
Pop. 5,400

Great Bend *(Barton)*

For more than a century, the "great bend" of the Arkansas River had been known as the grand feeding ground of the buffalo. The Arkansas River turns north in Ford County,

making a big bend in Barton County as it turns southward toward Oklahoma. The big bend of the Arkansas became a regular stop and mail station on the Santa Fe Trail. When a new town was located on the north bank of the Arkansas River at the apex of the bend, Hiram Bickerdyke christened it *Great Bend*.
PO: January 31, 1872–; Pop. 17,400; CS

Greeley *(Anderson)*

This small town was named for Horace Greeley before the county in western Kansas was named for him.
PO: April 23, 1866–; Pop. 405

Greeley County *(Established March 6, 1873)*

The most famous newspaper editor of his time, Horace Greeley of the *New York Tribune* said he wanted Kansas to be "untainted by the pestiferous blight of slavery." Highly partisan in politics and a founder of the Republican party, he ran for the presidency against Grant in 1872 and lost. Broken by a merciless campaign, personal problems, and business failure, Greeley died on November 29, 1872. Throughout the nation, admirers of Greeley named streets, towns, townships, and counties in his memory. Greeley County in Kansas was the last of the state's 105 counties to be created. County residents continued the Greeley theme with the names of *Greeley Center*, *Horace*, *Tribune*, and even *Hector*, the name of his dog. Greeley's successor as editor had a post office— *Whitelaw*—and a village—*Reid*—named for him.
Pop. 1,900

Green *(Clay)*

While Nehemiah Green, politician and Methodist minister, served as lieutenant governor, he offered a church bell to the first town given his name. Residents of Clay County named a town *Green;* the Methodist church received the promised bell.
PO: November 2, 1881–; Pop. 155

Greenleaf *(Washington)*

Named for A. W. Greenleaf, treasurer of the Union Pacific Railroad, Central Branch.
PO: February 2, 1887–; Pop. 462

Greensburg *(Kiowa)*

Jacob Barney and Edward Coates were constructing buildings in Janesville until D. R. "Cannonball" Green, who owned land adjacent to them, ended their project. Green operated a

successful stage coach line out of Kingman into western Kansas and led a group of men called the Greensburg Town Company. Green offered every prospective resident a free lot in Greensburg and said he would move any Janesville building free of charge. Barney lost his Janesville post office one night when the Greensburg group put skids under the building and moved it into Greensburg. This town claims having the "world's largest" hand-dug well, 32 feet wide and 192 feet deep. The Big Well is listed on the National Register of Historic Places. (For more on Green, *see* Cannonball Highway.)
PO: January 27, 1885–; Pop. 1,885; CS

Greenwich *(Sedgwick)* [GREEN-wich]

James R. Mead, originally from Greenwich, Connecticut, operated a trading post in the Towanda area. The small settlement of Greenwich was a few miles to the west. The naming may have been influenced by Mead's presence.
PO: September 3, 1874; Pop. 75

Greenwich Heights *(Sedgwick)*

Located near the corner of Greenwich Road and Pawnee east of Wichita, this community has increased in size in recent years due to the expansion of the Wichita metropolitan area.
PO: September 3, 1874–; Pop. 900

Greenwood County *(Established August 25, 1855)*

According to information from the Kansas State Historical Society, "this county lies almost entirely within one of the world's great beef cattle breeding grounds." As many as 75,000 head graze on the county's 739,000 acres. The county was named after Alfred Burton Greenwood, U.S. land commissioner under Presidents Pierce and Buchanan.
Pop. 8,600

Grenola *(Elk)* [gruh-NOH-luh]

In 1879 the Kansas Railroad laid track between two small settlements, Greenfield on the north and Canola on the south. Settlement leaders moved their homes and businesses to a central point near the railroad, then combined the first and last syllables to coin the name *Grenola*.
PO: July 17, 1879–; Pop. 335

Gridley *(Coffey)*

Walter Gridley promoted the Arkansas Valley Town and Land Company, managing to get a town named after himself.
PO: June 23, 1886–; Pop. 404

Grinnell *(Gove)* [gri-NEL]

A Union veteran, Captain Grinnell, is responsible for this place's name.
PO: June 6, 1870–; Pop. 410

Grinter House *(Wyandotte)*

Young Moses Grinter arrived in present Wyandotte County to establish the first ferry across the Kansas River. His ferry went into operation January 1831 and was used by the Delaware Indians and the military and later by immigrants to Oregon and California. Grinter is credited with being the first permanent white settler in present Wyandotte County. Known as a gentle and benevolent man, he lent large sums of money to his Delaware friends. The large two-story red brick house he built in 1857—the Grinter House—is listed on the National Register of Historic Places.

Gypsum *(Saline)*

A mill on Gypsum Creek shipped seven thousand tons of gypsum to Chicago to be used in the construction for buildings for the 1893 World's Fair. The nearby town of Gypsum, as well as Gypsum Creek, took the name of the natural resource.
PO: October 21, 1886–; Pop. 423

Haddam *(Washington)* [HAD-uhm]

Either J. W. Tabor or John Ferguson named Haddam; both men came from Haddam, Connecticut.
PO: August 10, 1864–; Pop. 239

Half Mound *(Jefferson)*

In the 1880s, the site was merely a side track and stopping place for trains on the Atchison, Topeka, and Santa Fe. The name *Half Mound* refers to a mound about two hundred feet above the prairie. The base covers about ten acres. The mound, composed of layers of limestone, is remarkably regular in contour.

Hallowell *(Cherokee)* [HAL-oh-wel]

Mine No. 19, near Hallowell, was once the state's largest producing coal field. Big Brutus, the giant power shovel that worked this mine, has become part of a coal mining museum and a monument to the once flourishing coal mining industry of southeast Kansas. James R. Hallowell, congressman, was remembered in the town name.
PO: February 6, 1878–; Pop. 120

Halstead *(Harvey)* [HAWL-sted]

Murat Halstead, war correspondent during the Civil War and editor and part owner of the *Cincinnati* (Ohio) *Commercial*, earned the admiration of H. D. Allbright, who named the new town site *Halstead*. The town is best known for its famous physician, Dr. Arthur E. Hertzler, author of the best seller *The Horse and Buggy Doctor* and founder of the Hertzler Clinic.
PO: April 2, 1873–; Pop. 1,994

Hamilton *(Greenwood)*

The small town was named for Alexander Hamilton, who served in George Washington's cabinet as the first secretary of the treasury of the United States.
PO: December 3, 1875–; Pop. 363

Hamilton County *(Established March 20, 1873)*

The county was also named for Alexander Hamilton.
Pop. 2,300

Hamlin *(Brown)*

Abraham Lincoln's vice president, Hannibal Hamlin, was an ardent opponent of the extension of slavery. Maine emigrant Edmund N. Morrill proposed Hamlin's name for the new town in Brown County.
PO: December 5, 1857–; Pop. 80

Hanover *(Washington)*

Gerat H. Hollenberg, born in the German state of Hanover, mined the California gold fields in 1849, left for Australia, went back to New York, and finally settled in Kansas, where he started a ranch on the Black Vermillion where westbound travelers on the Oregon Trail crossed the river. His Cottonwood Ranch became a station on the Pony Express Route.
PO: January 20, 1868–; Pop. 802

Hanston *(Hodgeman)*

Benjamin Hann planned the town of Hanston on his land.
PO: July 23, 1894–; Pop. 257

Happy *(Graham)*

Founders began the village on the banks of Happy Creek. Possibly the availability of water in this high, dry country influenced travelers to call the creek *Happy*.
PO: May 14, 1883–November 15, 1906

Hardtner *(Barber)* [HART-ner]

Hardtner came into being when Jacob Achenbach of Carrollton, Illinois, bought 6,300 acres from a Dr. Hardtner.
PO: July 12, 1887–; Pop. 336

Hargrave *(Rush)*

John Hargrave served as the first Rush County superintendent of schools.
PO: April 26, 1890–April 31, 1950

Harper *(Harper)*

Pioneers from Iowa who first settled the site called it *Cora City,* but changed the name to *Harper* after the county name.
PO: June 18, 1887–; Pop. 1,823

Harper County *(Established February 26, 1867)*

Fraud and deceit characterized organization of the county in 1873. A grocer and two soldiers of fortune who schemed to organize several counties in Kansas built a cabin in Harper County, called the site *Bluff City,* and petitioned for it to be the temporary county seat. They took enough names from a Cincinnati, Ohio, directory to show that they had the necessary six hundred inhabitants, and the governor declared the county organized. The trio then obtained bonds to build a county courthouse. A year later, a state committee investigation concluded that the county never had even forty inhabitants. The bonds and the petitioners disappeared. Legislators named the county for First Sergeant Marion Harper, Company E, Second Kansas, who died from wounds on December 30, 1863.
Pop. 7,600

Harris *(Anderson)*

In 1886, town founders named the place for A. A. Harris.
PO: February 3, 1887–; Pop. 80

Hartford *(Lyon)*

Harvey D. Rice and A. K. Hawkes named the town after Hartford, Connecticut, their home town.
PO: November 7, 1857–; Pop. 551

Harvey County *(Established February 29, 1872)*

Townships taken from Sedgwick, Butler, Marion, and McPherson counties combined to form Harvey County. Pro-

moters named it for Kansas Governor James Madison Harvey, with the hope of obtaining his support for their political plans. Harvey served as governor from 1869 to 1873 and as U.S. senator from 1874 to 1877.
Pop. 31,800

Harvey House Museum *(Marion)*

Before the railroads had dining cars, restaurants known as Harvey Houses were established all along the Santa Fe Railroad system by Frederick Harvey. The Harvey House at Florence, the second on the line, was the first one to offer sleeping accommodations in addition to a formal dining room. The Florence Harvey House operated from 1878 until March 1900. The museum opened in September 1971.

Harveyville *(Wabaunsee)*

The history of Harveyville dates back to 1854, when Henry Harvey and his two sons took land on Dragoon Creek. Harvey first came to the area as a Quaker missionary to the Shawnee Indians in 1840.
PO: August 21, 1869–; Pop. 280

Haskell County *(Established March 23, 1887)*

The respected politician Dudley Chase Haskell served in the Kansas House of Representatives in 1872 and from 1875 to 1876 and was a U.S. representative from 1877 to 1883.
Pop. 3,900

Havana *(Montgomery)*

The *Havana* in Kansas is named after the *Havana* in Illinois. Although the first farmers tried growing cotton, and Havana claimed it had the "northernmost cotton gin in the United States," the Havana farmers learned that the Kansas climate was not conducive to the successful raising of cotton.
PO: January 9, 1871–; Pop. 169

Haven *(Reno)*

Fred W. Ash, one of the founders, was a native of London, England. He came to Kansas in 1873, buying land in Haven township in 1878. When he and other local land owners Charles Peckham, William Astle, and Levi Charles learned that the St. Louis, Fort Scott, and Colorado Railway would pass through their county, they organized the Haven Town Company and bought a well-located town site. It was named *Haven* after a post office already in the vicinity. The more

H A V A N A

popular name *New Haven* occurs in ten eastern states and was once a place name in Kansas.
PO: April 10, 1873–; Pop. 1,125

Havensville *(Pottawatomie)*

At first the town was called *Havens* after Paul E. Havens, a director, secretary, and treasurer of the Kansas Central Railroad until the railroad was sold to Jay Gould in 1883. The post office called the place *Havensville*, so the town soon adopted that name. Except for damage done by fire and flood, Havensville remains much the same in appearance as it did at the turn of the century.
PO: March 5, 1878–; Pop. 183

Haviland *(Kiowa)*

The influence of an outstanding woman from another state prompted the choice of *Haviland* as the name for a new Kansas town. Laura Haviland and her husband Charles started several schools for indigent children and aided fugitive slaves before the Civil War. During the war, Laura Haviland (her husband died in 1845) traveled with the Union Army, helping to secure supplies for both soldiers and slaves and caring for wounded soldiers on battlefields, in hospitals, and in prisons. She visited Kansas to aid the black immigrants. Her humanitarian work was affiliated with both the Friends and Methodist churches.
PO: June 19, 1886–; Pop. 770

85

Hays *(Ellis)*

Founded in 1867, the town took its name from nearby Fort Hays. In those days, Hays was a wild town, filled with saloons and dance halls. Mrs. George Custer, wife of the famous Indian fighter, wrote: "There was enough desperate history in that little town in one summer to make a whole library of dime novels." Ten years later, however, the arrival of the Volga-Germans with their industrious, frugal, and dedicated natures made Hays a permanent settlement where the priorities were family, church, and community.
PO: October 28, 1867–; Pop. 16,301; CS

Haysville *(Sedgwick)*

The pretentious home of land baron Will Hays, known as the Hays Villa, was the center of the community social whirl in the 1880s. The village grew slowly until the 1950s, when housing development boomed. Ever since the Blood family brought in the first plantings in 1871, apple and peach orchards have been important to the Haysville economy. Haysville is recognized as the "Peach Capital of Kansas."
PO: February 22, 1877–; Pop. 8,006

Hazelton *(Barber)*

The Rev. J. W. Hazelton, founder of the town site in 1883, was apparently best known for his donation of a six-hundred-pound bell to a local girls' college.
PO: October 18, 1883–; Pop. 143

Healy *(Lane)*

O. H. Healey was the first to homestead in this area. The second *e* was dropped from the spelling of the town name.
PO: August 29, 1887–May 15, 1894; May 24, 1894–; Pop. 250

Heizer *(Barton)* [HEYE-zer]

D. H. Heizer was instrumental in founding Great Bend and was also an official of the Santa Fe Railroad.
PO: April 4, 1887–March 20, 1891, as Heizerton; March 20, 1891–May 15, 1954; Pop. 150

Henquenet Cave *(Dickinson)* [en-KEH-net]

The cave once served as a hideout for bandits who attacked travelers on the Santa Fe Trail. Gold is reportedly hidden in the cave. Auguste Henquenet, a small but zealous man, came to Hope after his service in the French army. He bought the land on which the cave stood.

Hepler *(Crawford)*

B. F. Hepler of Fort Scott was president of the town company that located Hepler.
PO: June 2, 1871–; Pop. 165

Herington *(Dickinson)*

In 1880, Monroe D. Herington shrewdly swapped a business lot in Illinois for 1,400 acres of land in Dickinson County. Herington contacted Marcus Low, manager of the railroad scheduled to come through the area, and offered a right-of-way for the railroad. Low accepted. Herington eventually became a railroad hub with six lines converging in the town.
PO: February 21, 1884–; Pop. 2,930

Herkimer *(Marshall)*

Settlers chose the name in memory of Herkimer County, New York.
PO: July 18, 1878–; Pop. 100

Herndon *(Rawlins)*

Hungarian immigrants wanted to name their post office *Pesth* after Budapest, the Hungarian capital. The Post Office Department did not like the name and suggested *Herndon* after William H. Herndon, who had read law with Abraham Lincoln.
PO: October 18, 1880–; Pop. 220

Hesston *(Harvey)*

This community northwest of Newton was named for Abraham Hess, its founder. Uncle "Abe" Hess supported the establishment of Hesston College by donating eighty acres and a team of mules. For many years the Hesston Corporation has been a major manufacturer of farm machinery, and another corporation, Excel Industries, manufactures commercial lawn mowers.
PO: December 16, 1887–; Pop. 3,013

Hewins *(Chautauqua)*

Politician and rancher Edwin Hewins was involved in the county seat fight that split Howard County into Chautauqua and Elk counties. It was said that his ranch stretched from Hewins to near Cedar Vale, a distance of about five miles.
PO: April 6, 1887–; Pop. 50

Hiattville *(Bourbon)*

James M. Hiatt once owned the site on which the town was built.
PO: April 2, 1872–; Pop. 100

Hiawatha *(Brown)*

The town was named by Dr. E. H. Grant, a man conversant with the fictional Mohawk Indian chief, Hiawatha, made popular by poet Henry Wadsworth Longfellow. *(See* Mount Hope Cemetery for the Davis Memorial located near Hiawatha.)
PO: July 13, 1858–; Pop. 3,702; CS

Highland *(Doniphan)*

William Sugg, of Highland, Illinois, named the site *Highland* in hopes of attracting Swiss settlers from the Illinois town to Kansas. The Kansas territorial legislature granted Highland a charter to establish a university that opened in 1858. Highland University is the oldest two-year college in Kansas.
PO: March 3, 1855–; Pop. 954

Highland Presbyterian Mission *(Doniphan)*

Iowa, Sauk, and Fox Indians of Missouri were removed by treaty to present Doniphan County in 1837. Accompanying them were Samuel and Eliza Irvin, Presbyterian missionaries who established a log-cabin mission and school. A three-story, thirty-two room stone and brick building was completed in 1846. Part of this building now houses a state museum.

Hill City *(Graham)*

In the fall of 1876, land speculator W. R. Hill located the town site of Hill City in the township of Hill City. Hill influenced blacks to settle in Graham County in 1877.
PO: September 20, 1878–; Pop. 2,028; CS

Hillsboro *(Marion)*

John G. Hill, owner of the town site, first called it *Hill City*. He changed to *Hillsboro* by the time the plat was filed June 24, 1879. Most of the people who settled the Hillsboro area were German Mennonite immigrants from Poland and Russia.
PO: August 29, 1879–; Pop. 2,717

Hillsdale *(Miami)*

After calling the community *Columbia,* then *Ten Mile,* the residents decided on the descriptive name of *Hillsdale.*
PO: April 7, 1870–; Pop. 300

Hodgeman County *(Established March 6, 1873)*

Captain Amos Hodgeman, Seventh Kansas Cavalry, worked as a carpenter in Leavenworth before dying of wounds suffered in battle in October 1863.
Pop. 2,200

Hog Back *(Ellis)*

The term is descriptive of the ridge of land with a sharp summit and sloping sides located in Ellis County. A similar landform in Douglas County was called *Hog Back Point* and *Hog Back Ridge.* It was later renamed *Mt. Oread* and became the site for the University of Kansas.

Hoisington *(Barton)* [HOYZ-ing-tuhn]

When the main western line of the Missouri Pacific Railroad was being built west from Kansas City and the construction crew reached a point near the present Hoisington, a company of Kansas men began planning the town. They took its name from the head of the company, A. J. Hoisington.
PO: April 14, 1887–; Pop. 3,678

Holcomb *(Finney)* [HOHL-kuhm]

A Holcomb native known as Mother Truitt described the naming of Holcomb to novelist Truman Capote: "Them days,

HOG BACK

we called this place Sherlock. Then along this stranger. By the name Holcomb. A hog-raiser, he was. Made money, and decided the town ought to be called after him. Soon as it was, what did he do? Sold out. Moved to California." *(New Yorker,* September 25, 1965, p. 154).
PO: December 3, 1909–; Pop. 816

Hollenberg *(Washington)*

The town is located about ten miles northwest of the Pony Express station from which it took its name.
PO: April 2, 1872–; Pop. 57

Hollenberg Pony Express Station *(Washington)*

Gerat Henry Hollenberg located this station on the St. Joe and Western Railroad on his own land in the spring of 1872. In the late 1850s, his Cottonwood Ranch had become *Cottonwood Station* for the Pony Express. The name of the station has been changed to *Hollenberg;* it is now a registered historic site and operated as a museum by the Kansas State Historical Society.

Holliday *(Johnson)*

Residents of this community named it after Cyrus K. Holliday, one of the most illustrious citizens in early Kansas. Holliday was one of the founders of Topeka, served as adjutant general of Kansas during the Civil War, and was the first president of the Atchison, Topeka, and Santa Fe Railroad.
PO: November 3, 1885–

Holton *(Jackson)*

Edward D. Holton, a wealthy merchant and banker from Milwaukee, sponsored six wagons of Wisconsin emigrants to Kansas in 1856. Journalist Edmund G. Ross led the colony, which chose the town site in Jackson County and, upon Ross's suggestion, named the town *Holton* in honor of their patron. The antislavery sentiments of the townspeople allowed Holton to become a station on the underground railroad before the Civil War. (Ross later served as a senator from Kansas and cast the deciding vote against impeachment of President Andrew Johnson.)
PO: August 5, 1858–; Pop. 3,132; CS

Holyrood *(Ellsworth)* [HAH-lee-rood]

The Corrigan family named the town *Hollyrood* for a place in Canada. According to local legend the name was spelled

Hollyrood until the wind blew one *l* off the railroad depot sign. The *l* was never replaced, and after fourteen years, the railroad officially accepted *Holyrood*.
PO: June 24, 1874–; Pop. 567

H O L Y R O O D

Home *(Marshall)*

When this town was first established it had the name *White's Quarry*. Then the name was changed to *Home City* and later shortened to *Home*.
PO: February 19, 1874–; Pop. 150

Hope *(Dickinson)*

Possibly Hope was named by Michigan immigrants after Hope, Michigan. Wayne Corley says that the local Methodist Ladies Society influenced the renaming of the community from *Wagram* to *Hope*.
PO: July 10, 1871–; Pop. 468

Horace *(Greeley)*

Several town sites in Greeley County were given names related to Horace Greeley, the New York newspaperman and proponent of western settlement. Greeley's mother chose the name Horace for him because she liked it and because another family member had the name. *(See* Greeley County.*)*
PO: February 10, 1886–; Pop. 137

Horse Thief Canyon *(Ellsworth)*

According to early stories, Pawnees stole 125 horses from the Cheyenne and hid them in the box canyon below Sentinel Rock, where three canyons come together. On a sandstone cliff in the canyon are carvings of thunderbirds, horses, buffalo, and hundreds of other objects put there thousands of years ago by Plains Indians. Mixed in among the ancient petroglyphs are modern-day carvings that are rapidly obliterating the art of the past. As the cliffs, too, are crumbling, little remains of what was once one of the finest collections of petroglyphs in the whole Middle West. There are also *Horse Thief Canyons* in Hodgeman, Scott, and Wallace counties.

Horton *(Brown)*

The name of the chief justice of the Kansas Supreme Court, Albert H. Horton, was given to the northeast Kansas town. Until the 1930s, large railroad shops of the Rock Island Railroad enhanced community prosperity.
PO: November 15, 1886–; Pop. 2,130

Howard *(Elk)*

Howard City, as it was first called, has been the county seat since March 11, 1875, after a bitter, no-bloodshed war. The town was once a part of Howard County, and therefore the name. The county had been named for General Oliver Otis Howard, a man of high ideals whose work with the freed blacks after the Civil War led to the naming of Howard University in Washington, D.C. In Kansas, Howard County was divided into Elk and Chautauqua counties, and only the town retains the general's name. Howard claims the first public school kindergarten in Kansas, established in 1906. Kansas was the third state in the nation to establish kindergarten training.
PO: February 14, 1870–; Pop. 965; CS

Hoxie *(Sheridan)*

Railroad contractor H. M. Hoxie of Des Moines, Iowa, received the contract to build the first five hundred miles of the Union Pacific Railroad. He later became vice president of the Missouri Pacific. He died before rails could be laid to the town named for him.
PO: October 12, 1886–; Pop. 1,462; CS

Hoyt *(Jackson)*

A lawyer who defended John Brown at Harpers Ferry and was a lieutenant colonel in the Fifteenth Kansas during the Civil War left his name on this town. George H. Hoyt also served as attorney general in Governor Harvey's administration.
PO: January 9, 1871–; Pop. 536

Hudson *(Stafford)*

Wisconsin emigrant Mr. Uptegraph could have named the town site on his land after himself. Instead, he chose to call it *Hudson*, after his former home in Hudson, Wisconsin.
PO: July 12, 1887–; Pop. 157

Hugoton *(Stevens)*

The town company that selected the town site near the center of the proposed county named it *Hugo* for Victor Hugo, the French author and poet. He died in 1885, the year the town was platted. But when the post office needed a name, it chose *Hugoton* to reduce confusion with Hugo, Colorado. In 1926, oil driller Walter L. Sidwell discovered gas near Hugoton. The field was officially opened to exploration and drilling in 1927 and developed into one of the nation's largest gas fields, under the name Hugoton Gas Field. The Gas Capitol Museum in Hugoton commemorates the event.
PO: April 1, 1886–; Pop. 3,165; CS

Humboldt *(Allen)*

A group of men of German birth organized a colony in Hartford, Connecticut, in the winter of 1856–1857. When they arrived in Lawrence in March 1857, they chartered the Humboldt Town Company. They traveled to Allen County, located a town site, and named it after Baron Alexander von Humboldt, the German philosopher, geographer, and scientist. Street names included Uhland, Herder, Schiller, Tritschler, Goethe, and Wieland.
PO: April 21, 1858–; Pop. 2,230

Hundred and Ten Mile Creek *(Franklin and Osage)*

The old crossing of the Santa Fe freight road located 110 miles from Independence, Missouri, was once a mail station that also offered coal, wood, water, grass, and entertainment to travelers. A similarly named creek—*One Hundred and Forty-two Mile Creek*—was located thirty-two miles down the road.

Hunnewell *(Sumner)*

This once "rip-roaring boom town" on the Oklahoma-Kansas border was named for H. H. Hunnewell, a director of the Santa Fe Railroad.
PO: August 12, 1880–March 31, 1960; Pop. 86

Hunter *(Mitchell)*

Hunter is one of the few towns started after the 1890s. It was named for Al Hunter, who came to Kansas from Marion County, Iowa. The post office was established in 1895, but the town was not chartered until 1915.
PO: May 14, 1895–; Pop. 135

Huron *(Atchison)*

Two men, Dr. Amarziah Moore and George W. Stabler, both claimed naming the town of Huron. Evidence supports Dr. Moore's claim; he named the town for his home county in Ohio.
PO: December 14, 1857–; Pop. 107

Huron Park *(Wyandotte)*

This park is located in the heart of downtown Kansas City. An 1855 treaty stipulated that the place was "permanently reserved and appropriated" as a burial ground for the Wyandots. At an earlier time, the Huron tribe had merged with the Wyandots. The Carnegie Library, Municipal Rose Garden, and Wyandot Cemetery are located within the park.

Hutchinson *(Reno)*

Founder Clinton C. Hutchinson, Indian agent, real estate speculator, and an agent for the Atchison, Topeka, and Santa Fe Railroad, followed the construction of the railroad westward through Kansas in 1871 to a site he thought suitable for a town. Hutchinson is nicknamed the "Salt City" because it was built above salt deposits reputed to be among the richest in the world. For many years Hutchinson's chief industry was the mining, processing, and shipment of salt. Morton, Carey, and Cargill have salt plants in Hutchinson.
PO: December 6, 1871–; Pop. 40,284; CS

Idana *(Clay)* [eye-DAN-uh]

Idana has been a school district, a post office, and a railroad station, but never an incorporated town. Two families, the Howlands and the Broughtons, bought a 320-acre tract together. The name came from combining Mrs. Howland's first name—Ida—with Mrs. Broughton's first name—Anna.
PO: April 27, 1882–; Pop. 100

Independence *(Montgomery)*

A group of Oswego residents led by R. W. Wright organized to start a town named *Independence* in Montgomery County. There they confronted other claimants, among them Frank and Fred Buner, brothers who called the place *Bunker Hill*, and George Brown, who had a site he called *Colfax*. The Oswego group triumphed. R. W. Wright had come from Independence, Iowa, which explains the name choice. Alf Landon, Kansas governor and 1936 Republican candidate for U.S. president, lived in Independence from 1904 until 1933. Author Laura Ingalls Wilder used an area fifteen miles south

of Independence as the setting for her book *Little House on the Prairie*.
PO: June 13, 1870–; Pop. 10,598; CS

Independence Creek *(Atchison)*

Explorers Lewis and Clark named the creek after their expedition camped on the creek banks on July 4, 1804, and celebrated Independence Day with "an evening gun and an additional gill of whiskey for the men."

INDEPENDENCE CREEK

Industry *(Clay and Dickinson)*

In an age when industriousness was admired, land speculator A. L. Beard decided to name the site *Industry*. It's possible that Illinois immigrants brought the name to Kansas.
PO: February 21, 1876–November 30, 1906; Pop. 50

Ingalls *(Gray)*

Asa T. Soule, a wealthy New York financier interested in Kansas, named the town site *Ingalls* after Kansas Senator John James Ingalls, a man widely known for his eloquent oratory and polished writing. Ingalls had left New England for the Kansas Territory, where he worked on the Kansas constitution and chose the motto for Kansas: *Ad astra per aspera* (To the stars through difficulties).
PO: May 8, 1888–; Pop. 274

Inman *(McPherson)*

Colonel Henry Inman was stationed at Fort Harker as quartermaster general at the close of the Civil War. From notes collected from his experience with the cavalry during the Indian wars, he wrote eight books on the West, mostly about Kansas and the Great Plains. Lake Inman is also named after the colonel.
PO: April 17, 1884–; Pop. 947

International Forest of Friendship *(Atchison)*

The forest was a Bicentennial gift to the United States from the international organization of women pilots, The Ninety Nines, Inc. The forest includes trees from all fifty states and from thirty-three countries. The Ninety Nines was founded in 1929 by Amelia Earhart, world-famous aviator, who was born in Atchison, Kansas.

Iola *(Allen)*

Citizens unhappy with the selection of Humboldt as the Allen County seat organized a town company to locate a new town. The carefully chosen, centrally located site belonged to company members F. Colborn and W. H. Cochrane. At the meeting held to select a name, several names were proposed, including *Iola*, the name of the wife of J. F. Colborn. Four miles from Iola is the boyhood home of military hero General Frederick Funston, a prominent figure in the Spanish-American War credited with capturing Emilio Aguinaldo, the leader of the Philippine insurrection. Later Funston served as the military commander who oversaw martial law following the 1906 San Francisco earthquake. He also saw service in the U.S. intervention in Mexico in 1914.
PO: October 25, 1859–; Pop. 6,938; CS

Iowa Point *(Doniphan)*

Once a booming town on the Missouri River, Iowa Point was established in 1855 on land given to the Reverend S. W. Irvin by the Iowa Indians. Population zoomed to an estimated three thousand within a year. However, the commercial life of the settlement suffered from the intense partisan strife between the free-state and proslavery settlers, so by 1857 Iowa Point began an abrupt decline.
PO: March 15, 1855–July 19, 1933

Iowa, Sac, and Fox Reservation *(Doniphan)* [SAK]

In 1837 the Sac (yellow earth people) and the Fox (red earth people) ceded their Iowa lands and accepted a tract of land in

Kansas. Through several negotiations, the reservation was reduced to 894 acres situated in Nebraska and Kansas. It is one of three Indian reservations remaining in Kansas out of a total of nineteen.

Isabel *(Barber)*

While Layton White was surveying a town site in Barber County, he received news of his daughter Isabel's birth. He named the town for her.
PO: May 24, 1887–; Pop. 137

Iuka *(Pratt)* [eye-U-kuh]

Town founders meeting together wrote possible town names on slips of paper and placed them in a hat. The first name drawn was *Iuka*, put there by a Civil War veteran of the Battle of Iuka, Mississippi.
PO: December 6, 1877–; Pop. 235

Jackson County *(Established February 11, 1859)*

The 1855 proslavery legislature honored the late Senator John C. Calhoun of South Carolina by naming the county after him. The choice was totally unacceptable to the free-state legislature of 1859, whose members considered the name suggestive of treason to the American nation. They renamed the county *Jackson*, after U.S. president Andrew Jackson, who boldly denounced Calhoun and his nullification proposal.
Pop. 11,900

Jacob's Mound *(Chase)*

At an elevation of 1,450 feet, Jacob's Mound was a prairie landmark on the old stage, freight, and immigrant trail between El Dorado and Emporia. Gabriel Jacobs left his name on the mound, a creek, and an early settlement.

I U K A

Jamestown *(Cloud)*

This settlement was named after James P. Pomeroy, vice president of the Union Pacific Railroad, Central Branch.
PO: October 8, 1878–; Pop. 440

Jarbalo *(Leavenworth)* [JAHR-buh-loh]

A member of the Alexander Doniphan expedition named the hilly area *Diablo Hills. Jarbalo* is said to be a corruption of the word *Diablo.*
PO: March 28, 1872–December 31, 1958; Pop. 100

Jarvis Creek *(Rice)*

A misspelling on a map turned this into *Jarvis Creek;* the settler intended to call it *Chavez* after Don Antonio Chavez, a Spanish trader who was murdered in 1841 as he was crossing the county with twelve thousand dollars in gold and silver. The Chavez party had camped along the creek and buried the bullion before being attacked by bandits. So far no one has reported uncovering the treasure.

Jefferson County *(Established August 25, 1855)*

The legislature named the county after former President Thomas Jefferson. The county claimed having the first real settler in Kansas—Daniel Morgan Boone, son of the legendary Daniel Boone. In 1827, the federal government chose Boone to instruct the Kansas Indians in the principles of agriculture. He lived with his family on the north bank of the Kaw River in extreme southern Jefferson County until 1835 or 1836, when the agency was abandoned.
Pop. 16,700

Jennings *(Decatur)*

Starting as *Slab City,* the name was changed to *Jennings* for Warren and Bedford Jennings, two local landowners.
PO: October 15, 1879–; Pop. 194

Jetmore *(Hodgeman)*

Colonel Abraham Buckner Jetmore, an attorney for the Atchison, Topeka, and Santa Fe Railroad, also directed the Kansas Freedman's Relief Association, which aided blacks seeking land in Kansas. The Prohibition party ran Jetmore as a candidate for governor of Kansas in 1884; he lost the race but is remembered in the town name.
PO: May 20, 1880–; Pop. 862; CS

JEFFERSON COUNTY

Jewell *(Jewell)*

The town, which takes its name from the county, evolved from the building of a large sod enclosure called *Fort Jewell* in 1870. Fortunately, it was never needed for defense.
PO: July 7, 1870–; Pop. 589

Jewell County *(Established February 26, 1867)*

A military associate called Lieutenant Colonel Lewis R. Jewell "the bravest man he ever met." Jewell, of the Sixth Kansas Cavalry, died of wounds suffered in action at Cane Hill, Arkansas, in November 1862.
Pop. 4,800

Johnson City *(Stanton)*

When laid out in 1885, the site was called *Veteran*. It was renamed to honor Colonel A. S. Johnson, land commissioner for the Atchison, Topeka, and Santa Fe Railroad and a member of the Johnson Town and Land Company.
PO: February 11, 1887–; Pop. 1,244; CS

Johnson County *(Established August 25, 1855)*

The Reverend Thomas Johnson, a Virginian and slave owner, came to Kansas in 1829 to establish the Shawnee Methodist

99

Mission. Between 1829 and 1858, he developed a training school and an experimental farm for training Indians. When Kansas became a territory, he served as president of the territorial council and a leader in the 1855 legislature. Although he was in sympathy with the South, he did not condone secession and remained loyal to the Union during the Civil War. Johnson was killed by an assassin in the doorway of his home in 1865. In the 1980s, Johnson County had the highest per capita income of Kansas's 105 counties: $16,190.
Pop. 307,600

Junction City *(Geary)*

A colonists' group successful in reaching the confluence of the Republican and Smoky Hill rivers after others had failed, chose the descriptive name of *Junction City*.
PO: June 30, 1858–; Pop. 21,100; CS

Kahola *(Chase)* [kuh-HOH-luh]

This small tributary of the Neosho arises in Chase County. The village of Kahola, on the Kaw Indian Reservation ten miles southeast of Council Grove, was burned in 1853 because of a smallpox epidemic. Kahola Lake and park are located twenty miles northwest of Emporia.

Kalvesta *(Finney)*

Kalvesta combines the Greek word *kalos,* meaning "good," and the Roman *vesta* pertaining to the Roman goddess of the hearth: thus the name "good home."
PO: September 18, 1866–

Kanopolis *(Ellsworth)* [kuh-NAH-puh-luhs]

The name combines the Greek word for "city"—*polis*—with the *Kan* of Kansas. The small village surrounded the site of Fort Harker, active in the 1860s. Because Kanopolis was the nearest town in the county to the dam built on the Smoky Hill River, both the reservoir and the dam are called Kanopolis.
PO: March 30, 1886–; Pop. 729

Kanorado *(Sherman)* [kan-oor-AY-doh]

Located on the border of Kansas and Colorado, the town name combines *Kan* with *orado.*
PO: September 9, 1903–; Pop. 217

Kansas [KAN-zuhs]

Controversy surrounds the origin of the state's name. Some say it was named for the Kansas River, which derived its name from the dominant tribe of Indians living in the territory when first visited by white men. David R. Atchison suggested the name *Kansas* to Stephen Douglas, author of the Kansas-Nebraska bill, saying that Nebraska was named for the Nebraska River, so Kansas should be named for the Kansas River. Both were Indian names. The Kansas River and the Kansas Indians were known to early French settlers. *Kansas* refers to "winds" or "wind people." Historian George Morehouse contends that Kansas is neither of Indian nor French origin but probably derived from the Spanish verb *cansar*, which means "to molest" or "to harass" and from *cansado*, which signifies a "troublesome fellow." To make things even hazier, Kansas has had numerous spellings: *Kanzas, Kansies, Kanzon, Konza, Konsas, Kanzan, Canceas, Cansez, Canzes, Canses,* and *Canzon!*
Pop. 2,363,208

Kansas City *(Wyandotte)*

A written description of the town site dates back to August 1806 when explorers Lewis and Clark passed through. They landed on an extension of land, called *Kaw Point,* between the Kansas and Missouri rivers. Clark wrote in his journal: "the Kansas is low at this time. About a mile below it we landed to view the situation . . . , which has many advantages for a trading house or fort." Several Kansas City, Missouri, businessmen organized the Kansas City, Kansas, town company in 1868. Through the years other small towns developed nearby; consolidation of these towns began in 1886. Riverview and Wyandotte were the first to merge, followed by Kansas City, Armourdale, and Armstrong. The name *Kansas City* prevailed over the suggested *Wyandotte* on the agreement that municipal bonds would sell better under the name of *Kansas City.* Later Rosedale, Argentine, and Quindaro merged with Kansas City.
PO: March 27, 1885–; Pop. 161,087; CS

Kansas River *(East Central Kansas)*

The river was named many years before the state and could be of either Spanish, Indian, or French origin. The French map makers marked the Kanza River in the late seventeenth century. The French shortened that to *Kaw,* a name used locally.

Kansas State Forest (Vieux Elm) *(Pottawatomie)*

This forest occupies a 1.5-acre tract and consists of only one spectacular tree, the largest American elm in the United States. This tree was 270 years old, 99 feet high, with a trunk circumference of 23 feet, 2 inches, as of January 1988. It was named for Louis Vieux, who settled with his family on the spot where the Oregon Trail crossed the Vermillion River and near where the great elm stands. Ironically, *vieux* means "old" in French.

Kanwaka *(Douglas)* [kan-WAH-kuh]

The Oregon-California Trail crossed through this township between the Kansas and Wakarusa rivers.
PO: April 7, 1857–April 14, 1900

Kaw Indian Mission *(Morris)*

The word *Kaw* is interchangeable with *Kansas* when referring to the Kansas Indians (the Kaws) or to the Kansas River (the Kaw). The federal government set aside a 22-square mile tract in Morris County for a reservation for the Kaws, who moved there in 1847. The Methodist Church missionaries operated a school for Indians between 1851 and 1854. Seth Hays moved to the reservation, where he set up a trading post at a site called Council Grove. The school building constructed for the Indians has been preserved and is now a museum.

Kearny County *(Established March 6, 1873)* [KAHR-nee]

This county was named for General Philip Kearny, noted for his dash and courage and idolized by his soldiers. He was killed at the battle of Chantilly, Virginia, in 1862. Philip Kearny is not to be confused with his more famous uncle, Stephen Watts Kearny, who marched with his troops down the Santa Fe Trail from Fort Leavenworth to Santa Fe during the Mexican War.
Pop. 3,700

Kechi *(Sedgwick)* [KEE-cheye]

This community northeast of Wichita was named for the Kechi Indians who were closely related to the Wichitas and Wacos. The word *Kechi* may mean "water turtle."
PO: May 29, 1888–; Pop. 288

Kennekuk *(Atchison)*

Kennekuk, religious leader and prophet of the Kickapoos, had formulated a religion of his own. The Catholics estab-

lished a mission for the Kickapoos but had so little success they closed the mission in 1840. Nearby, Kennekuk's church thrived with some three hundred members. During the territorial period, the town of Kennekuk catered to travelers on the California and Oregon Trail.
PO: June 8, 1857–October 20, 1900

Kensington *(Smith)*

The name *Kensington* as a Kansas place name was believed to have been the name of the wife of a railroad builder.
PO: January 7, 1888–; Pop. 681

Kickapoo *(Leavenworth)*

The Kickapoo Indians occupied the area on land allocated to them by the United States. Among the first trading posts in Kansas, Kickapoo became a bitter, but unsuccessful, rival for supremacy with the city of Leavenworth. *Kickapoo* refers to both a town and township in the county.
PO: January 24, 1855–; Pop. 100

Kickapoo Cemetery *(Leavenworth)*

This cemetery reportedly had its origins in a Methodist mission to the Kickapoo Indians established in the 1830s and a Catholic mission established in 1836. However, the oldest gravestone, dated 1857, is that of one of Kickapoo's mayors. The cemetery is a Kansas Historic Landmark.

Kickapoo Reservation *(Brown)*

The Kickapoo Indians still live on this reservation, which straddles the Delaware River in Brown County.

Kill Creek *(Johnson and Osborne)*

The Dutch immigrants to America called a creek or a stream *kill*, the Dutch word meaning "stream."

Kincaid *(Anderson)*

Robert Kincaid, of Mound City, promoted the St. Louis and Emporia Railway and also promoted the town carrying his name.
PO: November 9, 1885–; Pop. 192

Kingman *(Kingman)*

The county seat of Kingman County was named for Kansas Supreme Court Justice Samuel A. Kingman. He was also the first president of the Kansas State Historical Society. Salt mining appeared to be among the city's early industries, if this verse is to be believed:

> I sing of a city,
>   A rock crystal city,
> Kingman, the city of worth;
>   She sits in her splendor
>   The Crystal-salt vendor—
> Her mines can supply the earth.
> —Ellen Beebe, 1891

PO: March 23, 1873–; Pop. 3,563; CS

Kingman County *(Established February 29, 1872)*

Judge Samuel Austin Kingman, Chief Justice of the Kansas Supreme Court, was instrumental in organizing the county and in obtaining the charter for the town of Kingman.
Pop. 9,100

Kingsdown *(Ford)*

Two Englishmen had taken homestead in Sodville township. According to Ford County historian Ida Ellen Rath, one of them said: "How beautiful are the prairies," and the other replied, "Say, indeed, they remind me of the King's Down!"
PO: January 11, 1888–; Pop. 180

Kinsley *(Edwards)*

A colony from Massachusetts arrived in western Kansas in 1873 to establish the county seat town of Kinsley, funded partly with money from E. W. Kinsley of Boston and partly by Boston's Homestead and Colonization Bureau. Boston planners included orange groves for the new settlement!
PO: January 19, 1874–; Pop. 2,074; CS

Kiowa *(Barber)* [KEYE-oh-wah]

It was in Kiowa that Carrie Nation smashed her first saloon. The town was named for the Kiowa Indians.
PO: January 7, 1887–; Pop. 1,409

Kiowa County *(Established February 10, 1886)*

The county is named for the Kiowas, who were among the last of the Plains Indians to come to Kansas. They had the reputation of being great horsemen, horse breeders, and horse traders.
Pop. 3,900

Kipp *(Saline)*

The Missouri Pacific Railway employed a roadmaster named Kipp Cherry.
PO: September 18, 1890–October 19, 1957; Pop. 100

Kirwin *(Phillips)*

Colonel John Kirwin came to Kansas after the Civil War to build a stockade for the protection of the overland emigrants on their way to California.
PO: June 2, 1871–; Pop. 249

Kismet *(Seward)* [KIZ-met]

Local residents say that railroad builders who had difficulty crossing the Cimarron River called the town site *Kismet*. The word means "destiny" or "fate" in Arabic. Town founder A. C. Olin, a very religious man, built a Bible School and forbade liquor in the town. (A number of town charters prohibited the sale and consumption of liquor on town lots.)
PO: November 14, 1888–; Pop. 368

Konza Prairie *(Riley)* [KAHN-zuh]

The name *Konza* is one of more than a hundred variations on the spelling of the word *Kansas*. The 8,616-acre tract of tall-grass prairie was purchased by the Nature Conservancy and is used for research by Kansas State University.

Labette *(Labette)* [luh-BET]

The town took its name from the county.
PO: July 5, 1870–; Pop. 123

KISMET

Labette County *(Established February 7, 1867)*

The name was first applied to the stream running through the area, and then to the county when it was established. A man named Pierre Labette lived near the mouth of the stream early in Kansas history. An 1836 map called the stream *La Bete Creek.*
Pop. 25,700

La Crosse *(Rush)*

For several years La Crosse rivaled Rush Center for county seat designation; La Crosse finally won. W. S. Taylor brought the name *La Crosse,* which was given to both a township and town in the county, from his former home, La Crosse, Wisconsin. The town claims to be the "Barbed Wire Capital of the World" because of the interest in collecting barbed wire and in its Barbed Wire Collectors Association. The Post Rock Museum, also located here, is built of a special limestone from which fence posts were cut by pioneers in the timber-scarce West.
PO: April 23, 1877–; Pop. 1,618; CS

La Cygne *(Linn)* [luh-SEEN]

La Cygne took its name from the stream called *Marais des Cygnes.* This French translation of an Osage name for the stream means "marsh of the swans." *(See* Marais des Cygnes.)
PO: September 27, 1869–; Pop. 1,025

LA CYGNE

La Harpe *(Allen)*

The building of the Fort Scott, Wichita, and Western Railway was credited for the establishment of the town La Harpe, named for Bernard de La Harpe, an early explorer, and La Harpe, Illinois. The Kansas town is located in the geograph-

ical center of Allen County and at one time was said to be "right over the strongest gas pressure in the state." *(See* Gas.)
PO: November 2, 1881–; Pop. 687

Lake City *(Barber)*

Reuben Lake left Canada for the United States in time to fight in the Civil War. After the war, in 1873, he homesteaded in Barber County and built a sawmill. County residents elected him sheriff and county commissioner. Lake opened the Lake City post office, platted the town, added a hotel and brickyard, and even started a newspaper.
PO: December 9, 1873–; Pop. 70

Lake Quivira *(Johnson and Wyandotte)* [kwi-VEER-uh]

Quivira was a legendary land peopled by wealthy and refined citizens. Explorer Coronado searched for Quivira, expecting to find it in the heart of North America, more specifically in the great bend of the Arkansas River in Kansas. Cleve Hallenbeck, in his *Land of the Conquistadores,* claimed that the name *Quivira* was a contraction for Coronado's motto, *Quien Vivirá, Verá,* which means "He who lives, shall see." The Santa Fe Railroad promoted Lake Quivira as a summer resort. Lake Quivira is one of the more recently developed communities.
Pop. 1,087

Lakeview *(Douglas)*

The private resort stands on the south side of an oxbow lake formed when the Kansas River changed its course around 1853. Fishermen and hunters frequented the lake in the 1870s and later incorporated under the name Lakeview Fishing and Shooting Association. Its members claim to have the oldest sports club still in existence in Kansas. Before air conditioning, members used it as a summer haven from the heat.
PO: February 28, 1898–June 15, 1914

Lakin *(Kearny)*

Lakin was one of eight stations between Dodge City and the Colorado state line established by the Atchison, Topeka, and Santa Fe Railroad in 1872. At Lakin the crews dug a well and constructed a windmill, water tank, and coal bins. A box car was equipped for a depot. This station, destined to become the county seat, was named for David Long Lakin, a land commissioner and treasurer and a member of the board of directors of the Santa Fe.
PO: March 6, 1874–; Pop. 1,823; CS

Lancaster *(Atchison)*

Whether named by F. F. Stoner or by John W. Smith for their home town in Pennsylvania, the popular name given to the Kansas community came from England before being applied to several towns in the United States.
PO: March 3, 1858–; Pop. 274

Lane *(Franklin)*

Lane was a crossing on Pottawatomie Creek for the military trail connecting Fort Leavenworth and Fort Scott. The town site was first named for William Sherman, a victim of John Brown in the Pottawatomie Massacre. The name was changed during the Civil War to *Lane*, for James Henry Lane, the "tall, lean, lanky, swarthy and hungry looking man" known for his oratory. The name was also given to a spring, a fort, and a university in Kansas.
PO: December 21, 1855–January 28, 1863, as Shermansville; January 28, 1863–; Pop. 249

Lane County *(Established March 6, 1873)*

James Henry Lane, an outspoken leader of the Free-state party, led immigrants into Kansas by way of Iowa and Nebraska on a route that became known as Lane's Trail. He served as a U.S. senator from Kansas from 1861 to 1866, before committing suicide. Several years later the state legislature named the county for him.
Pop. 2,500

Langdon *(Reno)*

Langdon was platted in 1887 and named for a local store owner.
PO: June 20, 1881–; Pop. 84

Lanham *(Washington)*

The main street on this town is on the border between Kansas and Nebraska. Source of the place name is unknown.
PO: April 27, 1914–September 14, 1923; Pop. 40

Lansing *(Leavenworth)*

James W. Lansing founded the town, which was known as *Petersburg* before being changed to *Lansing* in 1875. The town is best known as the site of the Kansas State Penitentiary, which for many years had the reputation of being one of the most feared and hated prisons in the country. Men incarcer-

ated there called it the "Devil's Front Porch—the nearest thing to hell."
PO: November 1, 1875–; Pop. 5,307

Larkinburg *(Atchison and Jackson)*

After coming to Kansas in 1860, M. E. Larkin entered the livestock business. Later he served in the Kansas legislature. The post office began as *Larkin* but was changed to *Larkinburg* to avoid confusion with Lakin, Kansas.
PO: September 26, 1872–April 9, 1909 (Larkin); April 9, 1909–; Pop. 25

Larned *(Pawnee)*

The city of Larned took its name from nearby Fort Larned. *(See* Fort Larned.)
PO: August 15, 1872–; Pop. 4,811; CS

Latham *(Butler)* [LAY-thuhm]

Latham Young, a Chicago-based railroad commissioner for the St. Louis and San Francisco line, left his imprint on the small station in Butler County. It has also been said that it was named for Arlie Latham, shortstop of the St. Louis Browns baseball team of the 1880s.
PO: October 6, 1885–; Pop. 148

LANSING

Latimer *(Morris)*

After first being called *Far West,* the name was changed to
Latimer for one of the town promoters.
*PO: September 20, 1887–June 20, 1888, as Far West; February
5, 1889–April 15, 1895; November 2, 1895–January 6, 1961;
Pop. 31*

Lawrence *(Douglas)*

What shall we name it—New Boston, Wakarusa, Mount
Oread, Worcester? It is not surprising that Kansas' first Free-
state settlers instead chose Lawrence to honor the much-
admired Amos A. Lawrence of Massachusetts. Lawrence,
wealthy manufacturer and generous treasurer of the New
England Emigrant Aid Company, deplored naming the Kansas town for him, fearing that it "would give the appearance
of promoting my own celebrity . . . and would lessen my
own influence for the good of the cause." Lawrence settlers,
along with other Free-staters, rallied to the cause by making
Kansas a state free from slavery. The University of Kansas
was established there in 1866; Haskell Indian Institute, now
Haskell Indian Junior College, was started in 1884.
PO: January 13, 1855–; Pop. 55,700; CS

Leavenworth *(Leavenworth)*

If they had profits in mind, they had better call their town
Leavenworth rather than *New Town,* H. Miles Moore warned
the town association. Sale of lots, he said, could be stimu-
lated by leading outsiders to identify the town with the military post, the latter being in a very desirable location. Politically, early Leavenworth rivaled Atchison as a hotbed of proslavery sentiment. The new town prospered because of its
nearness to Fort Leavenworth and its location on the Missouri, and for nearly thirty years, from 1855 to 1885, surpassed all other Kansas cities in trade, industry, and population.
PO: May 31, 1871–; Pop. 35,100; CS

Leavenworth County *(Established August 25, 1855)*

One of the first counties organized in Kansas was named for
Fort Leavenworth, which was established in 1827. Carved out
of Delaware Trust lands belonging to the Delaware Indians,
the county claimed the state's first fort, the first post office on
the upper Missouri, the first Kansas newspaper, and the first
territorial governor's home.
Pop. 58,400

Leawood *(Johnson)*

The town, which has developed in recent years into a large suburb of Kansas City, was named for Oscar G. Lee, a retired policeman who made real estate investments.
Pop. 13,360

Lebanon *(Smith)*

Named by R. B. Ray for his former home of Lebanon, Kentucky, Lebanon is close to the center of the forty-eight contiguous states. The stone monument and plaque that mark the center are off by one-eighth of a mile because the farmer who owned the exact center did not want tourists tramping over his fields. Lebanon had the coldest recorded temperature ever in Kansas—minus 40 degrees Fahrenheit on February 13, 1905.
PO: February 16, 1876–; Pop. 440

Lebo *(Coffey)* [LEE-boh]

The naming of *Lebo Creek* preceded the naming of the town. Joe Lebo, once a captain in the Tenth Kansas Cavalry, lived on the creek, and thus the name.
PO: June 4, 1883–; Pop. 966

Lecompton *(Douglas)*

"The great metropolis of Kansas" was the founders' forecast for the town located on the Kaw halfway between Lawrence and Topeka. Judge Samuel Lecompte presided over the town company that surveyed the 600-acre tract, which they then officially named *Lecompton* for the judge. For three years, 1855–1858, Lecompton fulfilled the grandiose expectations of its founders. The proslavery leaders made it their territorial capital, and workers began excavating for the capitol and the governor's house, while nearly 5,000 residents supported a variety of businesses. Boomers of the town called it "the Wall Street of the West." With the triumph of Free-state forces, however, the capital was moved to Topeka. Businessmen and workers abandoned Lecompton for towns with more promising futures. Before its political heyday, the place was known as *Bald Eagle* for the eagles that roosted in the timber by the river.
PO: September 5, 1855–; Pop. 576

Lehigh *(Marion)*

Alden Speare, a Boston, Massachusetts, land speculator who founded several Kansas towns, platted Lehigh in 1881 on

land he owned in Marion County. The town may have been named for Lehigh, Pennsylvania. The majority of the farmers coming in the years between 1874 and 1885 were of German heritage—Mennonites from Russia, Adventists from the Volga River region in Russia, Lutherans from Germany, and Pennsylvania Germans.
PO: April 23, 1880–; Pop. 189

Le Loup *(Franklin)* [luh-LOOP]

The station on the Kansas City, Lawrence, and Southern Kansas Railroad was first named *Ferguson* after a local resident. Then its name was changed to *Le Loup,* a word meaning "the wolf" in French.
PO: May 8, 1879–February 15, 1954; Pop. 100

Lenexa *(Johnson)* [luh-NEKS-uh]

Once a "pretty little town" north of Olathe, the fast-growing, populous Kansas City suburb was named for Lenexa, wife of Blackhoof, a Shawnee chief. In recent years, Lenexa has called itself the "Spinach Capital" and commemorates the designation with an annual celebration.
PO: July 15, 1869–; Pop. 18,639

Lenora *(Norton)*

Controversy surrounds the source of the naming of Lenora. W. T. Andreas, in *History of Kansas* (1883), reported that it

LE LOUP

was named for Mrs. Lenora Hauser (Hanser), who settled there in 1873. Norton County historians, however, said that residents of the community wanted the name *Spring City*, but the U.S. Post Office insisted on the name *Lenora*.
PO: June 24, 1874–; Pop. 444

Leon *(Butler)*

Immigrants to this town site named it for their previous home in Leon, Iowa.
PO: March 28, 1882–; Pop. 667

Leona *(Doniphan)* [lee-OH-nuh]

Leona Shock, daughter of J. W. Shock, president of the town company, was the first child born in the new community.
PO: May 13, 1873–; Pop. 73

Leonardville *(Riley)*

The name *Leonardville* appealed to the large number of Swedes who settled the community. They said it was a *vackra namnet*, "a beautiful name." The Swedes liked it because it sounded like the Swedish equivalent of "lion's heart." The town actually got its name from Leonard T. Smith, president of the Kansas Central Railway Co.
PO: June 28, 1882–; Pop. 437

Leoti *(Wichita)* [lee-OH-ti]

Leoti is said to be an Indian word meaning "prairie flower." In a story, Prairie Flower was the name of a white girl captured and adopted by an Indian chief. Another version says the town was named for Mrs. Henry (Leoti) Kibbee.
PO: February 19, 1887–; Pop. 1,869; CS

Leoville *(Decatur)*

Joe Boeger suggested the name *Leoville* in honor of Pope Leo XIII.
PO: November 21, 1923–; Pop. 80

Lerado *(Reno)* [luh-RAY-doh]

Residents wanted the name *Laredo*, after the Texas town, but a clerical error at the Post Office Department changed it to *Lerado*. Lerado founder, Dr. John A. Brady, planted twenty thousand catalpa trees on the lots. Lerado never became the major railway stop Brady envisioned; it remains instead a rural neighborhood.
PO: May 2, 1884–February 13, 1904

Le Roy *(Coffey)* [luh-ROY]

Settlers from an Illinois town named *Le Roy* brought the name to the Kansas community.
PO: March 20, 1856–; Pop. 701

Lewis *(Edwards)*

Town founders named the site Lewis after M. M. Lewis, the editor of the *Valley Republican* (the *Kinsley Graphic*). The paper was printed in the county seat town of Kinsley.
PO: November 3, 1886–; Pop. 551

Lewis Point *(Atchison)*

Every steamboat captain coming down the Missouri watched for Lewis Point, the projection of land lying immediately above Oak Mills in far southeastern Atchison County. Calvin Lewis, a pioneer riverman, settled at the point. Steamboats stopped here frequently to take on wood fuel.

Liberal *(Seward)*

At a lonely ranch on the trail from Dodge City to the Texas Panhandle, genial ranch owner S. S. Rogers generously offered water to passing travelers. When asked what it cost, Rogers would reply, "Oh, that's all right, water's always free here." The response might be: "Well, that's right liberal." The place became known as "the liberal well" and then simply *Liberal*. The town's more recent claim to fame is its annual Pancake Day Race. Since 1950, the housewives of Liberal have competed with their counterparts in Olney, England, in a 415-yard pancake-flipping foot race on Shrove Tuesday. The friendly competition is part of an all-day celebration in Liberal attended by the British consul for the area and by Kansas state officials.
PO: June 14, 1886–; Pop. 14,911; CS

Liberty *(Montgomery)*

The settlements of Montgomery City and Verdigris City combined their town promotion efforts to start Liberty, a town with a name compatible with that of their neighbor, Independence.
PO: May 25, 1870–; Pop. 174

Liebenthal *(Rush)* [LEE-buhn-tahl]

The village of Liebenthal is the oldest of the villages founded by the German-Russian Catholics who settled in western

Kansas. The founders brought the name *Liebenthal,* which means "valley of love," from Russia.
PO: February 11, 1880–; Pop. 163

Lincoln *(Lincoln)*

The county seat of Lincoln County took its name from the county. The official name is *Lincoln Center.*
PO: November 29, 1878–; Pop. 1,599; CS

Lincoln County *(Established February 26, 1867)*

After George Washington's name, the most popular choice among political place names in the United States is *Lincoln,* for Abraham Lincoln. One of the twenty-two counties in the United States named *Lincoln* is in Kansas.
Pop. 4,000

LIBERAL

Lincolnville *(Marion)*

In 1872, founders named their town after former President Abraham Lincoln.
PO: December 31, 1868–; Pop. 235

Lindsborg *(McPherson)* [LINZ-berg]

"We decided to go to Kansas even before inspecting the territory," said one of the founders of Lindsborg. Besides, Kansas land was the cheapest offered to the Chicago-based First Swedish Land Company. S. P. Lindgren, S. A. Lindell, A. P. Linde, and J. O. Lindh of the first board of directors decided easily on the name *Lindsborg*. They used the first syllable of each man's surname and the suffix *borg,* which corresponds to *burg*. Lindsborg is known for its annual rendition of Handel's *Messiah,* presented each Easter since 1882.
PO: December 1, 1869–; Pop. 3,155

Linn *(Washington)*

Organized in a box car in 1877, Linn was first called *Summit* because it was the highest point railroad surveyors found on that branch of the Missouri Pacific. The name was changed to *Linn* when the town applied for a post office, and it was found that there was another post office called *Summit*. The source of the name is the same as for Linn County.
PO: January 25, 1888–; Pop. 483

Linn County *(Established February 26, 1867)*

The county got its name from physician and politician Dr. Lewis Fields Linn, who served as U.S. senator from Missouri from 1833 to 1843. While a senator, he was instrumental in the acquisition of the Oregon territory for the United States. Linn County claims to have had the first woman rural mail carrier in the United States. Mary Reynolds Hazelbaker began delivering mail in 1904 and stopped in 1933 when she retired at age 65.
Pop. 8,700

Linwood *(Leavenworth)*

The city of Linwood, situated at the junction of Big Stranger Creek and the Kansas River, was originally called *Journey-Cake,* after a chief of the Delaware tribe. Next it had the name *Stranger* and finally *Linwood* for the linden trees in the vicinity.
PO: December 20, 1877–; Pop. 343

Little Arkansas *(South Central Kansas)* [ahr-KANZ-uhz]

The Little Arkansas River arises in Rice County and joins the Big Arkansas in Wichita. The Osage called it *Ne Shuta Shinka,* meaning "the young" or the "little red water."

Little Balkans *(Southeast Kansas)*

The southeast corner of Kansas contains an astonishing fifty-two different ethnic groups, all brought to Kansas to work in zinc smelters and mine the coal that once dominated that regional economy. The term *Balkans* refers to the five countries occupying the Balkan Peninsula in Europe; "the Little Balkans" in Kansas had even greater ethnic diversity in a smaller space.

Little River *(Rice)*

The descriptive name of *Little River* was given to the town platted on the banks of the Little Arkansas River.
PO: June 1, 1880–; Pop. 529

Logan *(Phillips)*

One of the founders suggested the name of his Civil War commander, General John Alexander Logan of Illinois.
PO: March 1, 1872–; Pop. 720

Logan County *(Established March 4, 1881)*

This western Kansas county had been named for Kansas Governor John P. St. John. However, his presidential ambitions and his prohibition activities incurred so much hostility that the legislature renamed the county Logan, after Civil War Union General John Alexander Logan, an Illinois soldier and politician who served in the U.S. Senate from 1871 to 1877 and 1879 to 1886.
Pop. 3,500

London *(Sumner)*

Located on a well-traveled road between Wichita and Wellington, London became a trading center. The village no longer exists, but the township remains. A number of settlers of English ancestry settled Sumner County, leaving such names as *London, Avon, Oxford,* and *Wellington.*
PO: July 10, 1871–September 20, 1887

Lone Elm *(Anderson)*

Lone Elm, probably named for a tree on the site, began as a post office. Later, the town platted near the new railroad took the name.
PO: March 14, 1879–January 31, 1956; Pop. 55

Lone Star *(Douglas)*

Patrons could not think of a name for their new school. While standing outside after a meeting, someone pointed out a lone star shining in the evening sky and suggested the name *Lone Star*. The community also took the name.
PO: October 3, 1899–May 15, 1953

Lone Star Lake *(Douglas)*

In the 1930s, the Civilian Conservation Corps constructed the Lone Star Lake. A small resort community developed around it. The lake took its name from the town of Lone Star a few miles north.

Longford *(Clay)*

An English colony, sixty miles northwest of Dublin, Ireland, was known as *Longford*. A few of the colonists' descendants settled in southern Clay County in 1869, 1870, and 1871.
PO: May 27, 1875–; Pop. 109

Long Island *(Phillips)*

A group of Holland Dutch established a trading and shipping point for farmers and cattlemen in 1871. The name *Long Island* refers to its position between two creeks that run parallel to each other for several miles.
PO: May 16, 1872–; Pop. 187

Longton *(Elk)*

Longton began as *Elk Rapids*. In the county, the word *elk* was so popular as a place name that the post office ordered the name changed to avoid confusion. Local hardware merchant Herbert Capper, father of the future Senator Arthur Capper, suggested the name *Longton,* for his parents' home in England.
PO: August 24, 1870–; Pop. 396

Loretto *(Rush)*

The village of Loretto came into being in 1912 when the Catholic church divided Kansas into the Wichita Diocese and the Concordia Diocese. Members of the Pfeifer parish lived on both sides of the line. To avoid confusion, those in the Wichita Diocese broke away completely from Pfeifer to form a new parish. The Rev. Joseph Stuze named it *Loretto* after a city near the Adriatic Sea in Italy which has been a shrine of the Blessed Virgin Mary since 1295. The name has also been spelled with an *a, Loretta.*
Pop. 30

Lorraine *(Ellsworth)*

Railroad officials had numerous opportunities to name newly established stations and towns after themselves or their families. A Wichita-based railroad official named *Lorraine* for his daughter Lorraine Stanley.
PO: February 15, 1888–; Pop. 157

Lost Spring *(Marion)*

> Who spoke so soft the southwest Spanish tongue,
> And failed to find this fountain as of yore,
> They wailed their loss and from their lips was heard,
> "Oh, Agua Perdida, Oh, Water Lost!"
> —George Morehouse

Despite its occasional dry spells, Lost Spring had enough water to be a regular stopping place on the Santa Fe Trail from the 1830s through the 1860s. In 1846, the U.S. Army planted watercress and strawberries there for passing soldiers to eat to prevent scurvy. A ranch located there in the 1850s catered to gamblers and outlaws before closing in the late 1860s.
PO: August 29, 1861–May 23, 1864

Lost Springs *(Marion)*

This town is located one and a half miles east of the Lost Spring of Santa Fe Trail fame. Other springs in the area led to the multiple "springs" in the name. An oil scout visiting Lost Springs during the boom town years remembered: "Heck, I'll tell you how the town got its name. The springs were slipped out of the beds just before the customer arrived."
PO: July 9, 1879–; Pop. 94

Louisburg *(Miami)* [LOO-is-berg]

A year before the town site was surveyed, a settlement named *St. Louis,* or *Little St. Louis,* had developed a quarter of a mile east. When the site was platted, and the St. Louis settlement was included in the community, founders believed that St. Louis, Kansas, could be easily confused with St. Louis, Missouri, and therefore chose *Louisburg.*
PO: January 2, 1872–; Pop. 1,744

Louisville *(Pottawatomie)* [LOO-is-vil]

Established as a town site in 1857, Louisville was named after Louis Wilson. On the south side was Iron Springs, once a popular health resort.
PO: July 19, 1867–; Pop. 207

Lovewell *(Jewell)*

Former government Indian scout and hunter Thomas Lovewell and his family settled in the White Rock Valley in the spring of 1865. The nearby Lovewell Dam, located on White Rock Creek, was dedicated on June 5, 1958.
PO: August 20, 1895–; Pop. 25

Lucas *(Russell)*

The name *Lucas* came from Lucas Place in St. Louis.
PO: June 7, 1887–; Pop. 524

Ludell *(Rawlins)*

First it was *Prag*, then *Danuble*, then *Luella*. The U.S. Post Office department did not like the name *Luella*, so William H. Demmich, town site owner, changed it by saving the first syllable *Lu* and adding *dell*.
PO: May 9, 1881–; Pop. 90

Luray *(Russell)* [loo-RAY]

Postmaster John Fritts changed the name of the station from the feminine *Lura* to *Luray*.
PO: January 7, 1888–; Pop. 295

Lyndon *(Osage)*

Lawrence D. Bailey, judge of the state Supreme Court, was the town founder. He may have named it for Lyndon, Vermont.
PO: March 28, 1870–; Pop. 1,132; CS

Lyon County *(Established February 5, 1862)*

Once a part of Breckenridge County, the name was changed to *Lyon* in February 1862. Nathaniel Lyon, an abolitionist, was in command of Fort Riley in 1860 and led Kansas and Iowa regiments in the Civil War battle of Wilson's Creek. He was wounded there and died August 10, 1862.
Pop. 38,500

Lyons *(Rice)*

The city of Lyons was started by Truman J. Lyons in 1876. When Lyons arrived the community was called *Atlanta*. He bought the land where the city of Lyons now stands, laid out the town, and donated the ground for a court house square, public school grounds, and various business lots. Near Lyons stands a monument to the first Christian martyr on U.S. terri-

tory, Father Juan de Padilla, who came to the territory first with explorer Francisco de Coronado in 1541. They reputedly erected a cross near the location of present-day Lyons, then returned to Mexico. Father Padilla and a small group returned to Kansas the next year, and the Indians he knew welcomed him. When unfriendly Indians approached him, he urged his friends to flee and he alone would try to pacify them. The hostile Indians riddled his body with arrows. No one knows for sure where he died. Other monuments to Padilla stand in Council Grove and Herington.
PO: February 16, 1877–; Pop. 4,134; CS

Macksville *(Stafford)*

George Mack was one of the town company directors and also the first postmaster.
PO: March 14, 1879–; Pop. 546

Madison *(Greenwood)*

The name was given to a creek, a township, a golf course, and a town. All were named for the fourth president of the United States, James Madison.
PO: September 16, 1858–; Pop. 1,099

Mahaska *(Washington)* [muh-HAS-kuh]

Mahaska is the Indian version of the name of White Cloud II. A chief of the Prairie Sioux (Iowa), Mahaska had both his Indian name and English name used for towns in northeastern Kansas.
PO: December 22, 1887–; Pop. 119

Maize *(Sedgwick)*

Located in the midst of rich farm land, where corn and wheat were major crops, promoters found the Spanish name for Indian corn—*maize*—to be appropriate for their new station nine miles northwest of Wichita.
PO: February 1, 1886–; Pop. 1,294

Manchester *(Dickinson)*

Manchester is said to be named for Manchester, England. It may also have taken its name from any one of the fifteen Manchesters east of Kansas.
PO: October 28, 1889–; Pop. 98

Manhattan *(Riley)*

With their steamboat stranded on a sandbar near the junction of the Blue and Kansas rivers, a disappointed Cincinnati Kan-

sas Association gave up their dream of founding the town of Manhattan at the Smoky Hill and Republican rivers junction twenty miles farther upstream. Settlers on site near the stranded boat *Hartford* invited the Cincinnati group to join them. The on-site group consisted mostly of settlers from New England led by Isaac Goodnow and supported by the New England Emigrant Aid Company. When the Goodnow party had arrived in March 1855, they had found the site claimed by others. One group called its claim *Canton*, and another party called part of the site *Polistra*. All the early claimants organized the Boston Town Association and agreed to call the settlement *Boston*. Yet not all were happy with that name. When the Cincinnati group decided to join the Bostonians, the name was changed to *Manhattan* because, as Goodnow recalled in June 1855, a clause in the Ohio company's constitution required that the town where they settled be called *Manhattan*. Kansas State University is located in Manhattan. *(See* Aggieville.)
PO: September 4, 1856–; Pop. 32,644; CS

Mankato *(Jewell)* [man-KAY-toh]

H. R. Hills named the county seat of Jewell County after his former home in Mankato, Blue Earth County, Minnesota. *Mankato* was a Siouan name meaning "blue earth."
PO: April 1, 1880–; Pop. 1,205; CS

Manter *(Stanton)*

A Santa Fe Railroad official's name was used for this town.
PO: February 10, 1923–; Pop. 205

Maple Hill *(Wabaunsee)*

Mrs. Higgenbotham, acting postmaster, named the small community in Wabaunsee County for the small grove of maple trees growing on a knoll near where she worked.
PO: May 1, 1862–; Pop. 381

Mapleton *(Bourbon)*

A Vermont colony settled a town they named for the maples in the area.
PO: June 15, 1857–; Pop. 121

Marais des Cygnes *(Miami and Linn)* [mair-uh-duh-SEEN]

The translation from French is "marsh of the swans." The name is given to a waterfowl refuge area, a river, and a historic massacre site. Legend surrounds the name. An Osage story tells of two young lovers who disappeared mysteriously while canoeing in the river. As the horrified people looked upon the scene where the canoers had vanished, they saw two great white swans swim away together. Another story told of Evangeline of the Longfellow poem who walked to the top of a timbered mound overlooking the river and valley, saying "C'est le marais des cygnes." In the valley of the Marais des Cygnes there are more than 15,000 acres of ox-bows, natural lakes, and wetlands and an occasional swan. The river was originally called the *Osage*. The Kansas part was officially renamed *Marais des Cygnes,* but it remains the *Osage* in Missouri.

Marais des Cygnes Massacre Site *(Linn)*

In May 1858, thirty proslavery Missourians crossed over into free Kansas, gathered up eleven men, and shot them. Five died.

> From the hearths of their cabins,
>   The field of their corn,
> Unwarned and unweaponed,
>   The victims were torn—
> By the whirlwind of murder
>   Swooped up and swept on
> To the low, reedy fen-lands,
>   The Marsh of the Swans.
>   —John Greenleaf Whittier

Mariadahl *(Pottawatomie)* [muh-REE-uh-dahl]

Swedish settlers came to the Blue Valley in 1855. Their Lutheran congregation organized on October 14, 1863, making it the oldest Swedish Lutheran Church in Kansas. The church and the community took the name *Mariadahl* to honor Maria Nilson Johnson, the mother of settlers John and Peter Johnson. Construction of the Tuttle Creek dam and reservoir on their land forced descendants of the early settlers to move away.
PO: October 27, 1876–March 31, 1903

Marion *(Marion)*

The county seat town was first called *Marion Center.* Marion was one of twenty-eight Kansas towns that included the word *Center* in its name. Sometimes this meant the town was in the center of the county, and sometimes the *Center* was used for political-geographical emphasis. Once the town won the county seat designation, the name center was usually dropped.
PO: October 15, 1881–; Pop. 1,951; CS

Marion County *(Established August 25, 1855)*

When the county was named in 1855, the pro-South legislature named it for the American Revolutionary War hero Francis Marion, the "Swamp Fox," of South Carolina. At one time Marion County reached all the way to the Colorado and Oklahoma borders, but its size was reduced as other counties came into being.
Pop. 13,500

Marquette *(McPherson)* [mahr-KET]

The French name *Marquette* was hardly the most suitable one for this predominantly Swedish community. The town founder, Harrison S. Bacon, seeking a flour mill site, came to Kansas from Marquette, Michigan, in 1872. He helped organize the town in 1874. A committee in Illinois formed the Galesburg Land Company to secure land for Swedish immigrants. They purchased 14,080 acres in Saline and McPherson counties from the Kansas Pacific Railroad. This land, which was located along Dry Creek in Saline County and along the Smoky Hill River in McPherson County, extended from five miles south of Salina to three miles west of Marquette. Swedes began arriving in 1869, establishing the communities of Falun, Smolan, Assaria, Lindsborg, Fremont, and Marquette. Before the post office was named *Marquette,* it was called *Calmar* (December 1, 1871—August 11, 1873), after the town of Kalmar in southeastern Sweden.
PO: August 11, 1873–; Pop. 639.

Marshall County *(Established August 25, 1855)*

Francis J. (Frank) Marshall, one of the state's first settlers and a member of the first territorial legislature, was able to get a county named for him. In 1849 he began the operation of a ferry and trading post at Independence Ford on the Big Blue River nine miles below the Marysville crossing.
Pop. 12,900

Marysville *(Marshall)*

Francis Marshall not only got a county named for himself, he also got a county-seat town named for his wife, Mary. Although the Marshalls were proslavery people prior to the Civil War, they moved to Colorado rather than be forced to take sides. The Marysville post office is said to be the first in Kansas named for a woman.
PO: November 11, 1854–; Pop. 3,670; CS

Matfield Green (*Chase*)

David W. Mercer, coming to the county in 1858, named the post office and town of Matfield Green after a hamlet near his birthplace in the village of Five Oaks, County Kent, England. As a boy, he had attended cricket matches in Matfield Green. The name in Chase County has also been given to the I-35 Turnpike service area. A stone memorial to the famous Notre Dame football coach, Knute Rockne, stands south of the restaurant in the service area; another memorial stands at the site where the plane carrying Rockne crashed three miles northwest of there on March 31, 1931.
PO: January 11, 1867–; Pop. 71

Maxwell Game Preserve (*McPherson*)

Brothers John G. and Henry I. Maxwell became prosperous grain merchants, acquired large holdings of real estate, and shortly after the turn of the century developed an orchard considered one of the show places of central Kansas. In their wills, both brothers provided for the establishment of a wildlife preserve. The Kansas State Fish and Game Commission carried out their wishes. Buffalo, antelope, and other wildlife live on the 2,480 acres north of Canton in McPherson County.

May Day (*Riley*)

The rural community opened a post office about May 1, 1871, with the postmaster choosing the name *May Day*.
PO: April 13, 1871–February 15, 1954

Mayetta (*Jackson*) [may-ET-uh]

The town began as a trading center for farmers and Indians. Mrs. E. E. Lunger named the town in memory of her daughter Mary Henrietta.
PO: December 16, 1886–; Pop. 287

Mayfield (*Sumner*)

The origin of the name remains unclear. Possibly it was named for a pioneer named Mayfield. Or for the young niece of George Hutchinson, the town site owner. She enjoyed walking over the town site covered with wild flowers, so he could have called it *May's field—Mayfield*—for her.
PO: September 8, 1880–; Pop. 128

McConnell Air Force Base *(Sedgwick)*

The name was chosen to honor three Wichita flyers, Thomas L., Edwin M., and Fred McConnell, Jr., who did combat duty in the South Pacific during World War II. McConnell opened southeast of Wichita in 1951, becoming a training center for combat crews for the B-47 jet bomber and later the B-52.

MCCONNELL AIR FORCE BASE

McCracken *(Rush)*

The town was named after J. K. McCracken, close relative of the New York financier and railroad tycoon Jay Gould. McCracken, a pioneer in western Kansas, worked as the contractor in charge of building the Missouri Pacific Railroad through the town site.
PO: January 31, 1887–; Pop. 292

McCune *(Crawford)*

Isaac McCune founded the town in 1879 and also worked as the local postmaster.
PO: August 12, 1878–; Pop. 528

McDonald *(Rawlins)*

Rice McDonald gave land to the Burlington Railroad for a station and town in 1888.
PO: July 21, 1888–; Pop. 239

McFarland *(Wabaunsee)*

A Mr. Fairfield wanted the town he founded to be named for him, but because a *Fairfield* already existed in Russell County he recommended the name *McFarland* for his friend Judge J. N. McFarland of Topeka.
PO: December 19, 1887–; Pop. 242

McLouth *(Jefferson)* [muhk-LOWTH]

Amos McLouth came to Kansas to buy land in Jefferson
County, paying three dollars per acre in 1868. The development of the town of McLouth had raised the value to three
hundred dollars per acre by 1882.
PO: May 26, 1882–; Pop. 700

McPherson *(McPherson)* [muhk-FER-suhn]

Four towns competed for the McPherson County seat—
Gotland, Lindsborg, McPherson, and King City. The
McPherson Town Company offered a land site for the courthouse for a period of ten years. When the votes were
counted, McPherson had 605 votes out of a total of 934, and
the county offices moved from their temporary quarters at
Lindsborg to McPherson. Even though rumors of illegal votes
circulated, based on the fact that the vote cast exceeded the
county's population by nearly 200, no one challenged the
vote.
PO: January 21, 1873–; Pop. 11,753; CS

McPherson County *(Established February 26, 1867)*

James Birdseye McPherson, a general on the Union side, was
killed in action at Atlanta, Georgia, on July 22, 1864. McPherson graduated at the head of his class at West Point. An
equestrian statue of the handsome and popular military officer stands on the courthouse square in McPherson.
Pop. 28,000

Meade *(Meade)*

The county seat town took its name from the county.
PO: March 30, 1889–; Pop. 1,777; CS

Meade County *(Established January 8, 1873)*

"A tall, thin man, rather dyspeptic . . . lacking in cordiality
and disliked by his subordinates" had an admirer in Kansas
who named the county for him. The honored man, General
George Gordon Meade, commanded the Army of the
Potomac and was victorious at Gettysburg in 1863.
Pop. 4,800

Medicine Lodge *(Barber)*

Years before white settlers arrived, the Indians in the region
believed the site to be under the protection of the Great
Spirit. Prairie fires passed around the region, making it seem

that the waters of the Medicine River had the magic power to protect the green woodland on its banks. In October 1867, Medicine Lodge was the site of the Medicine Lodge Peace Treaty negotiated between the federal government representatives and the chiefs of the five plains tribes. Also, Medicine Lodge was the home of prohibitionist Carry Nation and the site of her first public demonstration (1899), when she and a few associates held a prayer meeting in front of a saloon.
PO: December 5, 1872–; Pop. 2,384; CS

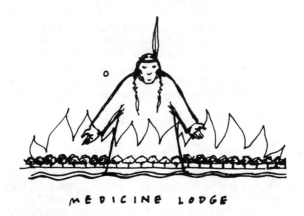

MEDICINE LODGE

Medicine Lodge River *(South Central Kansas)*

The Kiowas took medicine baths at the stream they called *A-ya-dalda-P'a,* or "timber-hill river." Settlers called it Medicine Lodge River.

Melvern *(Osage)*

Charles Cochran, one of the town company members who founded the town in 1870, was born at Malvern Hills, England. By mistake, the *a* was changed to *e,* and the name remained Melvern.
PO: June 13, 1870–; Pop. 481

Meriden *(Jefferson)* [MAIR-i-den]

When the pioneer Newell Colby moved from Meriden, New Hampshire, to Kansas, he named the town site for his previous home.
PO: December 19, 1873–; Pop. 707

Merriam *(Johnson)* [MAIR-ee-uhm]

This community, now a part of Greater Kansas City, was first known as *Campbellton,* for J. M. Campbell, one of its earliest residents. In 1881 the name was changed to *Merriam* for either G. F. Merriam, who served as township clerk in Johnson County in 1858, or for a man who obtained a railroad line for the town.
PO: May 18, 1881–July 31, 1960; Pop. 10,794

Miami County *(Established August 25, 1855)*

Among the first counties established, it carried the name *Lykins* until the 1861 legislature changed the name to *Miami* for the Miami Indians who had settled in that area. *Miami* was an Indian word for "mother."
Pop. 22,800

Midian *(Butler)* [MID-ee-uhn]

This place, no longer listed on maps, was once a prosperous oil boom town of some 4,000. In 1912, the Missouri Pacific Railroad built a siding three miles east of Towanda. Two officials, C. K. Bothwell and W. H. Mooney, who both served as potentate of Midian Shrine, suggested the name *Midian.* A few years later a group of eleven men organized an oil drilling company they called the Trapshooter Oil Co. and on May 15, 1917, brought in a gusher, Trapshooter No. 1, at Midian. Cities Service, a major leaseholder, built a company town, "a good one." P. F. Hartnett of El Dorado remembered Midian having a baseball team with Casey Stengel as one of the players. Years later, after oil well ownership changed, the town died. "But it was quite a town while it lasted."
PO: November 5, 1918–July 22, 1950

Midway *(Crawford)*

First known as *Hole-in-the-Prairie,* the site was renamed because it was midway between Fort Scott and Baxter Springs

MIDWAY

on the old Military Road that paralleled the Kansas-Missouri border. During the coal mining era, Midway was situated in the heart of the most accessible coal fields in southeastern Kansas. Other rural communities called *Midway* are found in Butler, Kingman, and Rawlins counties.
PO: May 7, 1871–July 15, 1912

Milan *(Sumner)* [MEYE-luhn]

Milan possibly came from Milan, Ohio, the home of Chief Quenemo, who had given his name to another Kansas town.
PO: February 15, 1875–; Pop. 135

Mildred *(Allen)*

Cement company president J. W. Wagner promoted a town in northeastern Allen County, naming it *Mildred* for his daughter.
PO: September 24, 1907–; Pop. 64

Milford *(Geary)*

The town site of Milford, founded as *Batcheller* (or *Bacheller*) in 1855, now stands near the waters of the largest manmade lake in Kansas, the 16,168-acre Milford Reservoir. The name *Milford* may be descriptive and derived from the saw and grist mill established here on the Republican River. The infamous Dr. John R. Brinkley put Milford on the map. He came to Milford in 1918 and opened a medical practice where he offered to restore male sexual vitality by transplanting goat glands. After a few "successes" he opened his own bank and started the first radio station in Kansas. The "goat gland doctor" waged a formidable campaign for governor in 1930 and 1932, using newspapers, his own radio station, an airplane, and a 16-cylinder Cadillac to carry his opinions to the people.
PO: February 3, 1868–; Pop. 465

Mill Creek *(Wabaunsee)*

After the federal government built grist mills on Beaver Stream to assist the Kansa Indians in milling grain, the name was changed to *Mill Creek*. With these mills came the first white men, mainly of French descent. Mill Creek arises in Milford township in the Flint Hills and meanders down to the Kansas River. It has clear water, a rock bottom, and a quick current typical of Flint Hills streams. Bedrock outcrops in the stream have formed a number of waterfalls, and in some places the current has cut pools down to twenty feet deep. The name Mill Creek has been given to fourteen sites or streams in ten different counties. The one in Wabaunsee is among the most scenic.

Miller *(Lyon)*

Founded in 1910 and named after the Miller Ranch, Miller never incorporated, never flourished, but has endured. In fact, it was designated a Bicentennial community in 1976.
PO: April 22, 1887–April 18, 1958; Pop. 70

Miltonvale *(Cloud)*

Milton Tootle of St. Joseph owned the land upon which the town was situated. The private junior college, Miltonvale Wesleyan College, closed several years ago.
PO: April 6, 1882–; Pop. 588

Mine Creek Battlefield *(Linn)*

On October 24, 1864, about 2,000 Union soldiers and 7,000 Confederate troops battled along a 1,100-yard stretch of Mine Creek, 2 miles south of the present town of Pleasanton. The Battle of Mine Creek was Kansas' largest Civil War engagement; in it the Union forces defeated the Confederates. Indians and French explorers both had mined lead near the creek before Kansas became a territory in 1854.

Mingo *(Thomas)*

This western Kansas town has the same name as a branch of the Sioux Indian tribe.
PO: April 4, 1894–May 15, 1940; Pop. 35

Minneapolis *(Ottawa)*

Captain A. D. Pierce from Minneapolis, Minnesota, gave the name to the county seat in Ottawa County. The Sioux word *minne,* meaning "water," has been combined with the Greek *polis,* meaning "city."
PO: January 11, 1868–; Pop. 2,075; CS

Minneola *(Clark)* [min-ee-OH-luh]

The town name came from combining the names of Minnie Davis and Ola Watson.
PO: April 23, 1888–; Pop. 712

Mission *(Johnson)*

Three Greater Kansas City residential districts—Mission, Mission Hills, and Mission Woods—are named for the historic Shawnee Methodist Mission started by the Reverend Thomas Johnson. In 1985, the affluent Mission Hills community, with a population of 4,130, ranked second in the state

with a per capita income of $48,966; neighboring Mission
Woods had only 213 people.
Pop. 8,800

Mission Creek *(Shawnee)*

First called American Chief Creek, the name was changed to
Mission Creek after the Indian mission buildings, located west
of present Topeka, were erected there around 1835. The early
settlement consisted of Frederick Chouteau's fur trading post,
a government blacksmith, a farm, and a few other employees
of the mission established under the charge of Rev. William
Johnson (brother of Thomas Johnson) and his wife. There are
four other *Mission Creeks* in Kansas; this one is located at the
western edge of Shawnee County.

Mitchell County *(Established February 26, 1867)*

Captain William Mitchell came with his parents from Massachusetts in 1855 to settle near Ogden, Kansas. He was killed
at Monroe's Cross Roads, North Carolina, shortly before the
end of the Civil War.
Pop. 8,300

Modoc *(Scott)* [MOH-dock]

The Indian tribal name became a place name for towns in
Illinois, Indiana, South Carolina, and California, as well as
Kansas.
PO: October 15, 1887–; Pop. 60

Moline *(Elk)* [MOH-leen]

O. B. Gunn, chief engineer of the Southern Kansas Railroad,
needed to locate a depot for the railroad. Two groups contested for the station and each brought signed petitions to
Gunn, who offered W. H. Lamb eight hundred dollars for his
eighty acres. Major J. F. Chapman, however, was credited
with naming the town *Moline*, probably for his former home,
Moline, Illinois. Until the mid-1980s, L. E. "Chig" Ames of
Moline was the owner of one of America's oldest Chevrolet
dealerships in the nation. His father, Ora R. Ames, began
selling Chevrolet cars in 1915.
PO: September 1, 1879–; Pop. 533

Monmouth *(Crawford)*

The oldest town in the county, named after Monmouth, Illinois, was located in the abundant coal-producing region.
PO: July 17, 1866–September 30, 1955; Pop. 30

Monrovia *(Atchison)*

Once a station on the Overland Stage route, the town of
Monrovia was platted in 1856 or 1857, making it one of the
oldest towns in Kansas. Solomon J. H. Snyder, landowner
and organizer of the Monrovia Town Company, chose the
name after Monrovia, Liberia, to symbolize his support of the
free-state principle. The Liberian town was named after President James Monroe.
PO: September 4, 1857–November 30, 1955; Pop. 25

Montezuma *(Gray)*

The town founder, familiar with the story of the Spanish
conquest of Mexico, named the town *Montezuma* for the emperor of the Aztecs and named the streets for historical figures associated with the conquest.
PO: August 21, 1886–; Pop. 730

Montgomery County *(Established February 26, 1867)*

The county was named after James M. Montgomery, a dis-
tant relative of Brigadier General Richard Montgomery of the
Continental Army, who was killed while leading an assault
against the English at Quebec, December 31, 1775. James M.
Montgomery was an outspoken abolitionist and preacher
who settled in Linn, Kansas. Montgomery County has been
home to a number of famous people: explorers Martin and
Osa Johnson, playwright William Inge, movie actor Tom Mix,
author Laura Ingalls Wilder, oil man Harry Sinclair, and
politicians Wendell Willkie and Alf Landon.
Pop. 43,000

Monument *(Logan)*

This town was born upon the arrival of the Union Pacific
Railroad in June 1868. Monument marked the 386th mile post
on the line. A second version of the source of the name says
that the town company had started to erect a monument in
honor of General John A. Logan. Costs were too great, and it
was never completed. Eventually the structure, damaged by
high winds, was considered unsafe and torn down. The settlement remains.
PO: June 16, 1868–September 25, 1868; May 19, 1880–; Pop. 70

Monument Rocks *(Gove)*

These "Kansas Pyramids" are a chalk formation carved and
shaped by the Smoky Hill River. The rocks rise steeply from
the High Plains, which in ancient times were a floodplain of

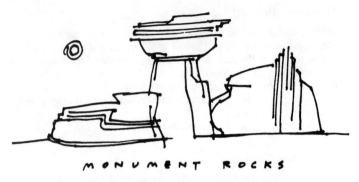

MONUMENT ROCKS

the Smoky Hill River. The land around the rocks is one of the richest fossil hunting areas in the world.

Moonlight *(Dickinson)*

Moonlight traces its beginnings to 1879 when a colony of seventy men and their families, all members of the Brethren church, moved west from Pennsylvania to Kansas. When a post office opened in the community in 1894, they named it *Moonlight* for Thomas Moonlight, a Kansas politician who served as secretary of the state of Kansas from 1869 to 1871.
PO: March 19, 1894–October 14, 1905

Moran *(Allen)* [mor-AN]

It could have been named for the Moran brothers of Chicago or for Daniel C. Moran, a New York financier of the Fort Scott, Wichita, and Western Railway.
PO: May 6, 1899–; Pop. 643

Morganville *(Clay)*

The town was founded by Ebenezer Morgan in 1870.
PO: August 2, 1872–; Pop. 261

Morland *(Graham)* [MOR-luhnd]

First it was *Fremont,* then *Kalula,* and finally *Morland* for a railroad official in 1892.
PO: February 4, 1892–; Pop. 223

Mormon Grove *(Atchison)*

While migrating from their eastern settlement to a new home west of the Rockies, many Mormons stopped at a spot four miles west of Atchison. They occupied the site at various times from 1845 to 1860. Because there was not enough lumber to build fences for livestock, they dug ditches around their 200-acre camp to keep the livestock from leaving. West of these pasture lands was their main settlement, at the grove of trees that came to be known as Mormon Grove.

Morrill *(Brown)*

T. J. Elliot named the town for his friend Edmund Needham Morrill of Hiawatha, Kansas. During his long and distinguished career, Morrill served as a territorial legislator, soldier, businessman, state senator, member of Congress, and governor of Kansas.
PO: December 14, 1870–; Pop. 336

Morris County *(Established February 11, 1859)*

The 1855 legislature created the county of Wise. The 1859 legislature changed it to Morris, after Thomas Morris, U.S. senator from Ohio.
Pop. 6,300

Morrowville *(Washington)*

Founded in 1884, the town was named for its founder, Cal Morrow, a politician. The Post Office Department appears to have been responsible for changing the name to *Morrowville*. It was said that asking for a ticket to Morrow confused people enough to change the name to *Morrowville*.
PO: June 9, 1884 to June 7, 1894, as Morrow; June 7, 1894–; Pop. 180

Morton County *(Established February 18, 1886)*

Named to honor Oliver Hazard Perry Throck Morton, Indiana governor (1861–1876) and senator (1867–1877).
Pop. 3,400

Moscow *(Stevens)* [MOS-koh]

No, it was not named for the city in Russia. One story said that it was named for Mosco, a Colorado pioneer. Another story claimed it was named for Moscoso, one of Coronado's men. A clerk added a *w* when officially recording the name.
PO: May 3, 1913–; Pop. 228

Mound City *(Linn)*

The county seat derived its name from proximity to a local landmark, Sugar Mound. Proud residents of Mound City boasted that their place was the "Eden of the West." In the

early years local mineral wells attracted hundreds of people afflicted with different ailments.
PO: February 1, 1859–; Pop. 755; CS

Mound Valley *(Labette)*

A range of moundlike hills exist in the vicinity.
PO: May 18, 1870–; Pop. 381

Moundridge *(McPherson)*

D. P. Jones was directing the construction of the Missouri Pacific Railroad through McPherson County when he suggested the name *Moundridge* after Mound township in which it is located and for its elevation. The majority of the town's early settlers were German Mennonites who came to Kansas in the 1870s from Europe, primarily Russia.
PO: February 17, 1887–; Pop. 1,453

Mount Hope *(Sedgwick)*

There are no "mounts" or even hills in the town twenty-five miles northwest of Wichita. Admirers refer to Mount Hope as the greenest town in Sedgwick County because stately cottonwood and maple trees line Main Street. The popular name *Mount Hope* was given to eighteen cemeteries in Kansas, including the one close to the town of Mount Hope.
PO: December 24, 1873–; Pop. 791

Mount Hope Cemetery *(Brown)*

Eleven life-size portrait statues carved in Italian marble perpetuate the memory of John M. Davis and his wife in this section of the cemetery at the southeast edge of Hiawatha. Italian artists used photographs of the Davises as models for their statues. A Vermont sculptor carved the final granite image of the husband. The couple, married for over fifty years, had no children.

Mount Jesus *(Clark)*

During the Indian Wars, Mount Jesus was also called *Lookout* or *Fire Mountain* and used as a signaling point. Major Henry Inman, who was traveling with Lt. Col. George Custer in 1876, has been credited with calling the site *Mt. Jesus* but never saying why.

Mount Oread *(Douglas)* [OR-ee-uhd]

The 1854 settlers of Lawrence cooked their first meal atop a barren, treeless ridge that offered a sweeping view of the valleys of the Wakarusa and Kaw rivers. On the first day there, Ferdinand Fuller of Worcester, Massachusetts, wrote "Mount Oread" on his tent after Mount Oread Seminary for Girls in his home town. (More than likely, seminary founder Eli Thayer knew that in Greek mythology oreads were nymphs of the mountains.) The high ridge dividing the river valleys had earlier been called *Devil's Backbone* and *Hog Back Ridge*, but the names were too coarse for New Englanders. *Mount Oread*, a name rooted in mythology and familiar to them, seemed more appropriate. The University of Kansas opened there in 1866 and has since become one of the most beautiful campuses in the United States.

MOUNT OREAD

Mount Pleasant *(Atchison)*

Thomas Fortune opened the first store in Mount Pleasant Township in 1854 and the post office in 1855. Pleased with his claim's high, agreeable location, Jed Ashcroft named it *Mount Pleasant*. In the future, both a town and township would use the name. Mount Pleasant, the town, claimed to have the first high school in Kansas, which opened in the fall of 1859. The name *Mount Pleasant* has been applied to six churches, six cemeteries, and two townships in Kansas.
PO: March 3, 1855–February 28, 1900

Mount Sunflower *(Wallace)*

Mount Sunflower, at an elevation of 4,039 feet, is the highest point in Kansas. It lies close to the Colorado-Kansas border. Don't expect a prominent mountain. The land rises gradually from a low of around 680 feet south of Coffeyville to around 4,000 feet at the Colorado border.

Mulberry *(Crawford)*

Wild mulberry trees grew throughout eastern and central Kansas. The town of Mulberry began as *Mulberry Grove*.
PO: May 21, 1892–; Pop. 647

Mullinville *(Kiowa)*

In the spring of 1884, twenty-five-year-old Alfred A. Mullin was following the stakes of the Wichita and Western Railroad survey searching for a town site. He came to a spot where the railroad and the trail from Hutchinson to Kinsley crossed. There he drove a stake to mark off his town site and built a store to sell goods to freighters traveling through.
PO: September 12, 1884–; Pop. 339

Mulvane *(Sedgwick and Sumner)* [muhl-VAYN]

Located on the Sedgwick-Sumner county line, Mulvane owed its beginning and early prosperity to the coming of the Santa Fe Railroad. It was named for Topeka bankers Joab and John Mulvane. Joab was also a director of the Santa Fe Railroad.
PO: September 1, 1879–; Pop. 4,254

Munden *(Republic)*

John Munden of Allegheny, Pennsylvania, owned the land used for this station on the Santa Fe Railroad.
PO: February 18, 1888–; Pop. 152

Murdock *(Kingman)*

The Murdocks, founders of the *Wichita Eagle* newspaper, and specifically the editor Marsh Murdock, inspired the town's name choice. The town was first called *New Murdock,* but that changed to *Murdock* after another place called *Murdock* closed its post office.
PO: March 17, 1884–January 4, 1910 (New Murdock); January 4, 1910–; Pop. 75

MUTE CREEK

Muscotah *(Atchison)* [muhs-KOH-tuh]

The Kickapoo or Potawatomi word *muscotah* means either "beautiful prairie" or "prairie on fire."
PO: December 23, 1861–; Pop. 248

Mute Creek *(Osage)*

The principal southern tributary of the Marais des Cygnes was said to be named for a deaf mute who held a claim on its banks during the settlement period.

Narka *(Republic)*

Although Narka was said to be a name of Indian origin, it was the name of a daughter of an official of the Chicago, Rock Island, and Pacific Railroad.
PO: November 29, 1887–; Pop. 120

Nashville *(Kingman)*

The name was taken from Nashville, Tennessee, or Nashville, Illinois.
PO: August 30, 1887–; Pop. 127

Natoma *(Osborne)* [nuh-TOH-muh]

The Indian word *natoma* means "newly born." R. F. Baldwin, an early settler and lawyer, chose the name.
PO: July 16, 1890–; Pop. 515

NATOMA

Nemaha County *(Established August 25, 1855)* [NEE-muh-hah]

The county was named for the Nemaha River in Nebraska, a branch of which drains the northern half of the county.
Pop. 1,121

Neodesha *(Wilson)* [nee-OH-duh-SHAY]

The Osage word *neodesha* meant "meeting of the water." Several Indian villages were located near the junction of the Verdigris and Fall rivers, and the name *Neodesha* was given to the trading post there. The first Kansas oil well to produce in commercial quantities, Norman No. 1, was drilled at Neodesha in November 1892. Standard Oil Company built its first Kansas refinery at Neodesha.
PO: June 13, 1870–; Pop. 3,414

N E O D E S H A

Neola *(Stafford)*

The first settlers came from Neola, Iowa. Fred Sherman, a Neola native, preferred to believe that the village was named after a resident's favorite milk cow, Neola.
PO: August 15, 1878–September 30, 1918

Neosho County *(Established June 3, 1861)* [nee-OH-sho]

This county started out as Dorn, but on June 3, 1861, its name was changed to that of the Neosho River, which had been

named by the Kansas Indians many years before white settlement. George Sibley of the Santa Fe Trail survey team mentioned the Nee Ozho River in his journal entry of August 5, 1825. *Ne* means "water" and *osho* means "stream in" or "stream with water in it." The Osages described the color of Neosho as "Water-Like-the-Skin-of-a-Summer-Cow-Wapiti." Pioneers sometimes referred to the river as *Noshow* because it occasionally went dry in the summer.
Pop. 18,967

Neosho Falls *(Woodson)*

The oldest town in Woodson County was named after the river that flows in a broad riffle over a rock ledge. Once a busy place with churches, businesses, and a lively population, Neosho Falls nearly washed away when heavy rains caused a ten-foot wall of water that roared through the town in July 1951. Businesses weren't rebuilt, and the population dropped from 1,000 to around 150.
PO: May 21, 1857–; Pop. 157

Neosho Rapids *(Lyon)*

After being called *Florence, Neosho City,* and *Italia,* the town took its present name in 1860, when Forrest Page platted the town. He located it on the Neosho River near a rapids that powered the local gristmill.
PO: February 27, 1863–; Pop. 289

Ness City *(Ness)*

The county seat town was named after the county.
PO: January 31, 1881–; Pop. 1,769; CS

NEOLA

Ness County *(Established February 26, 1867)*

The county was named for Corporal Noah V. Ness of the
Seventh Kansas Cavalry, who died August 22, 1864, of
wounds received in battle. Ness was the only corporal to be
honored by a county name in Kansas. The renowned scientist
George Washington Carver homesteaded land near Beeler in
Ness County.
PO: 4,498

Netawaka *(Jackson)* [NE-tuh-WAH-kuh]

The Pottawatomi word *netawaka* is said to mean "grand
view" or possibly a "high divide" from which one could get a
grand view. Before the Civil War, the northeastern Kansas
town was one of several clandestine stations on the underground railroad.
PO: January 20, 1868–; Pop. 218

New Albany *(Wilson)*

Pioneers from New Albany, Indiana, settled this town.
PO: May 2, 1866–; Pop. 78

New Cambria *(Saline)*

Merchant and farmer S. P. Donmyer, who was born in Cambria County, Pennsylvania, started New Cambria in 1872. He
was the first to open a store and keep a post office there. He
probably influenced naming the township Cambria, also,
when it was organized in 1878.
PO: June 25, 1873–; Pop. 175

New Gottland *(McPherson)* [GAHT-luhnd]

Swedish immigrants settled in this township in the 1870s.
They named it *Gottland* for the Swedish island province in
the Baltic Sea.
PO: January 31, 1872–June 22, 1883

New Salem *(Cowley)*

Founder J. J. Johnson platted only twelve square blocks for
New Salem in 1882. It was enough; the site never developed
beyond the twelve-block limit. The exact source of *New Salem*
remains unknown; however, the place name "Salem" occurs
in many states. *(See* Salem.)
PO: March 6, 1872–; Pop. 60

New Strawn *(Coffey)*

Enos Strawn came to Kansas from Indiana in 1855. He gave
the land for the town site in 1871. Because the original
Strawn was destined to be inundated by the John Redmond
Dam, in the early 1960s the town had to be moved to a new
site about four miles north of Burlington. The dam was completed in 1965.
PO: September 21, 1871–; Pop. 457

Newton *(Harvey)*

Railroad investors from Newton, Massachusetts, named
Newton, Kansas. This town became another in a series of
Kansas cattle towns. By July 1871 the Santa Fe Railroad had
extended its line to the settlement; it succeeded Abilene as
the terminus of the Chisholm Trail, and saloons, dancehalls,
and gambling houses sprouted overnight. Although this
phase of Newton's growth lasted only until January 1873,
when the railroad was extended to Wichita, an estimated fifty
persons met sudden death in its dancehalls and saloons.
After the cowboy era, Newton became an important division
point on the Santa Fe Railroad.
PO: June 6, 1871–; Pop. 16,332; CS

Nickerson *(Reno)*

As early as 1872, a depot was built at the site and named after
Thomas Nickerson, then president of the Atchison, Topeka,
and Santa Fe Railroad. For several years the town prospered
as a division point for the railroad.
PO: January 21, 1873–; Pop. 1,292

Nicodemus *(Graham)*

> Nicodemus was a slave of African birth,
> And was bought for a bag of gold,
> He was reckoned as part of the salt of the earth,
> And he died years ago, very old.
>
> —Anon.

The only surviving black colony in Kansas is Nicodemus.
Blacks settled there in 1877 and named the site to honor the
legendary slave Nicodemus, who arrived in America aboard
the second slave ship and later purchased his freedom. An
agricultural center, Nicodemus never had many more than
six hundred residents at a time. Nevertheless, it remains
unique, and its people honor the original spirit of the
pioneers with an annual celebration and reunion of hundreds

of black Americans who have roots in Nicodemus. The town is on the Kansas Register of Historic Sites.
PO: September 12, 1877–August 15, 1918; July 20, 1920–November 30, 1953; Pop. 100

N I C O D E M U S

Ninnescah River *(South Central Kansas)* [NIN-uh-scah]

The Osage-Siouan word *ninnescah* has been translated to mean "spring water," "running water," "white water," "clear water," and "good water." Between Hutchinson and Wichita the Ninnescah has been dammed to form the Cheney Reservoir. The name has been given to several townships in southern Kansas.

Niotaze *(Chautauqua)* [NEYE-oh-tayz]

The U.S. Post Office gets credit for coining this name. The original name of the town site was *Niota*, which was mistaken for *Neola* in nearby Labette County. The name was changed to *Newport*, but that did not work out. The postmaster restored the old name *Niota*, adding *ze* to make it *Niotaze*.
PO: April 21, 1890–; Pop. 104

Norcatur *(Decatur)* [nor-KAY-ter)

The town located on the border between Norton and Decatur counties combined syllables for its name.
PO: October 30, 1885–; Pop. 226

North Newton *(Harvey)*

This small town is located immediately north of Newton.
PO: December 1, 1938–; Pop. 1,222

Norton *(Norton)*

N. H. Billings moved to Norton County in 1872 and later presented a petition to the governor asking that the county be organized with Billingsville as the temporary county seat. A contemporary described Billings as a "character possessed of fair education, some legal lore, a deal of egotism, and some degree of cunning, . . . a man of overweening vanity." Through his efforts the county was hurried into a premature and somewhat fraudulent organization. In the meantime another group also seeking the county seat designation formed the Norton Town Association. Subsequent contention led to a long court fight. Finally, Billingsville was forced to reorganize and file its plat as an addition to the town of Norton. The town takes its name from the county.
PO: October 28, 1872–; Pop. 3,400; CS

Norton County *(Established February 26, 1867)*

The county underwent several name changes. The legislature of 1859 named the territory *Oro,* a name it retained until 1867. At that time Preston B. Plumb, speaker of the Kansas House of Representatives, suggested the name *Norton,* after Orloff Norton, Captain of the Fifteenth Kansas Cavalry, who was killed at Cane Hill, Arkansas, in 1865. Opposition to the name came in 1872 from N. H. Billings, who petitioned the governor asking that the county be organized with Billingsville as the temporary county seat. Billings, also a member of the legislature, succeeded in having the 1873 legislature change the county name from *Norton* to *Billings.* The 1874 legislature changed it back to *Norton.*
Pop. 6,689

NIOTAZE

Nortonville *(Jefferson)*

T. L. Norton, Jr., roadmaster for the Santa Fe Railroad, left
his name on this town.
PO: May 14, 1873–; Pop. 692

Norway *(Republic)*

Norwegian immigrants predominated in the community's
early years. Norway became a center also for Norwegians living in nearby Cloud and Jewell counties.
PO: October 3, 1870–; Pop. 50

Norwich *(Kingman)*

W. W. Robbins, of Norwich, Connecticut, joined with settlers
from Runnymede, Kansas, to found the town of Norwich.
Also, two men who started the Norwich Bank came from
Norwich, New York. The English word *Norwich* refers to a
village bounded by a protecting hedge or wall.
PO: July 24, 1885–; Pop. 476

Oak Hill *(Clay)*

The settlers named the town for the presence of many oak
trees in the area.
PO: April 21, 1894–; Pop. 36

Oak Mills *(Atchison)*

A lumber mill at the site sawed large amounts of oak lumber.
Oak Mills claimed to be located on the site of the first permanent community occupied by white men (French), who
erected buildings and transacted business with Indians and
other fur traders early in the nineteenth century. The name
Oak Mills wasn't applied until 1854.
PO: January 6, 1868–March 31, 1945

Oakley *(Logan)*

David D. Hoag, founder of the town, suggested that it be
named *Oakley* for his mother, Eliza Oakley Gardner Hoag.
PO: October 20, 1885–; Pop. 2,343; CS

Oberlin *(Decatur)*

A former resident of Ohio, John A. Rodehaver, named the
Decatur county seat town after the Ohio town of Oberlin.
PO: April 22, 1878–; Pop. 2,387; CS

Offerle *(Edwards)* [OHF-er-lee]

This site, located on the Santa Fe Trail southwest of Kinsley, Kansas, was named for Laurence Offerle, a Frenchman from Illinois who surveyed the town site, established the post office, and opened the first store.
PO: May 26, 1876–; Pop. 244

Ogden *(Riley)*

Major E. A. Ogden, an officer of the Engineer Corps, was appointed to a commission to select a site on the Smoky Hill River for a cavalry post. Major Ogden supervised the construction of the post building at the new Fort Riley in 1853; he later died of cholera at the fort in August 1855. The town of Ogden, a short distance east of Fort Riley, served as the county seat until a countywide election gave that designation to Manhattan. In 1858 Theodore Weichselbaum built a brewery at Ogden, employed a large force of workers, and sold his beer to saloons and sutler stores all over northeast Kansas. The old three-story stone brewery building has been converted to an apartment house.
PO: March 20, 1856–; Pop. 1,804

Oketo *(Marshall)* [oh-KEE-toh]

The Oto Indian chief, Arkaketah, left his name on a town in Marshall County. Pioneers abbreviated it to *Oketo*. The township carries the same name.
PO: May 7, 1873–; Pop. 130

Olathe *(Johnson)* [oh-LAY-thuh]

Dr. John T. Barton, formerly a surgeon to the Shawnee Indians, wanted to locate a town near the geographical center of Johnson County. He associated with others to form a survey party that included Dave Daughtery (also spelled Doughtery), a Shawnee Indian. When Barton reached the top of a hill, he sighted the land he wanted for the future county seat. Daughtery found the site attractive and exclaimed *o-la-the,* the Shawnee word for "beautiful." Dr. Barton liked the Indian name and chose it for the new town.
PO: May 4, 1857–; Pop. 37,258; CS

Olivet *(Osage)* [ah-li-VET]

Three men representing a company of shareholders founded the town of Olivet. Although their purpose was to make it a center of the Swedenborgian movement, this never happened. The name *Olivet* may have Biblical origins in the Mount of Olives.
PO: April 15, 1870–October 6, 1888; Pop. 65

Olmitz *(Barton)* [AHL-mits]

Forty-seven Moravian immigrants settled in Olmitz, a Kansas town that traces its name source to Olmütz in eastern Bohemia.
PO: April 11, 1881–; Pop. 140

Olpe *(Lyon)* [OHL-pee]

To please his German neighbors from Westphalia, August Flusche took a place name that they knew well from Olpe, Westphalia, Prussia.
PO: April 6, 1887–; Pop. 477

Olsburg *(Pottawatomie)* [OHLZ-berg]

The *Ols* part of the name possibly came from Ole Thrulson; *burgh* completed the name. It was spelled *Olesburgh* from 1873 to 1887.
PO: November 7, 1887–; Pop. 166

Onaga *(Pottawatomie)* [oh-NAY-guh]

Paul E. Haven of the Kansas Central searched the Pottawatomi headrights books looking for a name he could give to a railroad station. He found *Onago* and changed it to *Onaga.*
PO: December 3, 1887–; Pop. 752

Oneida *(Nemaha)* [oh-NEYE-duh]

Founder Cyrus Shinn and his associates, who came from Oneida, Illinois, platted and named the town.
PO: January 19, 1876–; Pop. 120

Opolis *(Crawford)* [OP-uh-lis]

This place, which lies on the line between Missouri and Kansas, was first called *Stevenstown,* then *Stateline.* The St. Louis and San Francisco Railway renamed it *Opolis,* a Greek name meaning "city."
PO: December 30, 1868–June 4, 1877 as Stevenstown; June 7, 1877–July 5, 1877 as Stateline; July 5, 1877–; Pop. 160

Oregon-California Trail *(Northeast Kansas)*

The thousands of emigrants who followed this trail to Oregon and California started out from St. Joseph or Independence in Missouri. The separate routes joined ten miles west of Marysville, Kansas, before continuing on to Nebraska and west. Historical markers along the route trace the Oregon-California Trail through the northeastern corner of Kansas.

Osage City *(Osage)* [oh-SAYJ]

Land speculator Dr. H. H. Rosenburg and Atchison, Topeka, and Santa Fe Railroad president J. T. Peters traveled to Osage County to select a town site. Peters proposed the name *Rosenburg*. John F. Dodd, Peters's land agent, suggested *Petersburg*. When the naming was referred to Dr. Rosenburg, he objected to each and instead offered the name *Osage* after the county. When the government issued a postmaster's commission to John F. Dodd, the Post Office Department added the word *city*.
PO: January 6, 1870–; Pop. 2,667

Osage County *(Established February 11, 1859)* [oh-SAYJ]

On February 11, 1859, the legislature changed Weller County to Osage, for the Osage Nation who moved to Kansas when Missouri became a state in 1821 and after the Osage River. Osage County was on part of former Osage land. The French travelers into the area spelled the word *Ouz haghi* or *Ousage*.
Pop. 15,319

Osage Mission *(Neosho)*

(See St. Paul.)

Osawatomie *(Miami)* [oh-suh-WAH-tuh-mee]

The word was formed by combining *Osa* of the Osage River with *watomie* of Pottawatomie Creek. The militant abolitionist John Brown brought notoriety to the town in 1856, when his forces defied the proslavery faction. His son Frederick was among those killed in the Battle of Osawatomie.
PO: December 21, 1855–; Pop. 4,459

Osborne *(Osborne)*

The town was settled by a Pennsylvania colony who named the first post office *Penn*. When the site became a candidate for the Osborne county seat, it was renamed *Osborne City*. The *City* was later dropped.
PO: January 24, 1872–; Pop. 2,120; CS

Osborne County *(Established February 26, 1867)*

The county is named for Vincent B. Osborne, sergeant in the Second Kansas Cavalry. After the war, Osborne settled in Ellsworth, where he practiced law and helped organize Ellsworth County. A bronze marker noting the geodetic center of the United States, the primary station for all North

American surveys, was located on a ranch in Osborne County in 1901 by the U.S. Coast and Geodetic Survey. Engraved on the bronze tablet is a cross-mark, and on the fine point where the lines cross depends the survey of a sixth of the world's surface.
Pop. 5,959

Oskaloosa *(Jefferson)* [ah-skuh-LOO-suh]

Jesse Newell and Joseph Fitzimmons laid out their forty-acre town with blocks, streets, and alleys modeled after the plat of Oskaloosa, Iowa, their hometown.
PO: November 25, 1856–; Pop. 1,092; CS

Oswego *(Labette)* [os-WEE-goh]

For many years this place was home of the Osage chief White Hair. His three wives are buried there. It was also the home of the notorious John Matthews, Indian trader and Confederate guerrilla leader. Up to 1865, the place was known as *White Hair's Village,* then the name was changed to *Little Town.* It kept that name until July 1866 when a majority of town company members voted for *Oswego* (several of the settlers were from Oswego County, New York).
PO: October 4, 1866–; Pop. 2,218; CS

Otis *(Rush)*

Otis came into being through the efforts of railroad town promoter Major Erastus C. Modderwell. He followed the Missouri Pacific line, promoting towns along the way. He bought land for this town site in Rush County and named it for his son, Otis Modderwell.
PO: August 12, 1887–; Pop. 410

Ottawa *(Franklin)*

The county seat of Franklin County was named for the Ottawa Indians whose reservation once occupied the surrounding area. The Reverend Jotham Meeker and his wife moved to the Ottawa reservation in 1837 and established the Ottawa Indian Baptist Mission. After Kansas opened to settlement, town promoters worked to obtain this desirable site at a natural ford of the Marais des Cygnes River. Ottawa became the county seat in 1864. After a treaty to move the Ottawas to Indian Territory in Oklahoma was signed February 23, 1867, white settlers moved in as the Indians moved out. Ottawa University incorporated in April 1865 and continues as one of the state's oldest universities.
PO: March 31, 1864–; Pop. 11,016; CS

ο T T A W A

Ottawa County *(Established February 27, 1860)*

The name *Ottawa* is derived from a word that signifies "to
trade" or "to buy and sell." The Ottawa Indians were known
among their neighbors as intertribal traders. The land comprising present Ottawa County had been reserved for the
Kansas Indians; however, they were moved farther south to
Council Grove in 1846.
Pop. 6,000

Overbrook *(Osage)*

Overbrook is on a ridge separating the waters of the Marais
des Cygnes and the Wakarusa. The name came from
Pennsylvania: both Pittsburgh and Philadelphia had suburbs
named *Overbrook*. The Kansas community was once a center
for bituminous coal mining.
PO: April 1, 1887–; Pop. 930

Overland Park *(Johnson)*

Overland Park is situated on a ridge 136 feet higher than the
highest point in Kansas City. W. B. Strang, the man who
built the interurban from Kansas City through Overland Park
to Olathe, got credit for naming the town that could overlook
Kansas City. It is now part of Greater Kansas City.
PO: February 5, 1910–July 31, 1960; Pop. 81,784

Oxford *(Sumner)*

The town of Oxford was organized by the Oxford Town and
Immigration Company founded at Oswego in 1871. The
founders bought the site, which had once been a favorite Indian campground. It was briefly called *Napawalla* until the
founders named the site after the great university in England,

hoping to make it an educational center. The town, however, remained very small, and its educational facilities were limited to primary and secondary public schools. The Oxford Mill remains a notable landmark in south central Kansas.
PO: October 27, 1879–; Pop. 1,125

O X F O R D

Ozawkie *(Jefferson)* [oh-ZAW-kee]

This community is named for a Sauk Indian, Osa Kiqug. The name could mean "yellow leaf" or "yellow earth." The original town site is now submerged under the waters of Lake Perry, and the buildings have been moved to the present Ozawkie.
PO: March 15, 1855–; Pop. 472

Palco *(Rooks)* [PAL-koh]

Two railroad officials, Palmer and Cole, could not agree on a station name until they decided to accept *Pal* from Palmer and *co* from Cole.
PO: November 6, 1888–; Pop. 329

Palmer *(Washington)*

In 1879, a few buildings were moved from Pete's Creek to a site two miles north next to the Union Pacific Railroad, Central Branch. E. A. Thomas laid out the town, naming it for J.

Palmer, the first superintendent of public instruction in the county.

Palmyra *(Douglas)*

Free-state advocates from New York and Ohio may have transferred the name *Palmyra* from their respective states. The planned town of Palmyra was absorbed into Baldwin. The name, however, remains on the township.
PO: June 29, 1857–May 22, 1862

Paola *(Miami)* [pay-OH-luh]

One of Kansas's first towns honored Baptiste Peoria, a linguist who knew several Indian languages in addition to English and French. Indians had difficulty pronouncing the *r* in Peoria, consequently the name became *Paola*. Peoria, who lived in the vicinity, was also a member of the Paola Town Company. In the 1870s and 1880s Paola was the first center of oil drilling and pumping in Kansas.
PO: February 13, 1856–; Pop. 4,557; CS

Paradise *(Russell)*

When James R. Mead entered the wooded valley of a creek flowing into the Saline River, he remarked to his hunting

PARADISE

153

companions: "Boys, we have got into Paradise at last." The hunter's paradise was full of elk, black-tailed deer, buffalo, beaver, otter, and wolves. The valley, the creek, and the town were all named *Paradise*.
PO: December 27, 1875–; Pop. 89

Pardee *(Atchison)*

In 1857, the Reverend Pardee Butler preached a sermon on the site. Although the politically active Butler hoped to make his namesake a thriving religious community, the town disappeared. A school in Atchison County honors his memory.
PO: August 6, 1858–March 31, 1903

Park *(Gove)*

This town was once known as *Buffalo Park*. The federal Post Office changed the name to *Park* in 1898. In the late 1880s Park served as a supply base for fossil collectors who searched the Cretaceous chalk for fossils.
PO: February 26, 1895–; Pop. 183

Park City *(Sedgwick)*

The first Park City platted north of Wichita disappeared in 1876. Many years later the name was revived for a suburb north of Wichita.
PO: April 21, 1871–April 24, 1876; Pop. 3,778

Parker *(Linn)*

J. W. Parker, of Atchison, owned the town site and sixteen quarter sections adjoining. Part of the land was planted to apple orchards.
PO: December 22, 1888–; Pop. 270

Parkerville *(Morris)*

The town tried unsuccessfully to get the county seat away from Council Grove by persuading transients to vote in the election. For a few years, 1870 to 1892, the place was called *Parkersville* for Charles G. Parker, a leading citizen and former freighter on the Santa Fe Trail.
PO: August 9, 1870–October 31, 1953; Pop. 42

Parnell *(Atchison)*

The distinction of being the first station on the Atchison, Topeka, and Santa Fe Railroad outside of Atchison went to Par-

nell. Local resident P. C. Hotham named the station for Private James L. Parnell of Company F, Thirteenth Kansas Volunteer Infantry, who lost his life at the Battle of Hoare Head, Arkansas, August 4, 1864.
PO: August 9, 1883–March 15, 1923

Parsons *(Labette)*

Levi Parsons, president of the Neosho Division of the Missouri Pacific Railroad Company and promoter of the Missouri, Kansas, and Texas (KATY), along with Bob Stevens, KATY general manager, selected a townsite in Labette County. "Here," they said, "we will build a city that will become the metropolis of this whole section of the country." They named it *Parsons City*, but the *City* was dropped. Several town streets bear the names of financial contributors.
PO: December 9, 1870–; Pop. 12,898

Partridge *(Reno)*

In 1886 the name was changed from *Reno Centre* to *Partridge*, the maiden name of the wife of an official of the Atchison, Topeka, and Santa Fe.
PO: May 24, 1886–; Pop. 268

Pawnee *(Geary)* [PAW-nee]

For four days in 1855, the stone building at Pawnee held the first territorial legislature; its only accomplishment was to agree to adjourn to the Shawnee Methodist Mission. Because the planned town of Pawnee was illegally within the boundaries of Fort Riley, it had no future. The territorial capital building has become a state museum.
PO: March 3, 1855–December 20, 1855

Pawnee County *(Established February 26, 1867)*

The Pawnees were a strong, warlike nation, claiming the region watered by the Platte from the Rocky Mountains to its mouth and also the country drained by the forks of the Kansas. Smallpox, other diseases, and warring Indians reduced their numbers from about 25,000 early in the nineteenth century to only 2,500 in 1873.
Pop. 8,085

Pawnee Rock *(Barton)*

The rock was a great landmark for Santa Fe Trail travelers in the nineteenth century. One of the first descriptions comes

from the journal of George Sibley, who recorded the survey
of the Santa Fe road from Fort Osage to Santa Fe in 1825. He
wrote about a "remarkable Rocky Point. . . . These Rocks are
very large and of a glossy black colour. Toward the River, the
face is nearly perpendicular. We rode upon the top which is
probably 50 feet above the plain below. . . ." Another person
wrote in 1839 that "Pawnee Rock springs like a huge wart
from the carpeted green of the prairie." The rock derived its
name from the fact that the Pawnees would meet in council
on top of the rock, which was 240 feet in circumference. The
once lofty summit has been stripped of most of its rock by
railroad builders and settlers. The four-acre site including
Pawnee Rock has become a State Historic Site; a road leads to
a shelter house and monument on the summit.

Pawnee Rock *(Barton)*

The town derives its name from the historic Dakota
sandstone cliff just north of the town.
PO: August 28, 1872–; Pop. 409

Paxico *(Wabaunsee)* [PAKS-i-koh]

In December 1886 surveyors staked out the town near the
railroad tracks. An old Potawatomi medicine man, Pashqua,
had lived on the north bank of Mill Creek for many years.
The town name is an anglicized version of his name.
PO: September 5, 1881–; Pop. 168

Peabody *(Marion)*

T. M. Potter knew that the Atchison, Topeka, and Santa Fe
Railroad was coming through his land, which was adjacent to
Coneburg. He sold many lots and men put up buildings, but
the town had no name until the railroad directors came
through on an inspection tour in May 1871. After being cor-
dially received and feasted by the local citizens, the directors
named the new town site for their treasurer, F. H. Peabody of
Boston. An appreciative Peabody erected a library building,
furnished it, and gave two thousand books and many periodicals to it, making it possible for Peabody to have the first free
public library in Kansas. (The Coal Creek Library, a subscrip-
tion library begun in 1859 at Vinland in Douglas County, is
said to be the first public library in Kansas.)
PO: October 31, 1871–; Pop. 1,474

Peck *(Sedgwick)*

Two major railroads, the Santa Fe and the Rock Island,
crossed on land belonging to George Peck. At this junction,

Peck's Palace Hotel welcomed train travelers, served them dinner for fifteen cents, and offered an overnight room for twenty-five cents.
PO: October 27, 1887–; Pop. 130

Penalosa *(Kingman)* [pen-uh-LOH-suh]

The name may have come from that of a governor of New Mexico, whose full name was Don Diego Dionisio de Peñalosa Briceño y Berdugo.
PO: May 13, 1887–; Pop. 31

Perry *(Jefferson)*

This town between Lawrence and Topeka was named for John D. Perry, president of the Exchange Bank of St. Louis and president of the Eastern Division of the Union Pacific. He was influential in getting the Union Pacific through Lawrence.
PO: October 11, 1866–; Pop. 907

Peru *(Chautauqua)* [puh-ROO]

Fourteen places in the United States had the name *Peru* before the name entered Kansas. E. R. Cutler, president of the town company, broke a naming tie by voting for the name of his former home, Peru, Illinois.
PO: January 27, 1870–; Pop. 286

Peters Creek *(Doniphan)*

Peter Cadue, a Frenchman, spent some time on this creek. Anothers Peters Creek is located in Kingman County.

Pfeifer *(Ellis)* [FEYE-fer]

Immigrants who came from Pfeifer, Russia, founded the new settlement of Pfeifer, Kansas, in August 1876. It was one of several settlements in Kansas named after Russian towns.
PO: March 15, 1887–; Pop. 100

Phillips County *(Established February 26, 1867)*

The county was named for a "gallant private soldier of the Union army" according to A. T. Andreas, *History of Kansas.* Wayne Corley says it was named in honor of William Phillips, a free-state man who was killed at Leavenworth in 1856 for refusing to leave Kansas when told to do so by the pro-slavery faction.
Pop. 7,406

Phillipsburg *(Phillips)*

The county seat of Phillips County is called "the city of the hills" because of its location on the uplands of Deer Creek. The name was not taken from the county name but rather from William Addison Phillips, a lawyer and journalist who worked for the *New York Tribune*. He wrote forceful editorials and articles about the struggle over slavery in Kansas. During the Civil War he was a colonel of the Cherokee Regiment; he later served as U.S. representative from Kansas and was influential in the development of Salina.
PO: December 23, 1872–; Pop. 3,229; CS

Pierceville *(Finney)*

Several railroad stations along the Santa Fe route were named for railroad officials. Charles W. Pierce and Carlos Pierce were remembered at this one. On July 3, 1874, a local historian recalls a band of Indians headed for Pierceville, and the townspeople scattered and hid in the gullies outside town. The Indians burned Pierceville to the ground. It took four years before the post office returned to Pierceville.
PO: June 10, 1873–July 2, 1874; July 24, 1878–; Pop. 100

Pilsen *(Marion)* [PIL-suhn]

The first Bohemian immigrants came to Marion County in 1874. The families agreed to name their community after their homeland city of Pilzeň, a large city in the Austrian state of Bohemia.
PO: March 17, 1917–March 8, 1957; Pop. 60

Piqua *(Woodson)* [PI-kway]

Motion picture comedian Buster Keaton was born in the rural village. While his father and Harry Houdini were staging an Indian medicine show in Piqua in the 1890s, a terrific wind storm blew their tent down. Mrs. Keaton was taken to a nearby church, where her son Buster was born. George A. Bowlus, one of the town founders, was born in Piqua, Ohio.
PO: March 13, 1882–; Pop. 100

Pittsburg *(Crawford)*

This community was first called *New Pittsburg* because the abundance of coal in the area made it similar to Pittsburgh, Pennsylvania. The *New* was dropped in 1880. The town became the coal mining metropolis of Kansas. Although at one time southeastern Kansas was one of the nation's leading mineral-producing regions, coal mining has declined in recent years. Pittsburg State University is located here.
PO: August 28, 1876–; Pop. 18,770

P I Q U A

Plains *(Meade)*

Situated on the plains of southwestern Kansas, the place was first called *West Plains,* a descriptive name.
PO: August 31, 1894–; Pop. 1,044

Plainville *(Rooks)*

The name is descriptive of the high plains area where it is located. Judge Darland had suggested the name *Plainville* to town planners.
PO: April 10, 1878–; Pop. 2,458

Planeview *(Sedgwick)*

Built in 1943 in view of the Boeing Airplane Company plant in Wichita that turned out B-29 bombers, Planeview was designed not for permanence or beauty but rather to provide emergency housing for aircraft factory workers. During World War II, it was a self-contained city one mile square, and at its peak population of twenty thousand, it became the state's largest public housing project and the seventh largest city in Kansas. By law the substandard, multiple-apartment buildings were to be removed within two years after the end of the war, but postwar housing shortages slowed removal or demolition of the buildings, and a number of the single-family houses, duplexes, and fourplexes remain some forty years later.

Pleasanton *(Linn)*

Incorporated in the spring of 1869, Pleasanton was named to honor General Alfred Pleasonton, who commanded the Union forces against General Price in the Battle of Mine Creek, October 26, 1864, the largest Civil War battle fought on Kansas soil. *(See* Mine Creek Battlefield.)
PO: August 10, 1859–; Pop. 1,303

Plevna *(Reno)* [PLEV-nuh]

Immigrants may have named this town and township after a province in Bulgaria or after Plevna, Indiana.
PO: October 25, 1877–; Pop. 115

Plymouth *(Lyon)*

Plymouth is among the oldest settlements in Lyon County, dating back to 1858. This town, which once stood on the frontier of Kansas settlements, was reportedly named for another pioneer town—Plymouth, Massachusetts.
PO: February 10, 1858–December 31, 1930; Pop. 100

Point of Rocks *(Morton)*

The name describes a well-known landmark on the Cimarron cutoff on the old Santa Fe Trail. The rugged bluff that rises near the Cimarron River was the westernmost landmark of significance on the trail in Kansas. With the bluff's good water supply from nearby Middle Springs, travelers used it for a campground.
PO: May 7, 1900–November 15, 1921

Pomona *(Franklin)* [puh-MOH-nuh]

Founder John H. Whetstone purchased fifteen thousand acres in Franklin County, where he planted an apple orchard that he named Pomona. The town he founded received the same name. The French word for "apple" is *pomme.*
PO: May 5, 1870–; Pop. 868

Portis *(Osborne)*

The town is named for Missouri Pacific Railroad vice president Portis.
PO: February 16, 1880–; Pop. 172

Port William *(Atchison)*

Port William's history can be traced back to the early French explorers and traders on the Missouri; the site was later

named for William Johnson, who crossed the Missouri River
to take a claim here. The town incorporated by the territorial
legislature in 1855 became a haven for blacks during and after
the Civil War, and many blacks living in northeast Kansas
can trace their ancestry to the Port William community.
PO: April 4, 1856–April 19, 1860

Potawatomi Indian Pay Station *(Pottawatomie)*
[po-tuh-WO-toh-mee]

This structure located near the old St. Mary's College campus
was built of stone in the 1850s and is the oldest building of
the St. Mary's Indian Mission. The one-story stone structure
was used as a pay station where government agents paid an-
nuities to Indians in exchange for reservation land. The site is
on the National Register of Historic Sites.

Potawatomi Indian Reservation *(Jackson)*

The largest of the three remaining Indian reservations in
Kansas once had its mission headquarters at St. Marys on the
Kansas River.

Pottawatomie County *(Established February 20, 1857)*

The county was named for the Potawatomi tribe of Indians
whose reservation embraced a large portion of the land in the
county. Only one *t* is used in the name when referring directly to the tribe and two *t*s when referring to a place name.
Pop. 14,782

P O M O N A

Potter *(Atchison)*

Joseph Potter, Fred Poos, and Henry Squires considered developing a nearby mineral springs into a resort. Nothing developed along that line. Instead, when the Santa Fe laid tracks through the area it named its station for Joseph Potter, who owned the station site land.
PO: February 29, 1888–; Pop. 115

Potwin *(Butler)*

Banker and land speculator Charles W. Potwin bought large tracts of land in Butler and Greenwood counties from railroad companies. At one time he owned twenty thousand acres in Butler County where the city of Potwin was established. Potwin also developed a residential section of Topeka. *(See* Potwin Place.)
PO: September 22, 1885–; Pop. 563

Potwin Place *(Shawnee)*

In 1869, Charles W. Potwin of Zanesville, Ohio, paid an "outrageous" price of two hundred dollars per acre for seventy acres northwest of the Topeka city limits. He platted Potwin Place in 1882, subdividing it into eighty large lots (122 1/2 ft. by 205 ft.). Circular parks marked each street intersection, and about two hundred native elm trees lined the streets. Potwin Place continues to be a handsome historic district in Topeka.

Powhattan *(Brown)* [pow-HA-tuhn]

The Indian name *Powhattan* was given to a town and township in Brown County. Powhattan was the father of Pocahantas.
PO: March 17, 1887–; Pop. 95

Prairie View *(Phillips)*

Prairie has been one of the most popular names, appearing as just *prairie* or in combination with other words in sixty-seven place names in Kansas.
PO: July 15, 1879–; Pop. 145

Prairie Village *(Johnson)*

Located within the Kansas City metropolitan area, Prairie Village developed from a city of the third class in 1951, with a population of 2,500, to the eighth-largest city in Kansas in just twenty years. Since 1971, population has declined from

30,000 to approximately 24,700. The name was originally descriptive.
Pop. 24,700

Pratt *(Pratt)*

Manipulation and multiplication of votes may have figured in Pratt's winning the county seat designation. Iuka and Saratoga had rivaled Pratt for the county seat.
PO: June 17, 1884–; Pop. 6,885; CS

Pratt County *(Established February 26, 1867)*

The county was named for Caleb Pratt, Second Lieutenant in the Second Kansas Cavalry, who was killed at the Battle of Wilson's Creek. The first organization was fraudulent, according to A. T. Andreas, who said: "It was accomplished by a party from Hutchinson who traveled through the country with a tent, going from county to county, organizing them as they went. Pratt was one of the counties thus organized." Not one bona fide settler lived in the county when the shysters sought organization, and the county waited until 1879 for official organization.
PO: 10,275

Prescott *(Linn)*

C. H. Prescott was auditor and treasurer of the Missouri River, Fort Scott, and Gulf Railroad. The town was called *Coal Centre* when laid out in 1870; its name was changed to *Prescott* in 1873.
PO: December 27, 1870–; Pop. 319

Pretty Prairie *(Reno)*

In the fall of 1872, forty-six-year-old widowed Mrs. Mary Collingwood, with visions of great opportunities on the free lands of western Kansas, sold her Indiana farm; with two new covered wagons, four horses, $2,200, and her six sons and three daughters, she left for the prairies of Kansas. The next spring she bought fourteen yoke of oxen and had her five oldest sons break the prairie. In the spring sun, the prairie looked so beautiful that she called the place *Pretty Prairie*. She gave the name to the post office she established in the front of her house.
PO: January 24, 1874–; Pop. 655

Princeton *(Franklin)*

E. M. Peck named the site for his home in Princeton, Illinois.
PO: March 28, 1870–; Pop. 244

Protection *(Comanche)*

The origin of the name is most often linked with the protective tariff, a much-discussed issue in the 1884 presidential campaign. Republican candidate James Blaine favored the tariff; however, Democrat Grover Cleveland, who favored free trade, won the election. Some of Protection's founders were strong Republicans.
PO: August 27, 1884–; Pop. 684

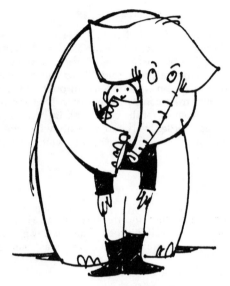

P R O T E C T I O N

Purcell *(Doniphan)*

Landowners usually welcomed railroad plans to buy land and lay tracks on their property. Not so John Purcell. When the Rock Island wanted to extend its line through Purcell's property, he fought them in court. They eventually worked out an agreement whereby the Rock Island could use the land if they named the station *Purcell.*
PO: May 16, 1887–June 11, 1956

Quenemo *(Osage)* [KWIN-uh-moh]

The source of the name is not clear. A. T. Andreas, in *History of Kansas,* wrote that several white traders worked on the site of the Sac and Fox Indian agency. One of them was John Goodell, who had married an Indian woman named Quenemo. Another version stated that the site was named

164

for "Old Joe" Quinemo; a third source said it was named for an Ottawa Indian who lived among the Sacs and Foxes.
PO: January 18, 1870–; Pop. 413

Quincy *(Greenwood)*

The community was named for an early resident.
PO: March 17, 1869–; Pop. 50

Quindaro *(Wyandotte)* [Kwin-DAR-oh]

One of the first towns founded in Kansas was named to honor Mrs. Abelard Guthrie, whose maiden name was Quindaro Brown. Her husband owned much of the land in the vicinity, and he often helped fugitive slaves over his land to safety. The town made a promising start in 1855 but declined quickly as people moved away during the Civil War. A black community developed around the deserted stone buildings of Old Quindaro. When Brown-Ferris Industries of Kansas City wanted to convert the site to a landfill, opponents petitioned to make it a Kansas Historic Site. The ruins of a few buildings remain.
PO: May 14, 1857–March 31, 1954; part of Kansas City

Quinter *(Gove)*

A group of Dunkards made Quinter their social and trading center. They named it for a Pennsylvania immigrant, the Reverend James Quinter, an elder in the Dunkard (Baptist Brethren) Church.
PO: March 31, 1886–; Pop. 951

Quivira National Wildlife Refuge *(Stafford)* [kwi-VEER-uh]

In the spring and fall thousands of migrating birds fly directly over Kansas, many of them stopping at the Quivira National Wildlife Refuge twenty miles south of Cheyenne Bottoms. Included among the birds are some of the endangered whooping cranes on their way to the Texas Gulf Coast. The 21,800-acre saltwater marsh contains two lakes and attracts some 250 species of birds annually.

Radium *(Stafford)*

In 1910 the Wellsville post office had its name changed to *Radium*. Perhaps the discovery of the radioactive metallic element radium in 1898 influenced the name change.
PO: October 17, 1910–; Pop. 47

Radley *(Crawford)*

Located in the once rich coal mining area of southeastern Kansas, this town was named for H. H. Radley, secretary of the Girard Coal Company that divided the town site into lots.
PO: October 30, 1913–; Pop. 100

Rago *(Kingman)* [RAY-goh]

Rago's most famous son, Clyde Cessna, showed more interest in flying than farming. From notes and his memory of a French monoplane, he built and flew his first monoplane on his forty acres near Rago in 1911. Seventeen years later, he and others started the Cessna Aircraft Company in Wichita. It became one of the world's major manufacturers of general aviation aircraft. As for Rago, the town took its name from the Rago Trading Post located southeast of the present town.
PO: April 13, 1883–; Pop. 40

Ramona *(Marion)*

The lilting Spanish name *Ramona* may have been on the mind of town planners because of the popular Helen Hunt Jackson novel *Ramona* (1884). More than likely, though, its origin lay in the history of land ownership dating back to the early 1800s when Spanish fur trader Manuel de Lisa acquired 6,439 acres in present Marion County. His widow, Mary Lisa, held title to half the grant until 1869. Through the name *Ramona*, settlers paid tribute to the first Spanish land holders in Kansas.
PO: August 9, 1887–; Pop. 121

Randall *(Jewell)*

First named *Vicksburgh*, the town's name was later changed to *Randall* to honor Edward Randall, the original owner of the site.
PO: October 24, 1881–; Pop. 154

Randolph *(Riley)*

In 1855, Gardner Randolph and his family came from Illinois to the Blue River Valley. It has been said that he planned to organize a slave plantation and make Kansas a slave state, but incoming settlers with contrary ideas squelched that plan. The elder Randolph became the first postmaster. The construction of Tuttle Creek Dam forced the relocation of the town from its original site. *(See* Fancy Creek.)
PO: August 8, 1856–February 29, 1960; Pop. 131

Ransom *(Ness)*

Ogdensburg changed its name to *Ransom* for General Thomas E. G. Ransom, a brilliant soldier who served with General William T. Sherman.
PO: September 18, 1888–; Pop. 448

Rantoul *(Franklin)* [ran-TOOL]

After hearing an inspiring speech delivered by U.S. Senator Robert Rantoul, Mrs. C. C. Cutler suggested that the local railway station be named *Rantoul*.
PO: September 10, 1862–; Pop. 212

Rawlins County *(Established March 20, 1873)*

The county was named for General John A. Rawlins, President Grant's secretary of war.
Pop. 4,105

Raymond *(Rice)*

Long ago, the cattle town of Raymond had the reputation of being the "wickedest" town in Rice County. Both town and township were named for a director of the Santa Fe Railroad, Emmaus Raymond.
PO: August 15, 1872–; Pop. 132

Reading *(Lyon)* [RED-ding]

Railroad man James Fagan, impressed with John McMann's land purchases in Kansas, named a station *Reading* for John McMann's Reading Iron Works in Reading, Pennsylvania.
PO: August 24, 1870–; Pop. 244

Redfield *(Bourbon)*

Dr. R. W. Lease honored his friendship with his colleague, Dr. Redfield, who lived in Fort Scott.
PO: May 22, 1872–; Pop. 185

Reece *(Greenwood)*

Town founder William Smith Reece was born in London, England, in 1843 and came to America in 1869. He acquired a 1,770-acre ranch in Greenwood County. He also imported thoroughbred horses, one of which was named Alhambra. When Reece platted the town, he named a street Alhambra in honor of his horse.
PO: January 29, 1883–; Pop. 60

Reno County *(Established February 26, 1867)*

The name honored General Jesse L. Reno, who died from wounds suffered in the Civil War.
Pop. 64,983

Republic *(Republic)*

A principal division of the Pawnee Indians, the Pawnee Republic, established a village in the vicinity many years before the whites arrived. It stood near the present town of Republic, and the Pawnee Indian Village Museum is outside of Republic.
PO: June 29, 1880–; Pop. 223

Republic County *(Established February 27, 1860)*

The county received its name, in part, because it was the first county in which the Republican River entered Kansas.
PO: 7,569

Republican River *(Northeastern Kansas)*

The Pawnee Indians who lived in southern Nebraska and northern Kansas were divided into four groups, one being the Republic. The first white men who had contact with them mistakenly thought that their form of government was republican. Before the French named the river *Republican* the Indians gave it a descriptive name. The river valley was a favorite grazing place for thousands of buffalo, who so polluted the river that the Indians called it *Manure River* or *Buffalo-Dung River*.

REPUBLICAN RIVER

Reserve *(Brown)*

The small town located near the Nebraska border was only six miles from the Sac and Fox Indian Reservation.
PO: October 5, 1882–; Pop. 105

Rexford *(Thomas)*

When Rexford was founded in the 1880s, the surrounding prairie was covered with bleaching buffalo bones. The first

settlers gathered the bones and sold them to fertilizer factories. A. F. and J. W. Rexford are remembered in the town name.
PO: August 18, 1888–; Pop. 204

Rhinoceros Hill Quarry *(Wallace)*

In this quarry are sedimentary deposits containing thousands of bones of rhinoceroses, birds, turtles, frogs, horses, saber-toothed cats, dogs, hoofed mammals, prongbucks, giant camels, peccaries, and llamas, all of which inhabited the Kansas savanna over six million years ago.

Rice County *(Established February 26, 1867)*

The most central Kansas county was named for Brigadier General Samuel A. Rice, who was killed at the Battle of Jenkin's Ferry in Arkansas on April 30, 1864.
Pop. 11,900

Richfield *(Morton)*

With dreams of future prosperity, pioneer A. T. Spotswood named the site *Richfield.*
PO: January 21, 1886–; Pop. 81

Richmond *(Franklin)*

John C. Richmond donated forty acres to the railroad with the provision that the town carry his name.
PO: April 12, 1870–; Pop. 510

Riley *(Riley)*

First known as *Riley Centre,* the town took its name from the county.
PO: April 19, 1870–; Pop. 779

Riley County *(Established August 25, 1855)*

The county took its name from the military post, Fort Riley. *(See* Fort Riley.)
Pop. 63,505

Riverton *(Cherokee)*

The river town is situated on the west bank of the Spring River.
PO: July 11, 1919–; Pop. 600

Robidoux Creek *(Marshall)* [ROH-bi-doh]

French fur trader Michael Robidoux of St. Joseph scratched his name on a rock at a ford known as the Lower Robidoux Crossing.

Robinson *(Brown)*

Despite the fact that he played a major role in the formation of Kansas, the state's first governor, Charles Robinson, had only a small town and township named for him. Before the town site name became *Robinson,* local residents called it *Lickskillet* because an old trapper placed dirty dishes outdoors for his dog to lick clean.
PO: June 30, 1858–; Pop. 324

ROBINSON

Rock *(Cowley)*

The nearness to Rock Creek is the reason for the naming of this town.
PO: August 12, 1870–June 2, 1871; June 7, 1872–; Pop. 90

Rock City *(Ottawa)*

Two and one-half miles southwest of Minneapolis, Kansas, are at least two hundred individual Dakota sandstone concretions. Some of these "dinosaur marbles" or "Jayhawk eggs" are perfect spheres; others are loaf shaped; some of the "eggs" are twenty-seven feet in diameter. Rock City is one of three National Natural Landmarks in Kansas.

Roeland Park *(Johnson)*

A prominent family named Roe donated land for the town
site, which is now part of Greater Kansas City. The place was
named Roeland Park in honor of the family.
Pop. 7,962

Rolla *(Morton)* [RAWL-uh]

Formerly known as *Reil,* after a Kansas pioneer, Rolla re-
ceived its name because of an error made by the Post Office
Department.
PO: August 31, 1907–; Pop. 417

Rome *(Sumner)*

One of the oldest towns in Sumner County was named by
Silas Omo, who donated land for the town site.
PO: January 6, 1874–December 30, 1933

Rooks County *(Established February 26, 1867)*

The Kansas legislature named the county in honor of a Kansas soldier, Private John Calvin Rooks, who died from a
wound suffered during the Battle of Prairie Grove, Arkansas,
December 7, 1862.
Pop. 7,006

Rosalia *(Butler)*

H. C. Stevens housed the post office in his home and named
it *Rosalia* for his wife. Both the township and town used the
name *Rosalia.*
PO: July 1, 1870–; Pop. 150

ROCK CITY

Rose Hill *(Butler)*

J. H. Lowery loved flowers and grew many on his Rose Farm. When a post office and town were established nearby, the founders chose the name *Rose Hill*.
PO: June 23, 1874–; Pop. 1,557

Rosedale *(Wyandotte)*

James G. Brown and A. Grandstaff platted Rosedale in 1872 in a peaceful valley that was almost totally surrounded by high, tree-covered bluffs. "A perfect bower of wild roses" grew in every ravine and crevice and covered every rock.
PO: August 22, 1872–July 14, 1902; part of Kansas City

Roseland *(Cherokee)*

Wild roses growing in Kansas have influenced the naming of streams, creeks, and towns.
PO: September 22, 1902–June 29, 1918; Pop. 119

Rossville *(Shawnee)*

In 1855 William Wallace Ross came to Kansas from Wisconsin. He and his brother Edmund, who joined him in 1856, worked as journalists in Topeka. William also served as a Potawatomie Indian agent in 1862. Edmund Ross, a U.S. senator in the late 1860s, cast the deciding vote against the impeachment of President Andrew Johnson.
PO: January 29, 1862–; Pop. 1,045

Round Mound *(Ellis)*

Rising five hundred feet from a generally flat countryside, Round Mound can be seen for miles. Indians used the elevation as a lookout point when the Union Pacific Railroad was building across the county. Years later, during an oil boom in the late 1920s, "thousands" drove to Round Mound to picnic and watch activities in the oil fields. Walter P. Chrysler, future head of Chrysler Motors, courted his girlfriend at the site; she was said to have danced "the skirt dance" on the tower atop Round Mound during this time.

Roxbury *(McPherson)*

E. W. Banks and B. B. Gates platted the town in 1871. After using the names *Bloomingdale* and *Colfax*, they decided in favor of *Roxbury*, after Gates's former home, Roxbury, Massachusetts.
PO: October 15, 1872–; Pop. 100

Rozel *(Pawnee)* [roh-ZEL]

Roseila, a daughter of the land grant agent, had her name given to this town. The name was later altered to *Rozel*.
PO: June 15, 1893–; Pop. 219

Runnymede *(Harper)*

Wheat fields cover the town site now, but once Runnymede resembled a thriving English village. Near the English-style houses were polo grounds, a steeplechase course, a race track, tennis courts, and a football field. Farms and orchards were modeled after English estates. An Irishman promoted all this British activity, persuading wealthy English families to send sons to the colony to learn American farming methods. In practice, Runnymede resembled a dude ranch. At one time one hundred young Englishmen lived in the settlement, but the colony failed within five years, and most of the men returned to England. The colony's Episcopal church was moved to Harper, where it is a museum.
PO: June 20, 1879–December 31, 1944

Rush Center *(Rush)*

Founders of Walnut City wanted to have the county seat and therefore dropped the name *Walnut City* in favor of *Rush Center*, for the county name. It didn't help: Rush Center lost the county seat battle to La Crosse.
PO: February 13, 1874–; Pop. 207

RUNNYMEDE

Rush County *(Established February 26, 1867)*

The county was named for Captain Alexander Rush of Company H, Second Kansas Colored Infantry. He was killed in the Battle of Jenkin's Ferry, Arkansas, on April 30, 1864. Colonel Samuel Crawford assumed command of the Second Kansas Colored Infantry. After he became governor of Kansas, Crawford named Rush County to honor the courageous captain.
Pop. 4,516

Russell *(Russell)*

Once known as *Fossil Station* because of rich fossil beds in the area, Russell was settled by an association from Wisconsin. Russell is the home of Senator Robert Dole. The town took the name of the county.
PO: January 21, 1871–; Pop. 5,427; CS

Russell County *(Established February 26, 1867)*

The county was named for Avra P. Russell, captain, Company K, Second Kansas Cavalry.
Pop. 9,100

Russell Springs *(Logan)*

The earliest known settler was William D. Russell, a cattleman who ran large herds of cattle on the open range and watered them at springs in the area. When the Butterfield Overland Dispatch drove stages over the Smoky Hill route in the 1860s, they located an "eating" station near the springs. First called *Eaton*, it was changed to *Russell Springs*.
PO: March 5, 1887–; Pop. 56; CS until 1963

Sabetha *(Brown and Nemaha)* [suh-BETH-uh]

According to legend, Sabetha was named by a young man who reached this point on his way to California in the 1850s. His ox died on this spot on the Hebrew Sabbath, so he named his camp *Sabetha*. The town could also have been named for a woman or for a temporary fort that was established on a Sunday.
PO: March 15, 1858–; Pop. 2,286

St. Francis *(Cheyenne)*

Some say that the town may have been named for Mrs. A. L. (Frances) Emerson. Her religious devotion to God and her sense of obligation to humankind led many to consider her a saint.
PO: April 18, 1888–; Pop. 1,610; CS

St. George *(Pottawatomie)*

While traveling from St. Joseph, Missouri to Manhattan, Kansas, a weary Mrs. George Gillespie refused to go any farther than what is now St. George. Other immigrants in the party agreed to stop and homestead there. Among her companions were her husband, George W. Gillespie, J. George Gillespie, and George Chapman.
PO: September 18, 1860; Pop. 309

St. Jacob's Well *(Clark)*

This spring is located in what geologists call a sink. St. Jacob's Well is a pool 125 feet wide that has never been known to go dry. The reference to Jacob's well may be a Biblical one. Kansas artist Margaret Whittemore has made the well widely known to Kansas through her painting *St. Jacob's Well.*

St. John *(Stafford)*

The county seat town was named for Kansas Governor John P. St. John.
PO: April 30, 1880–; Pop. 1,501; CS

St. Marys *(Pottawatomie)*

In 1848 Father Christian Hoecken, a Jesuit priest, established a mission on the Kansas River to educate the Potawatomi Indians. The first cathedral of the Catholic Church in Kansas was built here in 1849. Here, too, on a model farm and on individual Indian farms, Rev. John Duerinck introduced the use of cornshellers, cultivators, roller horse hayrakes, corncrushers, and the McCormick reapers in the 1850s.
PO: March 15, 1855–; Pop. 1,598

St. Paul *(Neosho)*

The name *St. Paul* had been used in Chautauqua and Sheridan counties before it came to Neosho County. Once known as the Osage Mission and Catholic Mission, the town became St. Paul to honor St. Paul of the Cross, founder of the Passionist Order, which had established a home in the Osage Mission. Father Paul Ponziglione, an Italian nobleman, was in charge of the mission for several years and wrote a prayer book in Osage.
PO: May 11, 1895–; Pop. 1,425

Salem *(Jewell)*

M. W. George and H. L. Browning moved to the area in 1871 and together started a steam sawmill. For their new town

they used the popular place name *Salem*, from the Hebrew word *Sholem*, meaning "peace" or "from Jerusalem."
PO: September 14, 1871–December 31, 1903

Salemsborg *(Saline)*

Swedish immigrants from Chicago and Galesburg, Illinois, homesteaded or bought land in Smoky View and Smolan townships in Saline County. They may have brought the name *Salem* from Illinois.
PO: April 28, 1875–January 31, 1902

Salina *(Saline)* [suh-LEYE-nuh]

The county seat of Saline County lies in a basin four miles southwest of the confluence of the Saline and Smoky Hill rivers. Its founder, William A. Phillips, called it *Saliena* in 1858, but the name became *Salina*.
PO: November 14, 1861–; Pop. 41,843; CS

Saline County *(Established February 15, 1860)* [suh-LEYN]

Saline County takes its name from the Saline River, which flows through the county.
Pop. 48,905

Salt City *(Sumner)*

The salty southeast corner of Sumner County contains several salt springs. Salt City stood near a ten-acre salt marsh.
PO: October 26, 1874–July 31, 1885

Sand Hills State Park *(Reno)*

This park contains about one thousand acres of rolling dunes, marshes, prairie, and woods. The land is similar to that encountered by travelers on the Santa Fe Trail.

Santa Fe Trail *(Northeastern to Southwestern Kansas)*

An international highway, a commercial and communication route, a military road, and an emigrant route—the Santa Fe Trail has been all of these. The main trail, often called Santa Fe Road in the early days, entered Kansas in Johnson County, and traversed the entire width of the state before exiting by one branch in Morton County and by another in Hamilton County.

Sappa Creek *(Decatur and Norton)*

In September 1878, Northern Cheyennes escaped from their Oklahoma reservation and headed north into Kansas and Nebraska. While being pursued by U.S. troops, they took revenge on innocent settlers, killing nineteen at Sappa Creek in 1878. *Sappa* is a Siouan word meaning "black" or "dark."

Satanta *(Haskell)*

Kiowa Chief Satanta was "the most dreaded warrior on the plains," said frontiersman James R. Mead. Satanta spoke for the dispossessed Indians at the Medicine Lodge Conference in 1867. While incarcerated in a Texas prison, he jumped from a high window to his death. *Satanta* means "white bear."
PO: January 13, 1885–; Pop. 1,117

Savonburg *(Allen)*

Swedes from Swedonia, Illinois, came to settle alongside other Scandinavians in the county. An early post office used the name *Savonsburg* before the town came into being.
PO: May 21, 1879–; Pop. 113

Saw Log Creek *(Ford and Hodgeman)*

To obtain wood for Fort Atkinson, wood gatherers went to the South Branch of the Pawnee River, where they stripped the trees of their smaller branches. They left the big trunks that they could not manage with their tools—thus the name *Sawlog Creek.*

Sawyer *(Pratt)*

J. W. Chamberlain named the town for Warren Sawyer, a director of the Santa Fe Railroad.
PO: June 18, 1887–; Pop. 213

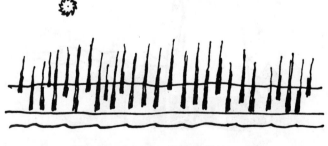

SAW LOG CREEK

Scammon *(Cherokee)*

Four brothers named Scammon owned and operated the first coal shaft in Cherokee County in 1874. Prior to that time, most coal mining had taken place at surface levels. The success of this shaft mine brought the opening of several more in Cherokee, Crawford, and Bourbon counties, where coal seams went as deep as 285 feet. Large numbers of immigrants with mining experience came from Italy, Austria, Yugoslavia, Germany, France, Belgium, Great Britain, and various parts of the United States.
PO: April 9, 1879–October 7, 1890, as Scammonville; October 7, 1890–; Pop. 501

Scandia *(Republic)*

In 1868 the Scandinavian Agricultural Society of Chicago, Illinois, sponsored settlers to Kansas. First called *New Scandinavia*, the name was later shortened to *Scandia*.
PO: June 24, 1869–June 7, 1876, as New Scandinavia; June 7, 1876–; Pop. 480

Schoenchen *(Ellis)* [SHEN-chen]

A group of Volga-Germans (Germans who had settled in Russia) left Russia for Kansas in 1875. Conflict divided the first colony that settled Liebenthal, and dissenters left to found a new town. The involved settlers came from Schoen-

S C H O E N C H E N

chen and Neu Obermonjour, Russia. Immigrants from each ancestral village agreed to name the new village *Schoenchen* and the church *St. Anthony* for the patron saint of Neu Obermonjour. The name *Schoenchen* means "little beautiful one" in German.

PO: March 10, 1902–June 15, 1917; May 18, 1938–; Pop. 209

Scipio *(Anderson)* [SIP-i-yoh]

The first settlers in the pioneer community came from Scipio, Indiana.

PO: September 6, 1859–March 15, 1905

Scott City *(Scott)*

The county seat, located in the exact center of the county, took its name from the county.

PO: March 24, 1880–; Pop. 4,154; CS

Scott County *(Established March 20, 1873)*

The memory of General Winfield Scott has been perpetuated in the county name.

Pop. 5,182

Scottsville *(Mitchell)*

The town was named for pioneer Tom Scott.

PO: November 12, 1978–; Pop. 56

Scranton *(Osage)*

The Burlington and Scranton Coal Company promoted the coal mining town in 1872, naming it after Scranton, Pennsylvania.

PO: September 6, 1872–; Pop. 664

Sedan *(Chautauqua)*

While Thomas Scurr was transporting a load of lumber needed for a store building in an as yet unnamed settlement in the fall of 1870, he was looking at a current magazine picture of the famous battle between France and Prussia at Sedan. Among the pictures was one showing a full view of the landscape. As Scurr came to the new village from the north and looked over the hills to the south, he commented to his companion: "Why this village looks just like this picture; let's call it Sedan." The famous clown, Emmett Kelly, was born in Sedan.

PO: April 5, 1871–; Pop. 1,579; CS

Sedgwick *(Harvey)*

Organizers of Sedgwick County planned to make it the county seat of Sedgwick County and named the town after the county. But when ten northern townships were assigned to Harvey County, Sedgwick found itself almost entirely within Harvey County boundaries.
PO: June 27, 1870–; Pop. 1,471

Sedgwick County *(Established February 26, 1867)*

The county was named in honor of Major General John Sedgwick, who died at the Battle of Spottsylvania, Virginia, on May 9, 1864. Sedgwick County contains Wichita, the state's largest city.
Pop. 366,531

Selden *(Sheridan)*

Town company members honored one of their own, Selden G. Hopkins.
PO: July 21, 1888–; Pop. 266

Seneca *(Nemaha)*

Finnley Lapping from Seneca, Ohio, named the Kansas town. The Indian tribal name *Seneca* came from New York.
PO: November 5, 1858–; Pop. 2,389; CS

Severance *(Doniphan)*

John Severance was one of three men who once owned the town site.
PO: December 29, 1869–; Pop. 134

Severy *(Greenwood)* [SEV-uh-ree]

Severy was another among the many Kansas towns named for directors and officials of the Santa Fe Railroad. Luther Severy of Emporia, Kansas, won this honor.
PO: July 25, 1882–; Pop. 447

Seward *(Stafford)*

The town of Seward was named for William H. Seward, U.S. senator and secretary of state in President Lincoln's cabinet. The widely separated town and county, each having the name *Seward*, have the same name source.
PO: September 20, 1878–; Pop. 88

Seward County *(Established March 26, 1873)*

In 1861, William Seward ardently supported Kansas state-hood. To honor him, the legislature changed the name of Godfrey County to *Seward* in 1861. In 1867, however, Seward's name was replaced by that of military hero General Oliver O. Howard. In 1873 the legislature moved the *Seward* name west to a county between Meade and Stevens.
Pop. 17,071

Shannon *(Atchison)*

The name of Wilson Shannon, who served as governor of the Kansas Territory from 1855 to 1856, is remembered in this rural community. The town did well until major fires in 1915 and 1918 destroyed nearly all the buildings.
PO: December 13, 1882–November 15, 1941

Sharon *(Barber)*

In Hebrew the word *sharon* means "plain," and the rolling plain along the Mediterranean from Joppa to Mount Carmel has the name *Sharon*. Because the town was founded by Campbellites, the name may have Biblical connections.
PO: November 30, 1880–; Pop. 283

Sharon Springs *(Wallace)*

This town was originally known as *Eagle Tail* after the creek which flowed nearby. Later the name was changed to *Sharon Springs* for some nearby sulphur springs and for Sharon Springs, New York.
PO: May 6, 1886–; Pop. 982; CS

Shawnee *(Johnson)*

The city of Shawnee, a part of Greater Kansas City, is located on land once belonging to the Shawnee Indians. The word *Shawnee* means "southerner."
PO: March 19, 1857–July 31, 1960; Pop. 29,653

Shawnee County *(Established August 25, 1855)*

Actual settlement of Shawnee County by whites began as early as 1830 on Mission Creek, where Frederick Chouteau established a trading post. The Shawnee Indians had been driven from their eastern homes by the Iroquois and the white man. Their reserve in Kansas was located south of the Kansas River in a strip about 25 miles wide and extending 150 miles west of the Missouri border. Thomas Johnson sug-

gested the name of *Shawnee* for the county in which he lived; however, it was named *Johnson*, for him, and the name *Shawnee* was given to the county where the state capital was located. Two creeks and two townships also carry the name *Shawnee*.
Pop. 154,916

Shawnee Methodist Mission *(Johnson)*

If judged by the number of Indians enrolled and buildings constructed, the Shawnee Methodist Mission superintended by the Reverend Thomas Johnson was one of the most active in Kansas. At one time, 300 to 400 Indian children resided at the Mission, which opened in 1830. A building constructed in 1841 and two others are National Historic Landmarks.

Sheridan County *(Established March 20, 1873)*

Sheridan was another county named to honor a Civil War officer. This time it was General Philip H. Sheridan.
Pop. 3,544

Sherman County *(Established March 20, 1873)*

Civil War General William Tecumseh Sherman left his name on this county, which borders Colorado.
Pop. 7,759

Shunganunga *(Shawnee)* [shun-guh-NUNG-guh]

The Sioux word means "the race course," certainly an appropriate name for a course run by high school cross-country teams. The name *Shunganunga* applies to a creek and a park. The word *shunga* refers to a small horse, perhaps a race horse.

SHUNGANUNGA

Silkville *(Franklin)*

Frenchman E. V. de Boissiere had high hopes of growing silk in Kansas and for a while his venture proved successful. In 1876, at the Centennial Exposition in Philadelphia, de Boissiere won first prize for his silk. Unfortunately, he could not compete with the cheap silk of foreign markets, so he stopped the production of silk in 1886. For several years afterwards, Silkville built a reputation for its excellent cheese and butter production. Silkville was located three miles west of Williamsburg.

Silver Lake *(Shawnee)*

Silver Lake was created when the Kaw River cut off an oxbow bend. Before Kansas opened to white settlement, the Potawatomi developed a community there. The occasional silvery appearance of the surface of the water may account for the name.
PO: June 2, 1855–September 8, 1957, as Hallett; July 10, 1868–; Pop. 1,350

Simpson *(Mitchell)*

After Alfred Simpson deeded a portion of land for the town site in 1882, the name was changed from *Brittsville* to *Simpson.*
PO: April 3, 1882–; Pop. 123

Sitka *(Clark)*

A man known only as Mr. Pratt had been working in a fish cannery in Sitka, Alaska, when he decided to head south for a warmer climate. He stopped here in 1884, stayed, and opened a post office. The railroad came through, enabling the town to become a major supply point for a part of northern Oklahoma as well as southern Kansas.
PO: March 11, 1886–; Pop. 30

Skiddy *(Morris)*

Skiddy derived its unusual name from Francis Skiddy, a New York socialite and railroad financier who had promised to build a town hall and library for any town named for him. Although Kansans in Morris County called their new town *Skiddy,* Francis Skiddy reneged on his promise. Disgruntled state representative Dr. Adams changed the name to *Camden* after Camden, New Jersey. The residents of Camden did not wish to share their name with seventeen or more other *Cam-*

dens in the United States and demanded that the name *Skiddy* be returned to them.
PO: November 16, 1869–March 11, 1879, to Camden; August 3, 1883–October 31, 1953, from Camden

Smallwood *(Ness)*

This town and community were founded with the hope that the rich farming region would make colonizer Dr. Samuel Grant Rodger and a group of Chicago working people wealthy. Rodger's assistant on the scene was C. A. Smallwood, who acted as groceryman, work supervisor, and advertising agent for the colony. Drought later forced many colonists to leave.
PO: January 9, 1874–May 21, 1875; CS

Smith Center *(Smith)*

Eager to derive benefits from being the county seat town, L. T. Reese started Smith Center. Eight miles to the west stands the cabin in which Dr. Brewster M. Higley wrote "Home on the Range."
PO: January 8, 1873–; Pop. 2,240; CS

Smith County *(Established February 26, 1867)*

County organizers L. T. Reese and associates used fraud and bribery to get the six hundred "residents" needed for county organization. The legislature named the county for Major J. Nelson Smith of the Second Colorado Volunteers, who was killed in battle in 1864.
Pop. 5,947

Smoky Hill River *(West and Central Kansas)*

The Indians considered the Smoky Hill River to be a part of the Kaw. The Smoky Hill arises in Colorado and flows eastward 310 miles before joining the Republican in Geary County, where it forms the Kaw River.

Smoky Hill Valley *(West and Central Kansas)*

Historians say that the Smoky Hill Valley was one of the best buffalo pastures in the Great Plains. Here Indians fought some of their bloodiest battles against invading whites. Fur traders, mountain men, explorers, and emigrants used the Smoky Hill Trail near the river through Kansas on their way to Colorado and other points west.

Smoky Hills *(Central Kansas)*

In the summer the dark shales and sandstones in the hills are covered by heat haze as viewed by persons approaching them from the east.

Smolan *(Saline)*

Swedes who moved to this area named their settlement after the province of Smoland in Sweden. The name means "small land." Smolan was one of several Swedish communities located in the Smoky Hill Valley from near Salina to Marquette.
June 15, 1887–; Pop. 169

Soldier *(Jackson)*

The Indians named Big Soldier Creek for the U.S. soldiers who traversed the areas. Settlers living in the vicinity of the creek named Soldier Township, and the town was named for the township.
PO: February 21, 1883–; Pop. 165

Soldier Creek *(Shawnee)*

As early as 1826, Major Langham and his troops camped on the banks of the creek. In later years, the creek banks were a favorite campground for soldiers traveling west of Fort Leavenworth. There are also *Soldier Creeks* in Kiowa, Nemaha, Jackson, and Osage counties. The creek in Osage County was named by C. H. Wittington in 1851 after he found a regiment of soldiers camping there. About half of the regiment was sick with cholera, and seventy-two soldiers had already died.

Solomon *(Dickinson)*

The town of Solomon stands at the mouth of the Solomon River. Solomon had large salt deposits nearby, and by the 1870s salt producers were making about ten thousand barrels of salt a year.
PO: August 24, 1894–; Pop. 1,018

Solomon River *(Northwest and Central Kansas)*

French fur traders named the river after Salmon, intendent of Louisiana. When explorer Zebulon M. Pike passed through the region in 1806, he referred to the stream as *Solomon's Fork*. The Indians called the river *Nepahalla, Wiskapalla,* or *Wisgapall,* all meaning "water on a hill."

South Haven *(Sumner)*

Shoo Fly City was not considered dignified enough for post office officials in Washington. The Wye brothers, formerly of South Haven, Michigan, proposed *South Haven* for Kansas.
PO: October 5, 1871–; Pop. 439

South Hutchinson *(Reno)*

This community is located just south of Hutchinson.
PO: August 22, 1887–July 19, 1898; Pop. 2,226

Spearville *(Ford)*

Boston financier, real estate speculator, and Santa Fe Railroad official, Alden Speare left his name on two Kansas towns— Alden and Spearville. When the land was first deeded as a town site, organizers spelled it *Speareville*. The middle *e* was dropped in the 1860s. The area became a first-class sheep raising center. Because of its several windmills, Spearville has been called the "City of Windmills."
PO: June 11, 1877–; Pop. 693

Speed *(Phillips)*

Dr. Chapman, a Kansas physician, suggested the name *Speed* to honor James Speed, President Lincoln's attorney general.
PO: March 28, 1895–; Pop. 41

Spivey *(Kingman)* [SPEYE-vee]

Colonel E. M. Spivey was president of the Arkansas Valley Town and Land company, which established the town in 1887. The first girl born in the town was given the name Spivey Belle Treadway.
PO: December 6, 1886–; Pop. 83

Spring Creek *(Throughout Kansas)*

Creeks are spring fed all over Kansas and the simplest, most obvious name for such a creek is *Spring Creek*. There are eighty-eight entries in the Kansas Geographic Names Alphabetical Finding List for streams or places designated *Spring Creek.*

Spring Hill *(Johnson)*

James B. Hovey named the town after Spring Hill, a suburb of Mobile, Alabama, noted for its beautiful gardens.
PO: September 9, 1857–; Pop. 2,005

Stafford *(Stafford)*

This town had hopes of becoming the county seat in Stafford County; however, St. John defeated Stafford for that privilege.
PO: June 7, 1878–; Pop. 1,425

Stafford County *(Established February 26, 1867)*

The Kansas legislature named the county after Captain Lewis Stafford who served in the First Kansas Infantry. After incarceration in Andersonville prison, Stafford was killed at Young's Point in Louisiana.
Pop. 5,539

Stanley *(Johnson)*

The station and community were named for Henry M. Stanley, the journalist who found the Scottish-born David Livingstone, the great explorer-missionary, in Africa in the nineteenth century.
PO: March 19, 1872–; part of Greater Kansas City.

Stanton County *(Established March 6, 1873)*

Edward McMaster Stanton served as secretary of war under Presidents Lincoln and Johnson.
Pop. 2,339

Stark *(Neosho)*

Originally named *Grant Center*, the town was confused with *Grand Center*. To eliminate the confusion, postmaster Frank Leighton suggested the name *Stark*, after his birthplace, Stark County, Illinois.
PO: January 7, 1886–; Pop. 143

Sterling *(Rice)*

This town with strong religious orientation was first called *Peace*. The name was changed to *Sterling* in 1876 by two young settlers from New York, who memorialized their father, Sterling Rosan. Sterling College is located here.
PO: August 1, 1871–; Pop. 2,312

Stevens County *(Established March 6, 1873)*

The county owes its name to Pennsylvania Congressman Thaddeus Stevens, strong opponent of slavery.
Pop. 4,736

Stockton *(Rooks)*

Settlers named their town *Stockton* because of its nearly perfect environment for raising livestock.
PO: April 25, 1872–; Pop. 1,825; CS

STOCKTON

Strawn *(See* New Strawn.)

Strawberry Hill *(Wyandotte)*

The area known as *Strawberry Hill* in Kansas City lies on the
bluffs overlooking the Kansas and Missouri rivers. Legend
says that wild strawberries once grew here. The area is
closely identified with the Slavs, especially Croatians, who
began settling the area in the late nineteenth century. Artist
Marijana Grisnik has told the story of the Croatian community through her paintings.

Strong City *(Chase)*

Located on the Santa Fe Railroad in 1872, about a mile and a
half north of Cottonwood Falls, the town was named *Strong
City* in 1881 after W. B. Strong, president of the railroad.
PO: April 1, 1951–; Pop. 675

Studley *(Sheridan)*

Abraham Pratt and James Taylor left northern England in 1878. They purchased land near the Solomon River, and Pratt named the town after Studley Royal, a park and king's hunting ground in England. Between 1878 and 1882, only men occupied the town. They welcomed Mrs. Abraham Pratt and her three daughters to Studley in 1882.
PO: December 4, 1894–; Pop. 50

Stull *(Douglas)*

The post office used the name of postmaster Silvester Stull.
PO: April 27, 1899–September 30, 1903; Pop. 40

Sublette *(Haskell)*

Founders honored trail guide, fur trapper, and trader William L. Sublette by naming the town for him. The streets were named for such other western frontiersmen as William Becknell, Kit Carson, "Buffalo Bill" Cody, and Zebulon Pike.
PO: January 2, 1913–; Pop. 1,293; CS

Sugar Creek Mission *(Linn)*

Jesuits opened this Catholic Mission to the Potawatomies in the late 1830s. The first nuns to work in Kansas, four sisters from the Society of the Sacred Heart, began their work among the Potawatomis in 1841. Seventy-two-year-old Mother Rose Philippine Duchesne led the group. Recognition of her pioneer efforts led to her canonization in July 1988.

STRAWBERRY HILL

Summerfield (Marshall)

Located on the Nebraska-Kansas border, the town was named for Elias Summerfield, an official of the Kansas City, Wyandotte, and Northwestern Railroad.
PO: February 11, 1889–; Pop. 225

Sumner County (Established February 26, 1867)

Massachusetts Senator Charles Sumner was physically beaten on the floor of the U.S. Senate in 1856 for his anti-slavery statements. The county named for him has often been a leading wheat-producing county in the state.
Pop. 24,926

Sun City (Barber)

Sun City was a cowboy town called simply *Sun* before *City* was added. Source of the name remains unclear. Locals say the town was so named because settlers arrived on Sunday at sunrise, or was it Sunday at sunset?
PO: August 19, 1873–; Pop. 89

SUN CITY

Susank (Barton)

In return for right-of-way privileges, the Santa Fe Railroad named the town after Ed Susank, the trustee of Union township.
PO: June 24, 1921–; Pop. 52

Swede Creek (Riley)

Scandinavian Peter Carlson settled near the creek in 1857.

Switzler Creek (Osage)

A man named Switzler died after a wagon rolled over him while he was descending the eastern bank of the creek where the Santa Fe Trail crossed the creek.

Sycamore *(Montgomery)*

The name probably came from the native sycamore trees.
PO: May 20, 1896–; Pop. 200

Sylvan Grove *(Lincoln)*

Impressed with the beauty of the area, William Clay Buzick, a
local editor, suggested the name *Sylvan Grove*.
PO: December 12, 1872–; Pop. 376

Sylvia *(Reno)*

Both Albert A. Robinson's wife and daughter were named
Sylvia. At the time of the naming, Robinson was working for
the St. Joseph and Denver City Railroad.
PO: April 23, 1887–; Pop. 353

Syracuse *(Hamilton)*

A colony from Syracuse, New York, settled Syracuse, Kansas.
PO: May 23, 1873–; Pop. 1,654; CS

Tampa *(Marion)*

No one seems to know for sure how Tampa got its name.
One story says the name was suggested by a railroad engineer who brought one of the first trains through. Considering the number of Hacklers living in the area in the 1880s, it
should have been called *Hackler* or *Hacklerville*. Widow T. J.
Hackler and her ten sons owned the property before selling
part of it to the Golden Belt Town Company, who planned
Tampa.
PO: April 17, 1888–; Pop. 113

Tecumseh *(Shawnee)* [Teh-KUM-suh]

The name perpetuated that of the famous Shawnee Indian
chief who led his braves in the Battle of Tippecanoe in 1811.
Tecumseh was the oldest town in the county and the county
seat from 1855 to 1858, when a county vote moved the county
seat to the more promising town of Topeka.
PO: March 3, 1855–; Pop. 600

Tescott *(Ottawa)*

The name was derived from that of T. E. Scott.
PO: June 22, 1893–; Pop. 331

Thayer *(Neosho)*

The town came into existence with the arrival of the Leavenworth, Lawrence, and Galveston Railroad and was named for Nathaniel Thayer, a financier of the railroad company.
PO: January 13, 1871–; Pop. 517

Thomas County *(Established March 6, 1873)*

The county was named for Brigadier General George Henry Thomas, who died in 1870.
Pop: 8,451

Thompson Creek *(Ellsworth)*

According to local stories, P. M. "Smoky Hill" Thompson not only hunted and killed buffalo, he broke a few to the plow using harnesses made of woven buffalo hair.

Thresher Machine Canyon *(Trego)*

Indians killed a crew of men transporting a thresher through the Cedar Bluff area. They burned the thresher and dumped it into this canyon.

Tiblow *(Wyandotte)*

Delaware Indian Henry Tiblow operated a ferry on the Kansas River. The site was close to Bonner Springs.
PO: June 20, 1866–July 9, 1886

Timken *(Rush)*

German immigrants Jacob and Henry Timken invested in land and livestock in Rush County, operating the Timken Ranch. When the Atchison, Topeka, and Santa Fe Railroad was built through the county, Henry Timken sold them the

TONOVAY

section of land on which the town of Timken is located. He then bought two thousand dollars worth of stock in the town company.
PO: July 23, 1888–; Pop. 99

Tipton *(Mitchell)*

Chris Reinking came to Kansas from Iowa in 1872. He and his neighbors called their village *Pittsburgh,* but because the name was already in use, Reinking suggested *Tipton,* the name of the county seat in his native county in Iowa.
PO: March 14, 1881–; Pop. 321

Tonganoxie *(Leavenworth)* [TAHN-guh-NOKS-ee]

In the 1850s a popular stopping place between Lawrence and Kansas City was a place belonging to a Delaware Indian, Tonganoxie. Later, when settlers moved in, William English built a grocery store and named the incipient village after the "great favorite" Tonganoxie. The name, which was said to mean "shorty," did not fit the tall Tonganoxie.
PO: March 16, 1863–; Pop. 1,864

Tonovay *(Greenwood)*

Local residents said that the town was first called *Ton of Hay,* after a wagonload of hay that they thought weighed a ton.
PO: March 17, 1886–November 30, 1912

Topeka *(Shawnee)* [toh-PEE-kuh]

Men of similar free-state political beliefs and economic ambitions joined forces to plan Topeka. They discussed the names *Webster* (after Daniel Webster) and *Mid-Continent* for the

TOPEKA

town, then chose *Topeka* because it had an Indian flavor. The name had an equal distribution of vowels and consonants, which gave it a "tripping and cadent sound." The favored definition of the word comes from the Indian term for "a place to dig wild potatoes." However, some believe an old Caddoan Indian word *ta-pa-ge*, meaning "noisy," might be more fitting, considering that the state legislature convenes at the capital city annually!
PO: March 3, 1855–; Pop. 115,266; CS

Toronto *(Woodson)*

Canadian settlers in Kansas named the town *Toronto*, perhaps after Toronto, Canada. The name has been interpreted to mean "meeting place," "gateway," and "a place of plenty."
PO: June 2, 1870–; Pop. 466

Toulon *(Ellis)* [TOO-lawn]

A group of homesteaders from Pennsylvania established the town in 1876. The name may have come from Illinois, where both a county and township were named Toulon.
PO: November 14, 1889–January 31, 1901

Towanda *(Butler)* [toh-WAHN-duh]

The town and township lie in the valley of the Whitewater River and are said to take their name from the Osage Indian word for "many waters." The name also could have been a transfer from Illinois or Pennsylvania. In the spring of 1863, James R. Mead built a trading post where he collected furs from hunters and Indians to sell in the east. His place served as dwelling, church, wayside inn, and Indian Agency and became a general supply point for the southwestern frontier. The post was widely known as *Meade's Ranche*, and the town of Towanda was built on a hill above the "Ranche."
PO: December 13, 1860–; Pop. 1,332

Trading Post *(Linn)*

Situated on the east bank of the Marais des Cygnes and four miles from the Missouri state line, Trading Post dates back to the 1830s when the fur trader Lewis Chouteau operated the post. Another man, Michael Giareau, had it in 1838. General Winfield Scott built a log fort there in 1842 before going on to build Fort Scott. Just before the Civil War, fugitive slaves entered Kansas through Trading Post.
PO: June 22, 1880–August 30, 1902

Treece *(Cherokee)*

Treece is one of several towns in the tristate district of Kansas, Missouri, and Oklahoma that went from boom to bust in the mining of lead and zinc. Mining operations ceased in the 1960s. Treece was established in 1916 on part of a farm belonging to D. S. Chubb and named for J. O. Treece, a real estate agent.
PO: December 10, 1917–; Pop. 194

Trego County *(Established February 26, 1867)*

The county was named for Captain Edgar P. Trego of Company H of the Eighth Kansas Infantry, who was killed in September 1863 at the Battle of Chickamauga.
Pop. 4,165

Tribune *(Greeley)*

The original name, *Cappapua*, gave way to *Tribune*. Nearly all the town sites in Greeley County had names relevant to Horace Greeley and his newspaper, the *New York Tribune*.
PO: March 26, 1886–; Pop. 955; CS

Trousdale *(Edwards)* [TROOS-dayl]

W. J. Trousdale established a post office here in 1886, but the town wasn't platted until 1915. An abandoned railroad, a failed bank, loss of the school to unification, and the closing of the post office have reduced Trousdale to a rural community.
PO: March 22, 1916–1974

Troy *(Doniphan)*

County Clerk James R. Whitehead gave the classical Greek name to the county seat. In the 1930s, Troy was a major shipping point for local fruit growers; the area contained an estimated ten thousand acres of apple orchards.
PO: March 16, 1857–; Pop. 1,240; CS

Turkey Creek *(McPherson)*

Wild turkeys ranged over much of Kansas in the nineteenth century. Twenty-six counties have a Turkey Creek. McPherson County has several Turkey Creek tributaries. One Turkey Creek crossing was a rest and watering stop on the Santa Fe Trail, especially at Fuller's Ranch. In the 1870s, Turkey Creek township became home to a group of Mennonites from the Crimea.

Turon *(Reno)*

Once known as *Pioneer City*, then *Cottonwood Grove*, Turon was named after Turin, Italy.
PO: December 2, 1881–; Pop. 481

Tuttle Creek Reservoir *(Pottawatomie and Riley)*

Mexican War veteran Henry Tuttle owned land along the creek that bears his name. Tuttle Creek flows into the Big Blue River. Tuttle Creek Dam, completed in 1963, was built to control flooding on the Big Blue.

Tyro *(Montgomery)*

This town was first known as *Fawn*. Why it became *Tyro* is unknown, but the name is fitting for a new town: *Tyro* is the Latin word for "novice."
PO: October 18, 1893–; Pop. 289

Udall *(Cowley)* [U-dahl]

Thirty acres belonging to P. W. Smith were used in platting the town named for Cornelius Udall. On the night of May 25, 1955, a tornado struck. The town's telephone operator, who died at the switchboard while trying to warn her neighbors, was one of eighty-three persons killed that night. The nearly demolished town has been rebuilt.
PO: September 4, 1879–; Pop. 891

Ulysses *(Grant)*

This town, named for General Ulysses S. Grant, is actually the second Ulysses. In 1888 the town fathers issued bonds and used the money to buy votes to elect Ulysses the county seat. Nearby Appomattox sued, and the Kansas Supreme Court ruled fraud. In 1890, more people moved to Ulysses

ULYSSES

and voted it the county seat. When the old bonds came due in 1908, Ulysses could not pay, so bondholders repossessed the town site. Next the citizens of Ulysses moved the town to a new site two and one-half miles away, where it remains.
PO: April 29, 1886–; Pop. 4,653; CS

Uniontown *(Bourbon)*

Many Union veterans settled in the area after the war. The name *Union* was popular for townships, schools, and cemeteries.
PO: March 10, 1873–; Pop. 371

Urbana *(Neosho)*

This small community was named for Urbana, Illinois.
PO: May 6, 1880–May 3, 1957; Pop. 50

Utica *(Ness)*

C. W. Bell named the post office *Utica* for his former home, Utica, New York.
PO: July 15, 1879–; Pop. 275

Utopia *(Greenwood)*

The town may have been named for the imaginary island described in Sir Thomas More's book *Utopia,* a place or state of political and legal perfection.
PO: May 6, 1880–February 28, 1935

UTOPIA

Valeda *(Labette)* [vuh-LEE-duh]

When it was established in 1881, the place had the name *Deerton*, then it changed to *Valeda*. The Latin word means "healthy" or "strong."
PO: *September 3, 1886–; Pop. 70*

Valley Center *(Sedgwick)*

Valley Center was proposed as the name for Wichita; the town of Valley Center is located in the valley of the Little Arkansas River, about ten miles northwest of Wichita.
PO: *April 25, 1872–; Pop. 3,300*

Valley Falls *(Jefferson)*

Early Kansas settlers didn't mind the name *Grasshopper* and gave it to this small settlement in Jefferson County in 1855. By 1863, residents had upgraded the name to *Sautrelle Falls*, ("sauterelle" is French for "grasshopper.") After the grasshopper plague of 1874, the distraught townspeople changed the offensive name to *Valley Falls* and changed the *Grasshopper River* to the *Delaware*. Some of the town streets bear names of the first female residents—Frances, Louisa, and Caroline.
PO: *December 21, 1855–October 12, 1863, as Sautrelle Falls; April 26, 1875–; Pop. 1,189*

VALLEY FALLS

Vassar *(Osage)*

The post office established on the site used the name *La Mont's Hill* for sixteen years before changing to *Vassar* in 1887. The reason for the name change and source remains unknown; perhaps the town founders named it for an Indian of this name.

PO: February 7, 1871–January 31, 1887, as La Mont's Hill; January 31, 1887–; Pop. 100

Verdigris River *(Southeastern Kansas)* [VER-duh-gris]

Either French explorers or the French Jesuits named the river *Verdigris* because of its gray-green color. The Verdigris flows through the lowest point in Kansas—680 feet.

Vegetarian Creek *(Neosho)*

Henry S. Clubb, an enthusiastic disciple of vegetarianism, organized sixty families to start a colony in Kansas where they could be "away from the contamination of flesh, alcohol and social vices" and where "the principle of the vegetarian diet can be fairly and fully tested, so as to demonstrate its advantages." A location in Allen County seemed the ideal place for such a colony. Colonists arrived in early 1856, but in less than a year, all but four families had given up and left. All that remains of the vegetarian experiment is the name given to this small creek and to the township—Cottage Grove.

VEGETARIAN CREEK

Vermillion *(Marshall)*

The town is named for the Vermillion River.
PO: May 2, 1870–; Pop. 191

Vermillion River *(Marshall)*

Meriwether Lewis called it the *Blackpaint River*. The French, however, named the river for its red sandstone bottom.

Vernon *(Woodson)*

Landowner Henry Foster named the town for his son Vernon. Cowley, Ness, Graham, and Finney counties also had places named *Vernon*. Only one survived—Vernon in Woodson County.
PO: January 31, 1887–August 15, 1953

Vesper *(Lincoln)*

A group of Pennsylvania Dutch settlers changed the name from the original *Nemo* to *Vesper*. The observation of an evening religious service may have been in their minds when they made the change.
PO: April 22, 1872–; Pop. 25

Victoria *(Ellis)*

London silk merchant George Grant came to Kansas in 1872 to seek property on which to establish a large cattle and sheep empire. He wanted English and Scottish immigrants to develop farms fronting Big Creek, which crossed the county from east to west. Victoria, named after Queen Victoria, would be the headquarters, with a railroad hotel and station, livestock corrals, and housing with 2,500 Englishmen. Grant is credited for the introduction of Aberdeen Angus cattle into the United States. Lack of financial backing, the harsh Kansas climate, grasshoppers, and adverse publicity about Kansas in the British Isles forced Grant into bankruptcy. Unable to farm successfully, the English left and were replaced by German Catholics from Russia. The later group developed the community of Herzog. The two towns combined in 1913 under the name *Victoria*.
PO: June 25, 1873–; Pop. 1,328

Vining *(Clay)*

Citizens finally settled on *Vining*, after using *Mulberry*, *Lookout*, and *Riverdale*. E. P. Vining, a freight agent for the Union Pacific Railroad, had granted special favors to the town.
PO: March 21, 1881–August 31, 1955; Pop. 85

Vinland *(Douglas)*

For years the community was generally known as *Coal Creek* because of its nearness to a creek showing deposits of soft coal along its banks. As early as 1859 a group of young people known as the Coal Creek Social Library Association started the first public library in Kansas "to prevent dancing from becoming the only amusement in the community." George Cutter's home housed the library, which began with ten volumes. Besides being the first librarian in the community, Cutter became the first postmaster, beginning in 1868. By then the settlement around his place was called *Vinland,* for William Barnes's vineyards. The Coal Creek Library remains a part of the Vinland community.
PO: September 25, 1868–April 30, 1954

Viola *(Sedgwick)*

The name given a township and town in the county was transferred from Viola, Illinois. The same name was used at one time for places in Elk and Ellis counties.
PO: May 27, 1899–; Pop. 199

Virgil *(Greenwood)*

The town was probably named after Virgil, New York, which in turn was named after the Roman poet who wrote the *Aeneid.*
PO: February 9, 1863–; Pop. 169

Vliets *(Marshall)* [vuh-LEETS]

An official of the Missouri Pacific Railroad named the station *Ewingsport,* but residents later changed the name to *Vliets* for a farmer who had land adjoining the railroad.
PO: November 11, 1887–; Pop. 35

Votaw *(Montgomery)*

Daniel Votaw, a Quaker, had dreams of making Votaw a black colony. Paul Davis, freedman and close friend of Votaw, brought a group of blacks from Shelby County, Texas, to establish the colony, which remained active until Davis's death in 1900. A devastating flood inundated the settlement in that same year. Votaw's residents moved, many of them going to Coffeyville, and no trace of the old community remains.

Wabaunsee *(Wabaunsee)* [wah-BUHN-see]

The town received its name more than three years before the county. In 1856 town planners envisioned a great city—the "New Haven of the West," with a park, steamboat landing, and tract for a university—that might even become the capital city. It never became more than a small town, but it was famous in Kansas history for its free-state activity. Rifles smuggled in with shipments of Bibles were intended to aid in the antislavery fight. *(See* the Beecher Bible and Rifle Colony.)
PO: December 29, 1855–January 31, 1944

Wabaunsee County *(Established August 30, 1855)*

The warrior chief of the Potawatomi never lived in Kansas, but his name is perpetuated in a county, township, town, and lake. Wabaunsee was born in Indiana in 1760 and died in 1845. He said: "The people will know me and always call me Wah-bahn-se," signifying "the dawn of day" or "causer of paleness." "When I kill an enemy, he turns pale, resembling the first light of the day."
Pop. 6,867

Waconda Springs *(Mitchell)* [wuh-KAHN-duh]

To the Pawnees, the Waconda Springs were sacred. White people used them as a resort and sanatorium. The springs were located in a mound that rose some thirty feet off the flat prairie around them. At the top was a pool of salt and mineral water more than sixty feet across, popularly believed to be bottomless, perhaps connected far underground with a channel to the sea. This idea was featured in a 1936 "Ripley's Believe It or Not" cartoon. The spring got its name from the Kaw word *Ne Waconda*, meaning "the Great Spirit" and "the Creator." The Kaws were the last tribe to worship the springs. Those who loved the spring, saddened by the federal government's decision to dam the Solomon River and thus cover Waconda Springs, kept the name Waconda for the lake behind the dam.
PO: April 23, 1908–July 15, 1955

WACONDA SPRINGS

Wagon Bed Springs *(Grant)*

On the Santa Fe Trail between the Cimarron cutoff on the Arkansas and the Cimarron River crossing in Indian Territory lay sixty miles of territory having no reliable water source. Late in the history of the trail, thirsty freighters sank a wagonbed in the quicksand of the dry Cimarron to get water. The springs are dry now.

Wakarusa River *(Douglas)* [wah-kah-ROO-sah]

Explorer Major Stephen Long referred to the *Warreruza* in 1819 and 1820. The word *wakarusa* intrigued early settlers. One account told of an Indian girl who rode her horse to the stream. She began to ford the river, going deeper and deeper until she was half immersed in the chilly water. She shouted *wa-ka-ru-sa,* supposedly meaning "hip-deep." Some say *Wakarusa* was an Indian word for "deep river" or "river of weeds." Another explanation says the river derived its name from wild plants partly covered with a fine hairy fiber that once grew along the banks. Yet another explanation is that *wakarusa* is an Indian name from the Sioux tribe in Kansas. White settlers used the name *Wakarusa* for a river, a valley, and a town in Shawnee County and for a township and valley in Douglas County.

WaKeeney *(Trego)* [wah-KEE-nee]

According to historian Craig Miner, one of the most ambitious colonial ventures organized for profit in western Kansas was that of the Warren Keeney Company. James F. Keeney, Chicago real estate developer, and his friend Albert Warren formed a partnership and acquired control of 340,000 acres of land in western Kansas. They planned an impressive depot and the town of WaKeeney. The colony grew rapidly in 1878, 1879, and early 1880 before drought struck and half the people returned east to their old homes.
PO: February 6, 1878–; Pop. 2,388; CS

Wakefield *(Clay)*

The town was named for Rev. Richard Wake, one of a group of founders in the Kansas Land and Emigration Company who laid out the town site August 26, 1869. Also, the secretary of the company came from Wakefield, England. Wakefield was one of several communities in Kansas established by immigrants from the British Isles. They welcomed a group of orphaned London children who boarded the train in New York for Kansas in 1869.
PO: December 22, 1869–; Pop. 803

Waldeck *(Pratt)*

George Waldeck owned land and built a large lake in the vicinity. He was the first man to introduce bass fish into this part of Kansas.
PO: August 10, 1889–February 14, 1903

Waldo *(Russell)*

Waldo took its name from a Union Pacific Railroad official.
PO: April 30, 1888–; Pop. 75

Waldron *(Harper)*

Howard Waldron owned a large ranch here in 1900, when the town was established near the Kansas-Oklahoma border.
PO: January 23, 1902–; Pop. 29

Wallace *(Wallace)*

This town did not take its name from the county, but rather from a railroad superintendent named George Wallace.
PO: August 15, 1872–; Pop. 86

Wallace County *(Established March 2, 1868)*

The county was named for Brigadier General William Harvey Lamb Wallace, who died April 10, 1862, from wounds received at Shiloh, Tennessee.
Pop. 2,045

Walnut *(Crawford)*

The word *walnut* appears in sixty-three place names in this state where black walnut trees thrive. The name is used frequently in townships. A post office called *Walnut* in 1870 stood a short way from the town site on the banks of Big Walnut Creek.
PO: April 4, 1877–; Pop. 308

Walnut Creek *(West Central Kansas)*

There are twenty-seven Walnut Creeks in Kansas. This one flows eastward from Lane County to Rice County, where it joins the Arkansas River. Santa Fe Trail surveyor George Sibley noted the creek in 1825, and travelers on the Santa Fe Trail often camped at the Walnut Creek Crossing. In the

1850s, William Allison and Francis Booth established a trading ranch at the crossing, selling supplies and provisions to travelers. The Kiowas called the creek *Tsodalhente-d Pa*, or Armless Man's Creek, for William Allison who had only one arm.
PO: August 22, 1853–November 20, 1857

Walton *(Harvey)*

A Santa Fe Railroad stockholder and businessman named Walton left his name on the small town.
PO: December 28, 1871–; Pop. 269

Wamego *(Pottawatomie)* [wah-MEE-goh]

The town was possibly named for either Henry or George Wam-me-go, Potawatomi Indians.
PO: October 11, 1866–; Pop. 3,159

Washington *(Washington)*

Town site promoters named the town after the first president of the United States.
PO: November 14, 1861–; Pop. 1,488; CS

Washington County *(Established February 20, 1857)*

According to onomastician John Rydjord, "George Washington's name was the most popular choice among political place names in the United States." The name *Washington* was used fifty-one times in Kansas place names. However, not all may be associated with George.
Pop. 8,543

Waterloo *(Kingman)*

The name, which came from Waterloo, Iowa, commemorated the allied victory over Napoleon near the Belgian village of Waterloo in June 1815.
PO: September 28, 1881–June 30, 1912; Pop. 30

Waterville *(Marshall)*

William Osborne of Waterville, New York, often visited Atchison, Kansas, where he owned the William Osborne Ferry in the town's early years. He also built the Central Branch Railway from Atchison to Waterville.
PO: February 18, 1868–; Pop. 694

Wathena *(Doniphan)* [wah-THEE-nuh]

Kickapoo Indian Chief Wathena (Wathenah), who owned the land in the town's vicinity until 1854, allowed the first settlers to hold church services in his wigwam.
PO: August 2, 1856–; Pop. 1,418

Wauneta *(Chautauqua)* [wah-NE-tuh]

Mrs. P. M. Calvert remembered the friendly tribe of Indians who raised her and chose the name Wauneta for the daughter of the chief.
PO: April 2, 1883–January 31, 1961

Waverly *(Coffey)*

When Andrew Pearson platted the town of Waverly, he suggested the name after his former home in Waverly, Indiana.
PO: June 10, 1878–; Pop. 671

Wayside *(Montgomery)*

Three names were submitted for consideration when the post office was established. The descriptive name of *Wayside* appears to have been the favorite. Reno County had a *Wayside* post office between August 23, 1880, and January 10, 1882.
PO: May 16, 1887–; Pop. 60

Wea Creek *(Miami)* [WEE-uh]

Wagoners using the trails between towns and forts often stopped along Wea Creek to grease their wagon axle housings with the thick, raw oil that seeped from many tar springs. The Kansas petroleum industry grew from the probings of George W. Brown in 1860 along Wea Creek to significant production after 1900. The Wea Indians had a reserve in the vicinity in the 1840s.

Webber *(Jewell)*

Webber was established when the Atchison, Topeka, and Santa Fe Railroad built through Jewell County. The town-site land once belonged to Dan Webber.
PO: February 21, 1889–; Pop. 53

Webster *(Rooks)*

Rooks County pioneer J. J. Griebel had an early Noah Webster dictionary that he referred to constantly. Wayne Corely said that it was Griebel's "opinion that accurate use of the

language was much to be preferred to mere religious faith." Griebel persuaded the residents to name the town *Webster*. The old Webster site was inundated by the Webster Reservoir, and the town moved to another site.
PO: December 8, 1879–June 30, 1953

Weir *(Cherokee)* [WEER]

T. M. Weir came from Pennsylvania to Kansas in 1871 to buy land. For many years Weir prospered from coal mining.
PO: January 15, 1875–; Pop. 705

Welda *(Anderson)*

The Kansas City, Lawrence, and Southern Railroad named the station on their line in 1870. A small town in Germany, which had the name *Welda*, may have been the source.
PO: June 23, 1874–

Wellington *(Sumner)*

The Wellington town site was selected in April 1871. One of the members of the town company, R. A. Davis, an Englishman and admirer of the Duke of Wellington, named the town after him.
PO: June 21, 1871–; Pop. 8,212; CS

Wellsford *(Kiowa)*

The name changed from *McDowell* to *Wellsford* in 1886, after F. M. Wellsford, a landowner. When the city fathers wanted to incorporate as a city of the third class in 1916, they lacked the necessary 250 human residents to qualify, so a number of dogs became "citizens for a day"!
PO: September 23, 1886–June 30, 1955; Pop. 30

Wells Overlook *(Douglas)*

At 1,060 feet, Wells Overlook is the highest of four limestone mounds in the Wakarusa Valley. In 1971 William H. Wells deeded the land for Wells Overlook Park to Douglas County. Wells had had aviation interests in Lawrence and Topeka.

Wellsville *(Franklin)*

Town founders honored D. L. Wells, the construction engineer for the Leavenworth, Lawrence, and Galveston Railroad.
PO: October 3, 1870–; Pop. 1,162

Weskan *(Wallace)*

This town is located about as far west as you can get in Kansas.
PO: August 12, 1887–; Pop. 300

West Mineral *(Cherokee)*

The only survivor among Mineral, East Mineral, and West Mineral is West Mineral. All three mining towns began side by side at approximately the same time in the late 1890s. The development of the Mineral mining district began with the building of a branch of the Missouri, Kansas, and Texas Railway from Parsons to this point. The Southwestern Development Company bought a total of twenty-two hundred acres of coal land, including the Mineral town site. They developed the site and built miners' houses and a company store. The company called its site *Mineral City,* but the post office shortened it to *Mineral.* Meanwhile, individuals could buy lots just west of the company property, and this west side became West Mineral. Another site developed into East Mineral. At the turn of the century, the side-by-side Minerals prospered with a population of approximately ten thousand. Twenty years later the coal mines closed, the population declined, and the towns consolidated into West Mineral. A few miles southwest of West Mineral stands Big Brutus, once the world's second-largest operating coal shovel. The 16-story high Big Brutus no longer shovels coal; it has been converted to a tourist attraction and is open year-round.
PO: January 23, 1899–; Pop. 229

Westmoreland *(Pottawatomie)*

Settler John McKimmans came to Kansas from Westmoreland County, Pennsylvania.
PO: June 30, 1858–; Pop. 598; CS

Westphalia *(Anderson)* [west-FAYL-yuh]

Westphalia is a German name transferred to various places in the United States. The Flusche brothers, from Westphalia, Iowa, named Westphalia, Kansas.
PO: June 12, 1880–; Pop. 204

Westwood *(Johnson)*

This residential area is part of Greater Kansas City. Its being west of Kansas City, Missouri, may have influenced its descriptive name.
Pop. 1,783

Westwood Hills *(Johnson)*

Also part of Greater Kansas City, Westwood Hills is located immediately east of Westwood.
Pop. 437

Wetmore *(Nemaha)*

W. T. Wetmore, vice president of the Central Branch of the Union Pacific Railroad, once camped at the spring near the town named for him.
PO: December 18, 1867–; Pop. 376

Wheaton *(Pottawatomie)*

Settlers from Wheaton, Illinois, named this settlement.
PO: October 17, 1883–; Pop. 90

White City *(Morris)*

The town site was named for F. C. White, superintendent of the Neosho division of the Missouri, Kansas, and Texas Railway (KATY). White had been ordered to "bull-whack" (whip) his construction crew in order to beat a competing railroad.
PO: January 2, 1872–; Pop. 534

White Cloud *(Doniphan)*

This old river town facing the wide sweep of the Missouri River was named for James White Cloud, chief of the Prairie Sioux (Iowas). Dr. Richard J. Gatling, later inventor of the famous Gatling gun, was one of the town company organizers.
PO: July 11, 1855–; Pop. 234

Whitewater *(Butler)*

The presence of the White Water River accounts for the town name. The post office started with the name *White Water* in 1871, then switched to *Ovo*, and back to *Whitewater* by 1950.
PO: August 7, 1871–December 7, 1871, as White Water; September 29, 1874–July 7, 1882, as Ovo; May 15, 1888–November 1, 1950, as White Water; November 1, 1950–; Pop. 751

White Woman Creek *(Western Kansas)*

Several places in Scott, Finney, Ford, and Hodgeman counties have the name *White Woman—White Woman Basin, White Woman Bottoms, White Woman Grave,* and *White Woman Creek.* Rancher Robert Wight told the story of Indians killing his livestock. While following their trail, he and his party discovered a wrecked government ambulance, its driver, and two soldiers horribly butchered and mutilated. The Indians had also captured a woman and carried her off with them. To end her suffering, she hanged herself from a tree on the banks of the creek. The Cheyennes called the place *White Woman Creek.*

Whiting *(Jackson)*

Kansas Senator Samuel Pomeroy named Whiting after his wife's maiden name.
PO: June 15, 1869–; Pop. 270

Wichita *(Sedgwick)* [WICH-i-tah]

For many years prior to the white man's coming, Indians had camped and traded at the junction of the Big and Little Arkansas rivers. During the Civil War, Wichita Indians left Indian Territory (present-day Oklahoma) to seek refuge at the junction. They stayed only three years, returning south after the war. The increasing number of traders and soldiers who traveled in the area called the site *Wichita town,* or just *Wichita,* because of the Indians there. *Wichita* was said to mean "scattered lodges." Town organizers in the late 1860s considered the names of *Beecher, Sedgwick, Hamilton,* and even *Opi Ela* (Elk Tooth) before accepting the name it had already carried for several years. During the late 1920s, Wichita boasted of being the "Air Capital" because of its growing dominance in the manufacture of general aircraft.
PO: February 17, 1869–; Pop. 279,272; CS

Wichita County *(Established March 6, 1873)*

Marsh Murdock, editor of the *Wichita Eagle,* named Wichita County. The city of Wichita is two hundred miles southeast of the county by the same name.
Pop. 3,041

Willard *(Shawnee)*

Willard began as a ferrying point on the Kansas River. The coming of the railroad in 1883 and success as a rural trading center brought prosperity to Willard until the 1930s. Over the years, fires, floods, and a changing economy have reduced Willard to a quiet country village.
PO: June 21, 1887–July 31, 1959; Pop. 128

Williamsburg *(Franklin)*

James Dane and William H. Scofield owned the town site.
Farmer Scofield named the town Williamsburgh after himself.
The *h* was dropped in 1894.
PO: April 10, 1869–; Pop. 362

Willis *(Brown)*

After the Civil War, Captain Martin Cleveland Willis served
with the Kansas Nineteenth Regiment. Later, he served two
terms in the state legislature.
PO: June 14, 1882–January 31, 1960; Pop. 85

Willowbrook *(Reno)*

According to a recent Associated Press article, Willowbrook
"has no post office, no police force or fire department. But by
an income definition, Willowbrook is the wealthiest city in
Kansas." The Census Bureau reported that in 1985 Willowbrook had the highest per capita income in Kansas, $51,666.
The community located a few miles northwest of Hutchinson
was founded by the Carey family, the salt manufacturers, in
the 1920s.
Pop. 80

Wilmore *(Comanche)*

Texas rancher C. C. Pepperd moved to Comanche County in
1874. When he heard that the Chicago, Kansas, and Western
Railroad was coming through his ranch, he and his foreman
Tom Wilmore organized a town company. C. C. and his
foreman flipped a coin to determine who would name the
town. C. C. won and named the town *Wilmore*.
PO: June 7, 1887–; Pop. 97

Wilsey *(Morris)*

J. O. Wilsey left Bloomville, Ohio, for this place in Morris
County.
PO: May 23, 1884–; Pop. 179

Wilson *(Ellsworth)*

Town founder Isaac Wilson named the town. Wilson attracted a large number of Bohemian immigrants; their descendants host a Czech festival each summer.
PO: June 24, 1873–; Pop. 978

Wilson County *(Established August 25, 1855)*

Army sutler and merchant Hiero T. Wilson was the first white settler in the Fort Scott area. He spoke Osage, Cherokee, and Creek.
Pop. 12,126

Winchester *(Jefferson)*

The honor of naming the town went to Alvin Best, the oldest man in the settlement. He came from Winchester, Virginia.
PO: March 15, 1858–; Pop. 570

Windom *(McPherson)*

The town's name, first *Laura*, was changed to *Windom* for William Windom, President Chester A. Arthur's secretary of the treasury.
PO: April 9, 1884–; Pop. 160

Winfield *(Cowley)*

The settlement was called *Legonda* when W. W. Andrews took a claim in 1869. He returned home to Leavenworth to get his family, persuading Mrs. Andrews to leave by saying that she could name the town *Winfield* for Winfield Scott, a Baptist minister in Leavenworth who was also scheduled to move to the new town. When she arrived and learned the name was already *Legonda*, a disappointed Mrs. Andrews

WINFIELD

wanted to return to Leavenworth. However, she learned that no name was official until voted upon by the residents. When an election was called and a formal ballot taken, followed by a dance, Mrs. Andrews's washstand drawer, with her key, was the ballot box. Apparently Mrs. Andrews stayed close to the ballot box, for she later remarked with a twinkle in her eye, "while they were dancing Legonda lost the day." A counting of the ballots favored *Winfield*.
PO: May 3, 1870–; Pop. 10,736; CS

Winona *(Logan)*

The Kansas Pacific called the freight center *Gopher* until the name was changed in May 1886 to *Winona* in honor of Mrs. Bill (Winona) Clark. The Clarks had a homestead north of the town site. Logan County historians say that *Winona* meant "little maid of the prairie" or "first born daughter" in an Indian language.
PO: December 27, 1886–; Pop. 258

Wolcott *(Wyandotte)*

The town was platted as *Conner* in 1868, but its name was changed to *Wolcott* in 1944 after the first general manager of the Kansas City Western Electric Railway.
PO: August 28, 1899–July 31, 1944, as Conner; part of Greater Kansas City

Wolf Creek *(Coffey)*

Wolf Creeks exist in thirty-two Kansas counties. At one time large numbers of wolves roamed Kansas, depending on the buffalo for sustenance. In the 1850s and 1860s hunters killed thousands of wolves for their hides. In recent years, Wolf Creek in Coffey County has made headlines as the site of the Wolf Creek Nuclear Power Plant.

Wonsevu *(Chase)* [WUHN-se-voo]

Mrs. Mariah Barnes named *Wonsevu* in 1885. The Indian word means "running deer."
PO: August 23, 1875–October 15, 1907

Woodbine *(Dickinson)*

Perhaps Woodbine was named for the Virginia creeper vine.
PO: January 31, 1872–; Pop. 172

Woodson County *(Established August 25, 1855)*

The county was named for Daniel Woodson, secretary of the territory of Kansas in 1855 and 1856.
Pop. 4,600

Woodston *(Rooks)*

Mr. Woods, a Stockton banker, offered five hundred dollars toward the building of a school house. Subsequently, the town developing near the school house was called *Woodston.*
PO: February 10, 1886–; Pop. 157

Wright *(Ford)*

Robert M. Wright was only twenty-six years old when he operated a ranch at Cimarron Crossing in 1867. Repeated Indian raids forced him to abandon the ranch, but not Kansas. He loved the excitement of living on the frontier and became one of the founders of Dodge City. During September 1872, he began building a stockyard in the vicinity of a site that would be named for him.
PO: March 24, 1886–; Pop. 150

Wyandotte County *(Established January 29, 1859)*
[WEYE-uhn-daht]

The village of Wyandotte preceded the establishment of the county. Wyandot Indians lived in the area. Wyandotte County, with only 151 square miles, is the smallest county in Kansas. The addition of the *te* to *Wyandot* may have been a clerical error.
Pop. 172,335

Xavier *(Leavenworth)*

A religious community was founded by Sister Xavier Ross in 1942. The Mother House of the Sisters of Charity of Leavenworth is here.
PO: September 22, 1942–

Xenia *(Bourbon)* [ZEE-nee]

Platted in 1858, Xenia was among the early towns of the territorial period. Several pioneers from Ohio took land in the township, and the name came from Xenia, Ohio. Xenia, Kansas, also shares its name with Xenia, Illinois.
PO: November 29, 1858–August 31, 1926; Pop. 20

Yates Center *(Woodson)*

Two facts led to christening the town *Yates Center*. This location is in the geographical center of the county and its original owner's name was Abner Yates.
PO: June 12, 1876–; Pop. 1,998; CS

Yoder *(Reno)*

Many Old Order Amish in the community still drive horses and buggies rather than cars and dress in a conservative, uniform style. Eli Yoder, of the Pennsylvania Amish, settled in an area east of Hutchinson. He served as the first postmaster and offered free land to the railroad for a station on the condition that the station and small town be named for him.
PO: November 25, 1889–; Pop. 150

YODER

Zarah *(Barton)* [ZAR-uh]

Kansas had two Zarahs, one a "hog ranch" and the other more respectable one in south central Kansas. The "hog ranch" in Barton County catered to the needs and pleasures of soldiers stationed at nearby Fort Zarah. The village offered drinking, gambling, prostitution, and a post office for two years. Fort Zarah was named by General Samuel R. Curtis for

ZARAH

his son Major H. Zarah Curtis, who had been killed in a Civil War encounter in 1863.
PO: July 6, 1871–April 2, 1873

Zeandale *(Riley)*

J. H. Pillsbury gave the name, which was a combination of the Greek work *zea,* meaning "corn," and the English word *dale*—thus corn-dale or corn-valley. Zeandale is just south of Manhattan, Kansas.
PO: June 29, 1857–March 16, 1868; August 27, 1884–December 31, 1944; Pop. 50

Zenda *(Kingman)*

A post office name changed from *Rochester* to *Zenda* after the publication of the popular novel *The Prisoner of Zenda.*
PO: October 7, 1899–; Pop. 146

Zenith *(Stafford)*

The vice president of the Atchison, Topeka, and Santa Fe Railroad, A. A. Robinson, established a town five miles west of Sylvia. Upon the urging of H. S. Thompson, one of the Sylvia town-site owners, he named the new site *Zenith.*
PO: February 25, 1902–

Zurich *(Rooks)* [ZOOR-ik]

Zurich is located on the high plains of central western Kansas, far from its onomastic ancestor, Zurich, Switzerland. *PO: January 2, 1880–; Pop. 185*

ZURICH

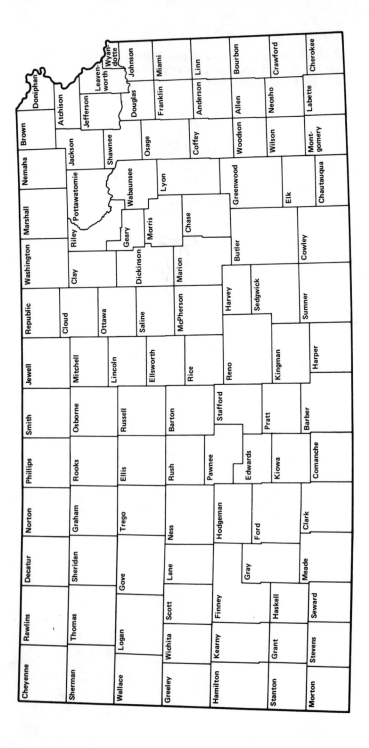

Index of Counties

ALLEN: Elsmore, Gas, Humboldt, Iola, La Harpe, Mildred, Moran, Savonburg, Vegetarian Creek

ANDERSON: Colony, Garnett, Glenloch, Greeley, Harris, Kincaid, Lone Elm, Scipio, Welda, Westphalia

ATCHISON: Arrington, Atchison, Cummings, Dalby, Donaldville, Effingham, Everest, Farmington, Good Intent, Huron, Independence Creek, International Forest of Friendship, Kennekuk, Lancaster, Larkinburg, Lewis Point, Monrovia, Mormon Grove, Mount Pleasant, Muscotah, Oak Mills, Pardee, Parnell, Port William, Potter, Shannon

BARBER: Flower Pot Mound, Hardtner, Hazelton, Isabel, Kiowa, Lake City, Medicine Lodge, Sharon, Sun City

BARTON: Albert, Cheyenne Bottoms, Claflin, Dubuque, Ellinwood, Galatia, Great Bend, Heizer, Hoisington, Olmitz, Pawnee Rock, Susank, Walnut Creek, Zarah

BOURBON: Bronson, Fort Scott, Freedom Colony, Fulton, Garland, Gilfillan, Hiattville, Mapleton, Redfield, Uniontown, Xenia

BROWN: Everest, Fairview, Hamlin, Hiawatha, Horton, Kickapoo Reservation, Morrill, Mount Hope Cemetery, Powhattan, Reserve, Robinson, Sabetha, Willis

BUTLER: Andover, Augusta, Beaumont, Benton, Brainerd, Cassoday, Douglass, Elbing, El Dorado, Freedom, Latham, Leon, Midian, Potwin, Rosalia, Rose Hill, Towanda, Whitewater

CHASE: Bazaar, Cedar Point, Cottonwood Falls, Elmdale, Jacob's Mound, Kahola, Matfield Green, Strong City, Wonsevu

CHAUTAUQUA: Cedar Vale, Chautauqua, Elgin, Hewins, Niotaze, Peru, Sedan, Wauneta

CHEROKEE: Baxter Springs, Carona, Columbus, Crestline, Faulkner, Galena, Hallowell, Riverton, Roseland, Scammon, Treece, Weir, West Mineral

CHEYENNE: Bird City, St. Francis

CLARK: Ashland, Big Basin, Englewood, Minneola, Mount Jesus, St. Jacob's Well, Sitka

CLAY: Athelstane, Clay Center, Fancy Creek, Green, Idana, Industry, Longford, Morganville, Oak Hill, Vining, Wakefield

CLOUD: Ames, Aurora, Clyde, Concordia, Glasco, Jamestown, Miltonvale

COFFEY: Burlington, French Ridge, Gridley, Lebo, Le Roy, New Strawn, Waverly, Wolf Creek

COMANCHE: Coldwater, Protection, Wilmore

COWLEY: Arkansas City, Atlanta, Burden, Cambridge, Dexter, Geuda Springs, New Salem, Rock, Udall, Winfield

CRAWFORD: Arcadia, Arma, Beulah, Cato, Cherokee, Crawford County State Park, Farlington, Franklin, Frontenac, Girard, Hepler, McCune, Midway, Monmouth, Mulberry, Opolis, Pittsburg, Radley, Walnut

DECATUR: Dresden, Elephant Rock, Jennings, Leoville, Norcatur, Oberlin, Sappa Creek

DICKINSON: Abilene, Buckeye Township, Carlton, Chapman, Enterprise, Henquenet Cave, Herington, Hope, Industry, Manchester, Moonlight, Solomon, Woodbine

DONIPHAN: Bendena, Denton, Doniphan, Elwood, Highland, Highland Presbyterian Mission, Iowa Point, Iowa, Sac, and Fox Reservation, Leona, Peters Creek, Purcell, Severance, Troy, Wathena, White Cloud

DOUGLAS: Baldwin City, Big Springs, Bismarck Grove, Black Jack, Clinton, Clinton Lake, Eudora, Kanwaka, Lakeview, Lawrence, Lecompton, Lone Star, Lone Star Lake, Mount Oread, Palmyra, Stull, Vinland, Wakarusa River, Wells Overlook

EDWARDS: Belpre, Kinsley, Lewis, Offerle, Trousdale

ELK: Elk Falls, Grenola, Howard, Longton, Moline

ELLIS: Cathedral of the Plains, Catherine, Ellis, Fort Hays, Hays, Hog Back, Pfeifer, Round Mound, Schoenchen, Toulon, Victoria

ELLSWORTH: Carneiro, Ellsworth, Holyrood, Horse Thief Canyon, Kanopolis, Lorraine, Thompson Creek, Wilson

FINNEY: Friend, Garden City, Holcomb, Kalvesta, Pierceville

FORD: Bloom, Boot Hill, Bucklin, Dodge City, Ford, Fort Dodge, Kingsdown, Saw Log Creek, Spearville, Wright

FRANKLIN: Centropolis, Hundred and Ten Mile Creek, Lane, Le Loup, Ottawa, Pomona, Princeton, Rantoul, Richmond, Silkville, Wellsville, Williamsburg

GEARY: Camp Forsyth, Fort Riley, Grandview Plaza, Junction City, Milford, Pawnee

GOVE: Gove, Grainfield, Grinnell, Monument Rocks, Park, Quinter

GRAHAM: Bogue, Happy, Hill City, Morland, Nicodemus

GRANT: Wagon Bed Springs, Ulysses

GRAY: Cimarron, Copeland, Ensign, Ingalls, Montezuma

GREELEY: Horace, Tribune

GREENWOOD: Climax, Eureka, Fall River, Hamilton, Madison, Quincy, Reece, Severy, Tonovay, Utopia, Virgil

HAMILTON: Coolidge, Syracuse

HARPER: Anthony, Attica, Bluff City, Danville, Freeport, Harper, Runnymede, Waldron

HARVEY: Burrton, Dutch Avenue, Emma Creek, Halstead, Hesston, Newton, North Newton, Sedgwick, Walton

HASKELL: Satanta, Sublette

HODGEMAN: Hanston, Jetmore, Saw Log Creek

JACKSON: Circleville, Danceground Cemetery, Delia, Denison, Holton, Hoyt, Larkinburg, Mayetta, Netawaka, Potawatomie Indian Reservation, Soldier, Whiting

JEFFERSON: Delaware River, Grantville, Half Mound, McLouth, Meriden, Nortonville, Oskaloosa, Ozawkie, Perry, Valley Falls, Winchester

JEWELL: Burr Oak, Esbon, Formosa, Jewell, Lovewell, Mankato, Randall, Salem, Webber

JOHNSON: Countryside, De Soto, Edgerton, Fairway, Gardner, Holliday, Kill Creek, Lake Quivira, Leawood, Lenexa, Merriam, Mission, Olathe, Overland Park, Prairie Village, Roeland Park, Shawnee, Shawnee Methodist Mission, Spring Hill, Stanley, Tiblow, Westwood, Westwood Hills

KEARNY: Deerfield, Lakin

KINGMAN: Cunningham, Kingman, Murdock, Nashville, Norwich, Penalosa, Rago, Spivey, Waterloo, Zenda

KIOWA: Belvidere, Greensburg, Haviland, Mullinville, Wellsford

LABETTE: Altamont, Bartlett, Bender Mounds, Chetopa, Edna, Labette, Mound Valley, Oswego, Parsons, Valeda

LANE: Amy, Dighton, Healy

LEAVENWORTH: Basehor, Easton, Fairmount, Fall Leaf, Fort Leavenworth, Jarbalo, Kickapoo, Kickapoo Cemetery, Lansing, Leavenworth, Linwood, Tonganoxie, Xavier

LINCOLN: Barnard, Beverly, Denmark, Lincoln, Sylvan Grove, Vesper

LINN: Blue Mound, Boicourt, La Cygne, Marais des Cygnes, Marais des Cygnes Massacre Site, Mine Creek Battlefield, Mound City, Parker, Pleasanton, Prescott, Sugar Creek Mission, Trading Post

LOGAN: Monument, Oakley, Russell Springs, Winona

LYON: Admire, Allen, Americus, Bushong, Emporia, Hartford, Miller, Neosho Rapids, Olpe, Plymouth, Reading

MARION: Alexanderwohl, Antelope, Burns, Canada, Chingawassa Springs, Crystal Spring, Durham, Florence, Goessel, Harvey House Museum, Hillsboro, Lehigh, Lincolnville, Lost Spring, Lost Springs, Marion, Peabody, Pilsen, Ramona, Tampa

MARSHALL: Alcove Spring, Axtell, Beattie, Blue Rapids, Frankfort, Herkimer, Home, Marysville, Oketo, Robidoux Creek, Summerfield, Vermillion, Vermillion River, Vliets, Waterville

MCPHERSON: Canton, Conway, Elyria, Emma Creek, Fremont, Galva, Inman, Lindsborg, Marquette, Maxwell Game Preserve, McPherson, Moundridge, New Gottland, Roxbury, Turkey Creek, Windom

MEADE: Fowler, Plains, Meade

MIAMI: Bucyrus, Fontana, Hillsdale, Louisburg, Marais des Cygnes, Osawatomie, Paola, Wea Creek

MITCHELL: Asherville, Beloit, Cawker City, Glen Elder, Glen Elder Dam, Hunter, Scottsville, Simpson, Tipton, Waconda Springs

MONTGOMERY: Caney, Cherryvale, Coffeyville, Dearing, Elk City, Havana, Independence, Liberty, Sycamore, Tyro, Votaw, Wayside

MORRIS: Council Grove, Delavan, Diamond Spring, Dunlap, Dwight, Kaw Indian Mission, Latimer, Parkerville, Skiddy, White City, Wilsey

MORTON: Cimarron National Grasslands, Elkhart, Point of Rocks, Richfield, Rolla

NEMAHA: Bern, Capioma, Centralia, Corning, Delaware River, Goff, Oneida, Sabetha, Seneca, Wetmore

NEOSHO: Chanute, Earlton, Erie, Galesburg, Osage Mission, St. Paul, Stark, Thayer, Urbana, Vegetarian Creek

NESS: Bazine, Beeler, Brownell, Ness City, Ransom, Rantoul, Smallwood, Utica

NORTON: Almena, Clayton, Devizes, Edmond, Lenora, Norton, Sappa Creek

OSAGE: Arvonia, Burlingame, Carbondale, Dragoon Creek, Hundred and Ten Mile Creek, Lyndon, Melvern, Mute Creek, Olivet, Osage City, Overbrook, Quenemo, Scranton, Switzler Creek, Vassar

OSBORNE: Alton, Downs, Kill Creek, Natoma, Osborne, Portis

OTTAWA: Ada, Bennington, Culver, Delphos, Minneapolis, Rock City, Tescott

PAWNEE: Burdett, Fort Larned, Garfield, Larned, Rozel

PHILLIPS: Agra, Glade, Kirwin, Logan, Long Island, Phillipsburg, Prairie View, Speed

POTTAWATOMIE: Belvue, Emmett, Flush, Fostoria, Havensville, Kansas State Forest, Louisville, Mariadahl, Olsburg, Onaga, Potawatomi Indian Pay Station, St. George, St. Marys, Tuttle Creek Reservoir, Wamego, Westmoreland, Wheaton

PRATT: Byers, Cairo, Coats, Cullison, Iuka, Pratt, Sawyer, Waldeck

RAWLINS: Atwood, Herndon, Ludell, McDonald

RENO: Abbyville, Arlington, Buhler, Castleton, Dutch Avenue, Haven, Hutchinson, Langdon, Lerado, Nickerson, Partridge, Plevna, Pretty Prairie, Sand Hills State Park, South Hutchinson, Sylvia, Turon, Willowbrook, Yoder

REPUBLIC: Agenda, Belleville, Courtland, Cuba, Munden, Narka, Norway, Republic, Scandia

RICE: Alden, Buffalo Bill's Well, Bushton, Chase, Cow Creek Crossing, Frederick, Geneseo, Jarvis Creek, Little River, Lyons, Raymond, Sterling

RILEY: Aggieville, Bala, Blue Mont, Fancy Creek, Fort Riley, Konza Prairie, Leonardville, Manhattan, May Day, Ogden, Randolph, Riley, Swede Creek, Tuttle Creek Reservoir, Zeandale

ROOKS: Ash Rock, Damar, Palco, Plainville, Stockton, Webster, Woodston, Zurich

RUSH: Alexander, Bison, Hargrave, La Crosse, Liebenthal, Loretto, McCracken, Otis, Pfeifer, Rush Center, Timken

RUSSELL: Bunker Hill, Dorrance, Dubuque, Garden of Eden, Gorham, Lucas, Luray, Paradise, Russell, Waldo

SALINE: Assaria, Bavaria, Brookville, Coronado Heights, Falun, Gypsum, Kipp, New Cambria, Salemsborg, Salina, Smolan

SCOTT: El Cuartelejo, Modoc, Scott City

SEDGWICK: Andale, Anness, Bentley, Cheney, Clearwater, Clonmel, Colwich, Derby, Eastborough, Furley, Garden Plain, Goddard, Greenwich, Greenwich Heights, Haysville, Kechi, Maize, McConnell Air Force Base, Mount Hope, Mulvane, Ninnescah River, Park City, Peck, Planeview, Valley Center, Viola, Wichita

SEWARD: Kismet, Liberal

SHAWNEE: Auburn, Berryton, Cedar Crest, Dover, Forbes Field, Mission Creek, Potwin Place, Rossville, Shunganunga, Silver Lake, Soldier Creek, Tecumseh, Topeka, Willard

SHERIDAN: Hoxie, Selden, Studley

SHERMAN: Edson, Goodland, Kanorado, Mt. Sunflower

SMITH: Athol, Cedar, Gaylord, Kensington, Lebanon, Smith Center

STAFFORD: Hudson, Macksville, Neola, Quivira National Wildlife Refuge, Radium, Seward, St. John, Stafford, Zenith

STANTON: Johnson City, Manter

STEVENS: Feterita, Hugoton, Moscow

SUMNER: Argonia, Bartlett Arboretum, Belle Plaine, Caldwell, Chikaskia, Conway Springs, Geuda Springs, Hunnewell, London, Mayfield, Milan, Mulvane, Oxford, Rome, Salt City, South Haven, Wellington

THOMAS: Brewster, Colby, Gem, Menlo, Mingo, Oakley, Rexford

TREGO: Collyer, Thresher Machine Canyon, WaKeeney

WALLACE: Fort Wallace, Mount Sunflower, Rhinoceros Hill Quarry, Sharon Springs, Wallace, Weskan

WASHINGTON: Barnes, Clifton, Greenleaf, Haddam, Hanover, Hollenberg, Hollenberg Pony Express Station, Lanham, Linn, Mahaska, Morrowville, Palmer, Vining, Washington

WABAUNSEE: Alma, Alta Vista, Beecher Bible and Rifle Church, Dragoon Creek, Eskridge, Harveyville, Maple Hill, McFarland, Mill Creek, Paxico, Wabaunsee

WICHITA: Leoti

WILSON: Altoona, Benedict, Buffalo, Coyville, Fredonia, Neodesha, New Albany

WOODSON: Neosho Falls, Piqua, Toronto, Vernon, Yates Center

WYANDOTTE: Argentine, Armourdale, Bonner Springs, Delaware, Edwardsville, Grinter House, Huron Park, Kansas City, Lake Quivira, Quindaro, Rosedale, Strawberry Hill, Tiblow, Wolcott